Bilingual English-Spanish Assessment™ (BESA™)

MANUAL

Bilingual English–Spanish Assessment™ (BESA™)

MANUAL

by

Elizabeth D. Peña, Ph.D., CCC-SLP
University of California
Irvine

Vera F. Gutiérrez-Clellen, Ph.D., CCC-SLP
San Diego State University
San Diego, California

Aquiles Iglesias, Ph.D., CCC-SLP
University of Delaware
Newark

Brian A. Goldstein, Ph.D., CCC-SLP
La Salle University
Philadelphia, Pennsylvania

and

Lisa M. Bedore, Ph.D., CCC-SLP
Temple University
Philadelphia, Pennsylvania

Baltimore • London • Sydney

Paul H. Brookes Publishing Co.
Post Office Box 10624
Baltimore, Maryland 21285-0624
USA

www.brookespublishing.com

Typeset by Absolute Service, Inc., Towson, Maryland.
Manufactured in the United States of America by
Potomac Printing Solutions, Inc., Landsdowne, Virginia.

Case examples are derived from the authors' research. Pseudonyms have been used and identifying details have been changed to protect confidentiality.

The research for the BESA was supported by the National Institute on Deafness and Other Communication Disorders: Contract No. N01-DC-8-2100 Development and Validation of a Language Test for Children Speaking Non-Standard English: A Study of Bilingual Hispanic Children. The opinions expressed are those of the authors and do not represent views of the Institute or U.S. Department of Health and Human Services.

Also available: *BESA Stimulus Book* (978-1-68125-281-0), *BESA English Protocol* (978-1-68125-282-7), *BESA Spanish Protocol* (978-1-68125-283-4), *Bilingual Input-Output Survey (BIOS)* (978-1-68125-284-1), and *Inventory to Assess Language Knowledge (ITALK)* (978-1-68125-285-8). Visit www.brookespublishing.com/BESA for more information.

Library of Congress Cataloging-in-Publication Data

Names: Peña, Elizabeth D., author.
Title: BESA Manual / Elizabeth D. Peña, Ph.D., CCC-SLP, University of California, Irvine, Vera F. Gutierrez-Clellen, Ph.D., CCC-SLP, San Diego State University, San Diego, California, Aquiles Iglesias, Ph.D., CCC-SLP, University of Delaware, Newark, Brian A. Goldstein, Ph.D., CCC-SLP, La Salle University, Philadelphia, Pennsylvania, and Lisa M. Bedore, Ph.D., CCC-SLP, Temple University, Philadelphia, Pennsylvania.
Description: Baltimore, Maryland : Brookes Publishing, 2018. | Includes bibliographical references and index.
Identifiers: LCCN 2018000395 | ISBN 9781681252803
Subjects: LCSH: Education, Bilingual—United States. | Spanish language—Study and teaching (Early childhood)—United States. | Communicative disorders in children—Study and teaching. | English language—Study and teaching—Foreign speakers. | Education, Bilingual—Ability testing. | Educational evaluation. | BISAC: EDUCATION / Evaluation. | EDUCATION / Bilingual Education. | EDUCATION / Special Education / Communicative Disorders.
Classification: LCC LC3731 .P463 2018 | DDC 370.117/50973—dc23 LC record available at https://lccn.loc.gov/2018000395

British Library Cataloguing in Publication data are available from the British Library.

10 9 8 7 6 5 4 3 2 1

2022 2021 2020 2019 2018

Contents

About the Authors

Elizabeth D. Peña, Ph.D., CCC-SLP, Professor, School of Education, University of California, Irvine, 3000C Education, Mail Code: 5500, Irvine, CA 92697

Dr. Peña is Professor in the School of Education at the University of California, Irvine. Her work focuses on differentiating language impairment from language difference in bilingual children. Her assessment work employs a variety of methods, including standardized and dynamic assessment. She is interested in how children from diverse linguistic backgrounds learn new language skills and how they lexicalize their conceptual knowledge across two languages, and she has published extensively in these areas. She is a Fellow of the American Speech-Language-Hearing Association.

Vera F. Gutiérrez-Clellen, Ph.D., CCC-SLP, Professor Emerita, School of Speech, Language, and Hearing Sciences, San Diego State University, 5500 Campanile Drive, San Diego, CA 92182

Dr. Gutiérrez-Clellen is Professor Emerita in the School of Speech, Language, and Hearing Sciences at San Diego State University. Her research focuses on the development of assessment measures for bilingual Spanish–English children and the evaluation of language intervention approaches for Latino children with language impairments.

Aquiles Iglesias, Ph.D., CCC-SLP, Professor and Founding Director, Speech-Language Pathology Program, University of Delaware, 540 South College Avenue, Newark, DE 19713

Dr. Iglesias is Professor and Founding Director of the Speech-Language Pathology Program at the University of Delaware. He was formerly a professor at Temple University and held various administrative positions. His major area of research is cultural and linguistic diversity, with a concentration on language acquisition in bilingual children. Dr. Iglesias contributed to the development of Systematic Analysis of Language Transcripts (SALT; Miller & Iglesias, 2012) for bilingual children, and he developed the Quick Interactive Language Screener™ (QUILS™; Paul H. Brookes Publishing Co., 2017) and the Quick Interactive Language Screener: English–Spanish™ (QUILS:ES™; Paul H. Brookes Publishing Co., in press). He has numerous publications focusing on the development and assessment of bilingual (Spanish–English) children. He is a Fellow of the American Speech-Language-Hearing Association and received its highest award, Honors of the Association.

Brian A. Goldstein, Ph.D., CCC-SLP, Provost and Vice President for Academic Affairs, Professor of Communication Sciences and Disorders, La Salle University, 1900 West Olney Avenue, Philadelphia, PA 19141

Dr. Goldstein is Provost and Vice President for Academic Affairs and Professor of Communication Sciences and Disorders at La Salle University in Philadelphia. He received master's and doctoral degrees in speech-language pathology from Temple University and a bachelor's degree in linguistics and cognitive science from Brandeis University. He has published extensively in the area of speech sound development and disorders in bilingual populations.

Lisa M. Bedore, Ph.D., CCC-SLP, Professor and Chair, Communication Sciences and Disorders, College of Public Health, Temple University, 1701 N. 13th Street, Weiss Hall 113, Philadelphia, PA 19122

Dr. Bedore is Professor and Chair of the Communication Sciences and Disorders Department at Temple University in Philadelphia. She is a bilingual speech-language pathologist by training. Her research interests focus on understanding the nature of language impairment in bilingual children and the factors that influence language outcomes for bilingual children. Many of her publications focus on the relationships between bilingual language experience and language performance in bilingual children. A key practical application of this work is the identification of clinical markers of language impairment that can be applied to assessments such as the BESA.

Acknowledgments

We wish to express our deep appreciation to all of the students, clinicians, and researchers who have assisted us throughout the project. Each of them has contributed his or her unique expertise in making this a valid, reliable, and user-friendly assessment. Input from clinicians and researchers was sought and received throughout—from selecting the illustrations to providing guidance on the appropriateness of individual statistical analyses. A special thanks goes to the students at San Diego State University, Temple University, and The University of Texas at Austin who spent numerous hours putting together all of the materials, testing the children, and assisting with the data analysis. The clinicians involved at different stages of the project kept us grounded, provided us with great insight as to what would work best, and constantly prodded us to keep on going and publish a test that would allow them to make appropriate diagnosis. Researchers throughout the country have been our sounding board, and many have used our experimental version. Their insight and commitment to excellence is deeply appreciated.

We also owe a debt of gratitude to those who have come before us. Development of a bilingual test to identify language impairment has been a goal for several decades. Early efforts focused on developing local norms for measures adapted from available tests. From this early work—including our own—we learned what might work and what might not.

In addition, since the late 1990s, there has been an increasing interest in bilingualism and cross-linguistic differences and similarities in language acquisition. We were able to draw on this research to inform our questions, interpret our findings, and make systematic predictions. We thank all of those who have come before us because their research allowed us to further the quest for development of a bilingual test.

Although many have contributed to this endeavor, there are some individuals whom we wish to specifically acknowledge. We want to thank the members of the advisory board, who met with us each year of the project, for their wisdom, insights, and guidance:

- John Baugh
- Nan Bernstein Ratner
- Alicia Paredes-Scribner
- Nicki Nelson
- Bruce Tomblin
- Barbara Pearson

- Jon Miller
- Elena Plante

We are grateful to our consultants, who provided their expertise:

- Barbara Davis
- Darrell Sabers

Colleagues contributed data for the norms and/or data for the validity and reliability studies:

- Thomas Bohman
- Ron Gilliam
- Zenzi Griffin
- Rochel Lazewnik
- Laida Restrepo

Our doctoral students and research associates played key roles in coordinating data collection and analyses:

- Jissel Anaya
- Gabriela Simon-Cereijido
- Ellen Kester
- Barbara Hidalgo-Sotelo
- Leah Fabiano-Smith
- Anita Mendez Perez

Finally, we acknowledge the critically needed funding provided by the National Institute on Deafness and Other Communication Disorders: Contract No. N01-DC-8-2100 Development and Validation of a Language Test for Children Speaking Non-Standard English: A Study of Bilingual Hispanic Children. This contract represented a commitment to addressing inequities in assessment and treatment of communication disorders in Latino bilingual children in the United States. Through this 6-year project, we were able to make significant progress toward documenting bilingual language development and language impairment.

CHAPTER 1

Overview and Rationale for the BESA

The *Bilingual English–Spanish Assessment*™ (*BESA*™) was developed in response to the need for valid, reliable instruments for assessment of speech and language ability, along a continuum, in Spanish–English bilingual children ages 4 through 6 years. The BESA consists of two questionnaires, one activity, and three subtests in two languages. The questionnaires provide speech-language professionals with information about the child's language environment as well as aspects of parent and teacher concern. The Pragmatics activity provides an opportunity for the examiner to interact with the child and observe language use. The three subtests address the language domains of morphosyntax, semantics, and phonology in Spanish and English. Each component may be used independently or combined as part of an assessment battery; all subtests are norm referenced. The BESA should be administered by experienced Spanish–English bilingual speech-language professionals to ensure that valid results are obtained and interpreted accurately.

BESA COMPONENTS AND SUBTESTS

The BESA is a comprehensive assessment of a child's speech and language abilities in English and Spanish. Two ancillary questionnaires (BIOS and ITALK), should be completed to document language exposure and use while also allowing the examiner to develop a profile of parent and teacher concerns. BESA subtests address domains of phonology, morphosyntax, and semantics separately for both Spanish and English. There are three standardized and norm-referenced subtests addressing language ability and one criterion-referenced activity allowing observation of pragmatic language. Depending on whether both languages are tested and which subtests are included, administration of all BESA components may take between 1 hour (for one language) and 2 hours (for both languages).

Bilingual Input-Output Survey (BIOS)

The *Bilingual Input-Output Survey (BIOS)* helps the examiner to know when and in what context each of the child's two languages were used on a year-to-year basis. It is typically completed as part of an interview by the examiner. In this survey, parents are asked about the language exposure history of the child. In addition, parents and teachers are asked what language the child hears and uses during a typical school day and during a typical weekend day on an hour-by-hour basis. This information provides clinicians with information about relative use and exposure to each language and should be used prior to assessment to guide whether to test children in Spanish, English, or both. The parent survey (BIOS-Home) takes 10–15 minutes to complete; the teacher survey (BIOS-School) can be completed in 5–10 minutes.

Inventory to Assess Language Knowledge (ITALK)

The *Inventory to Assess Language Knowledge (ITALK)* addresses relative use of a child's two languages and five areas of speech and language development (vocabulary, grammar, sentence production, comprehension, and phonology) in Spanish and English. It is completed by the examiner as a parent and teacher interview. Parents and teachers are asked to identify the child's perceived level of performance in each language. Given before the BESA, the ITALK provides a summary of parent and teacher concerns that can be used to guide target areas of assessment. Results of the inventory can be used to interpret diagnostic results from BESA or other speech and language tests. The ITALK can be completed in 10 minutes or less.

BESA Pragmatics Activity

The Pragmatics activity is based on Fey's (1986) model of assertiveness and responsiveness. In an interactive format, children are asked to "help wrap a present" with the examiner. Through this realistic situation, obligatory contexts are set up to elicit different assertive and responsive acts. The Pragmatics activity utilizes English, Spanish, or both languages together (via code-switching), depending on the child's preferred language of interaction based on results from the BIOS and ITALK. The activity should be used to identify children who may encounter difficulties in situations that require the children to be active participants (e.g., in the classroom). If administered at the beginning of a battery of tests, the Pragmatics activity provides an excellent opportunity to establish rapport with the child and will also provide clinicians with an indication of how collaborative and interactive the child will be during the rest of the assessment. This activity takes 5–10 minutes to complete.

BESA Phonology Subtest

The Phonology subtest is a single-word phonological assessment. Its primary purpose is to differentially diagnose typical from atypical phonological skills in Spanish–English bilingual children. Analyses are also included that allow the examiner to profile a child's phonological skills in each language. The assessment includes two measures. The Spanish measure assesses phonological production of 28 Spanish words. The English measure assesses phonological production of 31 English words. The Phonology subtest takes 10–15 minutes to administer in each language, depending on the individual child (20–30 minutes total).

BESA Morphosyntax Subtest

The Morphosyntax subtest employs cloze and sentence repetition tasks to target grammatical morphemes and sentence structures that were predicted to be difficult for children with language impairment (LI) in English or Spanish (Bedore & Leonard, 1998, 2001; Leonard, 2014). Forms tested in English include plural –s, possessive –s, past and present tense, third-person singular, progressives, copulas, auxiliary do + negatives, and passives as well as sentence repetition items to test complex verb forms, conjunctions, and embedded prepositions and noun phrases. Forms tested in Spanish include articles, progressives, clitics, and subjunctives using a cloze procedure. Preterite, complex verb forms, and conjunctions are included using sentence repetition. For each language, a grammatical cloze subscore, a sentence repetition subscore, and a total score that is a composite of those two subscores are derived. The Morphosyntax subtest takes approximately 15 minutes to administer in each language (30 minutes total).

BESA Semantics Subtest

The Semantics subtest targets six tasks: analogies, characteristic properties, categorization, functions, linguistic concepts, and similarities and differences. These six item types were based on the literature describing acquisition of semantic breadth and depth in order to tap into how children organize and gain access to their lexical system (Peña, Bedore, & Rappazzo, 2003).

The English Semantics subtest has a total of 25 items: 10 receptive and 15 expressive. The Spanish Semantics subtest also has 25 items: 12 receptive and 13 expressive. Scoring allows for code-mixing—giving children credit for a correct response in either language. Subscores are provided for semantics receptive and semantics expressive, and a total semantics score is also provided for each language. The Semantics subtest takes about 15 minutes to administer in each language (30 minutes total).

USES OF THE BESA

The BESA is designed to be used with children who speak English, Spanish, or both. The BESA subtests are psychometrically sound and yield scaled and standard scores for each of the domain tests (phonology, morphosyntax, and semantics). The BIOS and ITALK questionnaires provide criterion-based guidelines to determine language(s) of testing and to develop an assessment strategy. The tests can be used together for a complete speech and language battery, or tests specific to the diagnostic question can be selected. Presently, the test is appropriate for children between the ages of 4;0 and 6;11. The BESA can be used to

1. Identify LI in bilingual and monolingual Latino children
2. Document progress in speech and language related to intervention
3. Document the dominant language in each domain, including morphosyntax, semantics, and phonology
4. Conduct research studies of bilingual children with and without language impairment

Identification of Language Impairment

The BESA is specifically designed to assess speech and language in English–Spanish bilingual children's two languages. The primary use of the BESA is to identify phonological and/or language impairment in bilingual and English language learner (ELL) children via a standardized protocol. The objective scores obtained on the BESA across three domains can be used in combination with clinical observations and language samples, as well as with other standardized measures, to identify children with speech and/or language impairment. Through use of a combination of BESA subtests, clinicians can document children's speech and language strengths and weaknesses.

Documentation of Progress

A second use of the BESA is to monitor children's progress in speech and language. After initiation of a speech and language intervention program, children's progress should be regularly documented. It is recommended that more sensitive daily probes be used to monitor children's session-to-session progress and that this information be used to make decisions about the direction of the intervention. The BESA, however, is sensitive to year-to-year changes in children's speech and language growth and the particular language in which progress is being made. Thus, in addition to more sensitive measures of daily progress, the BESA can be used at broader intervals (e.g., annually or semiannually) to gauge progress in a specific program of intervention, to document continued need for intervention, and to document achievement of treatment goals for exiting services.

Documentation of Language Input and Output

Documentation of a bilingual student's dominant language is a challenge in school settings. Many children who have exposure to more than one language demonstrate mixed dominance, whereby they perform higher in one language in one domain but higher in the other language in a different domain. It is therefore important to know what a child's relative dominance is across different domains of speech and language. This information can be useful for planning intervention as well as for planning educational programming for bilingual children. The BIOS-Home and BIOS-School surveys together provide an objective measure of children's input and output of Spanish and English. This information helps speech-language pathologists, parents, teachers, and administrators to know how much the child hears and uses each language and in what contexts. This information is independent of performance, which can be affected by child characteristics such as language ability. In addition to the BIOS, the Spanish and English standardized test scores can be compared directly for phonology, morphosyntax, and semantics to determine a child's best language for a particular domain. If children's standard scores across domains are within 5 points of each other, we consider them to be balanced.

Research Uses

There are a number of ways that the BESA subtests can be used in research. ITALK can be used to gain parent and teacher observations about the child's performance across five domains of speech and language in Spanish and English as part of qualifying data for a study. BIOS can be used to document weekly input and output in Spanish and English as a way of grouping children by language experience and/or by year of first exposure. For bilingual children with LI, BIOS provides a measure that is independent of their test performance on speech and language tasks.

The three domain subtests can be used together or independently to assess children's speech and language. These can be used to qualify children for a study or to group children by ability.

As of this writing, we have conducted and published several studies with the longer, experimental versions of BESA subtests (Peña, Bedore, & Kester, 2016). In addition, researchers across the country have used the experimental versions of BESA in studies of bilingual Spanish–English speakers (Castilla, Restrepo, & Perez-Leroux, 2009; Fabiano-Smith & Barlow, 2010; Kapantzoglou, Fergadiotis, & Restrepo, 2017; Restrepo, Morgan, & Thompson, 2013; Rodriguez, Bustamante, Wood, & Sundeman, 2017). Researchers in Spanish-speaking countries are in the process of using the Spanish version of these measures in research studies (Auza, Harom, & Murata, 2018; Jackson-Maldonado, Hoist, Mejia, Peña, & Bedore, 2015). The BESA (or BESA subtests) has been included in two evidence-based reviews (Dollaghan & Horner, 2011; McLeod & Verdon, 2014). We hope to see continued use of the BESA in research; this can only help to improve the measure.

NEED FOR BILINGUAL ASSESSMENT INSTRUMENTS

Spanish speakers are the largest language minority in the United States, and they make up 79% of school-age English-language learners. Typically, these children begin to learn English when they enter preschool. Evaluation of these children is particularly challenging, because diagnostic assessments cannot rely solely on the child's proficiency in the second language. School-based speech-language pathologists who work with young bilingual/bicultural children are highly aware of the need for more information about bilingualism (Caesar & Kohler, 2007; Winter, 1999). Speech-language pathologists know that they need to assess and treat these children in different ways. Some speech-language pathologists prefer to err on the side of providing intervention for children who may not need it, whereas others are less likely to refer for services if the child is younger (presumably related to needing time to develop bilingual competence).

In general, a challenge for test developers in the field of speech-language pathology has been to develop tests with good classification accuracy. For English monolingual children, there are a handful of available tests that provide sufficient evidence about reliability, validity, and classification accuracy for clinical use (Betz, Eickhoff, Sullivan, Nippold, & Schneider, 2013; Friberg, 2010; McCauley & Swisher, 1984a, 1984b; Spaulding, Plante, & Farinella, 2006). For bilingual children, however, there are very few assessment tools and fewer with evidence about reliability and validity.

Important considerations for the development of language tests for bilingual children are their cultural and linguistic appropriateness as well as the extent to which they address variability in children's first and second language experiences. Early attempts to develop tests for other language groups included translation, but it is generally agreed that translated tests do not have the same psychometric properties as the original test (Arnold & Matus, 2000; Bracken & Barona, 1991; Peña, 2007). In addition, to identify speech and language impairment, it is critical that the test is developed based on the markers of the target language that are likely to help make diagnostic decisions. Translated tests from English may emphasize forms that are not clinically sensitive in another language. Another challenge in the assessment of bilinguals is that children vary greatly in the amount and kind of experiences they have in each language. It is difficult to know in what language bilinguals should be tested, and if they are tested in both languages, there are few guidelines for combining the results of testing in the two languages. In the development of the BESA, we addressed many of these issues in order to help clinicians make accurate, reliable diagnostic decisions.

Testing Bilingual Children

The BESA is based on the growing literature on the acquisition of Spanish in the United States where children are exposed to or learning English, and on the literature on LI in each language. Data on Spanish-speaking children with LI show that the elements that may discriminate children with LI from their typically developing peers are different in Spanish and English (see Leonard, 2014 for an overview of cross-linguistic differences). Thus, to create a test with a comparable level of difficulty in English and Spanish, language-specific item sets are needed. For example, a study of children's performance on vocabulary tests shows that tasks used to assess vocabulary may not be as familiar to Latino children as to mainstream children (Peña & Quinn, 1997). In addition, children may demonstrate their knowledge in different ways. Such a result means it is necessary to build tests around tasks that are familiar to test takers. Given the variability in bilingual speakers' knowledge, a test (and scoring procedure) that permits speakers to demonstrate their knowledge on a variety of item types, while also offering response alternatives regarding content and code-switching, has the potential to reveal the child's true language abilities.

THEORETICAL BACKGROUND

Normal Bilingual Acquisition

In Bialystok's description of the conditions under which bilingual children acquire language, she stated that "monolingual and bilingual children move in different cognitive worlds, experience different linguistic environments, and are challenged to communicate using different resources remaining sensitive to different abstract dimensions" (2001, p. 88). It is important to understand the context in which children are learning each language and the particular demands of those languages. To develop effective bilingual language assessment instruments, it is important to identify linguistic markers (e.g., grammatical forms, semantic knowledge) that differentiate between children with and without LI in each of their two languages.

As a group, bilingual children vary greatly in the amount and types of experiences that they have in each language. This is a special challenge for developing language assessment tools for bilingual language learners. Some children start learning two languages from birth; others start learning their second language later, when they start school. Yet other children may start getting exposed to their second language via older siblings. Different contexts for hearing and using two language results in considerable variability among children. It is important to document both similarities and differences in monolingual and bilingual language development in the areas of pragmatics, phonology, morphosyntax, and semantics.

Pragmatics is the ability to use language in social communication, conveying the communication needs and intentions of the speaker and the listener. According to Fey (1986), the speech acts used in conversations can be categorized as assertive and responsive acts. *Assertive acts* comprise the ability to initiate topics and various forms of requests or statements about events. *Responsive acts* comprise responses to a communication partner. Both assertive and responsive acts can be verbal or nonverbal.

Most research on phonological development has taken place with monolingual English speakers. There are fewer studies focusing on Spanish–English bilingual children. Overall, findings from existing studies on bilingual children indicate that phonological development is similar, although not identical, to that of monolingual speakers (Fabiano-Smith & Barlow, 2010; Gildersleeve-Neumann & Wright, 2010; Grech & Dodd, 2008; Xuereb, Grech, & Dodd, 2011). Although there are studies indicating that monolinguals exhibit a more rapid rate of acquisition compared to bilinguals, the phonological skills of bilinguals are still within developmental expectations compared to monolingual children (see Goldstein & Gildersleeve-Neumann, 2012). More specifically, the trajectory of phonological development for bilingual children is not remarkably different from that of monolingual speakers in either language. Their phonologies exhibit the same universal properties that monolingual children show. They initially exhibit stops, nasals, glides, and simple syllable structures and develop anterior sounds before posterior ones and sonorants before obstruents. As children get older, their phonological systems become attuned to the specific ambient languages they are acquiring, and they are able to separate the two languages. As is the case with monolingual speakers, their phonological system has largely developed by age 7 to 8 years, and they are able to produce phonologically long and complex syllables and words.

A common hallmark of typical phonological development in second language learners is cross-linguistic influence (Wilson, Davidson, & Martin, 2014). For example, the

Spanish flap might be used in an English production such that "rake" /ɹek/ is produced as [ɾek]. These effects are often bidirectional, not only from Language A to Language B but also from Language B to Language A. For example, the Spanish word "flor" /floɾ/ may be produced with the English –r, yielding [floɹ].

Grammar emerges as children have increased exposure to each of their languages, resulting in the production of longer and more complex sentences (Deuchar & Quay, 2000). Bilingual children produce many of the same types of grammatical errors as monolinguals (Bland-Stewart & Fitzgerald, 2001; Gutiérrez-Clellen, Restrepo, & Simon-Cereijido, 2006; Gutiérrez-Clellen & Simon-Cereijido, 2007; Gutiérrez-Clellen, Simon-Cereijido, & Wagner, 2008; Restrepo & Kruth, 2000). Yet knowledge of linguistic rules in each language may differ to some extent between monolinguals and bilinguals. For example, Punjabi–English bilingual school-age children used English-influenced word order when speaking in Punjabi (Martin, Krishnamurthy, Bhardwaj, & Charles, 2003). These cross-language influences are also observed in adults. For example, Montrul (2002) found that adult Spanish–English bilinguals who acquired both languages before age 7 use the imperfect/preterite distinction differently across languages than do monolingual Spanish speakers.

Work with Spanish-speaking children who are exposed to English shows that by age 8 to 9 years, children produce complex noun phrases, relative clauses, and greater clausal density, and they use these structures to make effective use of nominal, pronominal, elliptical, and demonstrative reference in narrative tasks (Gutiérrez-Clellen & Iglesias, 1992). These are skills that are evident in English learning as well. Complex semantic knowledge in narratives is reflected in bilingual children's use of mental-state verbs to express subtle differences in characters' perceptions of events in a story in Spanish as well as in English (Gutiérrez-Clellen, 2002; Silliman, Huntley Bahr, Brea, Hnath-Chisolm, & Mahecha, 2001). At the same time, bilinguals do not demonstrate the exact same set of skills as do their monolingual peers. For example, in a study of Spanish–English bilingual children's narrative production, Fiestas and Peña (2004) found that children told stories of similar length and number of propositions, but the specific story components they included were related to the language in which the story was told.

In development, bilingual children acquire the same kinds of words and structures as do their monolingual peers—even if the specific words they know vary. For example, similar to monolingual development, bilingual toddlers demonstrate rapid growth in vocabulary knowledge. Bilingual children use many of the same lexical constraints to narrow down word meaning as do their monolingual peers (Frank & Poulin-Dubois, 2002; Merriman & Kutlesic, 1993; Poulin-Dubois, Frank, Graham, & Elkin, 1999), but they may not know the same words in each language. For example, depending on their experiences, children may provide the words *banana*, *orange*, and *apple* in English but *papaya*, *mango*, and *piña* (*pineapple*) in Spanish. From infancy through adulthood, bilinguals demonstrate shared and unique vocabulary (Deuchar & Quay, 2000). Gaps in vocabulary can be problematic for school-age children who must use specific words in academic tasks (Carlo et al., 2004). However, bilinguals may use their knowledge of vocabulary in one language as a bootstrap to facilitate word learning in the other (Gawlitzek-Maiwald & Tracy, 1996; Ordóñez, Carlo, Snow, & McLaughlin, 2002).

Variation in Bilingual Language Proficiency as a Function of Exposure

A unique aspect of bilingual language development is proficiency as a function of language learning experiences. The amount of time children use and hear each language influences children's language performance. For example, Anderson (1995, 2001) documented gradual decreases in accuracy of number and gender agreement, as well as decreasing syntactic complexity, in case studies of children who used more English than Spanish over time. Montrul (2002) found that young adults who acquired English between birth and 7 years used the imperfect/preterite distinction less accurately than did individuals who immigrated to the United States and started to acquire English between 8 years and college age. Differing degrees of exposure may also affect access to lexical semantic knowledge. Kohnert and colleagues observed age-related changes in Spanish–English bilinguals' ability to produce and comprehend words in English and Spanish from the age of 5 through young adulthood (Anderson, 2001; Kohnert & Bates, 2002; Kohnert, Bates, & Hernández, 1999; Kohnert, Hernández, & Bates, 1998).

Exposure to each language may also influence performance differently across domains. For example, Bohman, Bedore, Peña, Mendez-Perez, and Gillam (2010) found that language use was significantly correlated with grammatical production, whereas hearing and using a language were significantly correlated with measures of semantics. Similarly, Bedore et al. (2012) found that across different levels of first- and second-language exposure, children varied on their performance on semantics and morphosyntax tasks. This level of variation in bilinguals may result in "mixed" language performance in which children are stronger in one language in one domain but in the other language in another domain. Our research (e.g., Bedore, Peña, Gillam, & Ho, 2010; Bedore, Peña, Griffin, & Hixon, 2016) documents that about 66% of the bilinguals we tested showed mixed dominance. These findings are consistent with other language pairs as well; for example, French–English bilinguals (Paradis, Crago, Genesee, & Rice, 2003).

LANGUAGE IMPAIRMENT IN BILINGUALS

Bilingual children with speech and language impairment have many of the same difficulties in the domains of speech and language as monolingual children. Children with LI may have difficulties with grammatical morphology and language productivity. Some children have additional difficulties with comprehension of language. Furthermore, children with LI are characterized by their difficulties in learning, organizing, and retrieving words, and making lexical-semantic associations. Sometimes children with LI have difficulties using language appropriately, and this may result in communicative breakdowns when interacting with adults and peers. In the speech area, children may have difficulty producing all the sounds of their language, making it difficult to understand what they are saying.

It is difficult to determine whether speech and language errors made by bilinguals are due to language differences or to speech and language impairment (Botting, Conti-Ramsden, & Crutchley, 1997; Damico, Oller, & Storey, 1983; Schiff-Meyers, 1992). Differences in grammar, distributed semantic knowledge, cultural experience, and sound systems can affect bilinguals' performance on assessments focusing on pragmatics, phonology, morphosyntax, and semantics. Research over the last 10 years has demonstrated an increased focus on understanding the nature of speech and language impairment in bilingual children (Blom & Boerma, 2017; Goldstein & Gildersleeve-Neumann, 2012; O'Toole & Hickey, 2013; Paradis, Jia, & Arppe, 2017; Peña & Bedore, 2009).

Pragmatics and Language Impairment

Although there is some contradictory evidence about the existence of pragmatics deficits in children diagnosed with specific language impairment (SLI), there are subsets of language-impaired children who demonstrate difficulty in responding to and expressing communicative intent. The work of Bonifacio et al. (2007) clearly demonstrated that children who are both less assertive and less responsive are likely to be at greater risk for LI, because their lack of assertiveness and responsiveness limits the quantity and quality of their interactions with others.

Phonological Impairment in Bilinguals

There are relatively few studies examining phonological skills in bilingual children with phonological disorders. Not surprisingly, bilingual children with phonological disorders exhibit more errors, lower consonant accuracy scores, and higher percentages of occurrence for phonological error patterns than do either typically developing bilingual children or typically developing monolingual children of either language (Goldstein, 2000). Moreover, the types of errors the bilingual children exhibited are similar to those produced by monolingual speakers with phonological disorders. Such types include errors on fricatives, clusters, and liquids. Typical error patterns are cluster reduction, unstressed syllable deletion, and liquid simplification. Bilingual children also show error types not typically associated with typically developing monolingual or bilingual speakers, such as backing and initial consonant deletion. It should be noted, however, that bilingual children will not necessarily exhibit error types with the same frequency in each language. For example, in Spanish–English bilinguals, final consonant deletion will be higher in English than in Spanish, because Spanish contains fewer final consonants in its inventory (Goldstein et al., 2008).

Phonology and Language Impairment

The earliest signs of LI are often delays in the onset of speech and language. At preschool and early school age, children who demonstrate deficits in vocabulary and grammar also demonstrate weak phonological skills (Shriberg & Austin, 1998). Phonological impairment has been associated with deficits in grammatical production, a hallmark deficit of LI (Cooperson, Bedore, & Peña, 2013; Shriberg & Austin). Common phonological processes such as weak syllable deletion are associated with lower-than-expected production of grammatical forms (Aguilar-Mediavilla, Sanz-Torrent, & Serra-Raventós, 2007; Royle & Stine, 2013). Often, children with LI demonstrate single-word receptive vocabulary within the average range for their age. However, comparisons with typically developing children show that their scores are often significantly below those of their typical peers (McGregor, 2009).

Morphosyntax and Language Impairment in Bilinguals

In the area of morphosyntax, findings indicate that bilingual children with LI demonstrate patterns of impairment similar to but not exactly like those of their monolingual peers with primary LI. For example, Salameh, Håkansson, and Nettelbladt (2004) followed Swedish–Arabic bilingual preschoolers with and without LI over a 1-year period. Although children with LI demonstrated delays in both languages, their development followed the predicted trajectory in each of their languages. These findings appear to be similar across many other language pairs as well. Paradis and colleagues (2003) compared the grammatical errors of French–English bilingual children to those of their monolingual peers in each language. The bilinguals with LI produced errors in tense-related morphemes in each of their languages.

There are also some error patterns, however, that are somewhat different from those of monolingual children with and without LI. Jacobson and Schwartz (2002) reported that in English, bilingual school-age children with LI produced qualitatively different errors in verb marking than did their typically developing peers. Typically developing bilingual children overregularized irregular verbs (e.g., *runned* for *ran*). In contrast, children with LI used the unmarked form (e.g., *run* for *ran*). Restrepo and Kruth (2000) compared the language skills of two 7-year-olds (one with and one without LI) who had begun to acquire English at school entry. In spite of the similar patterns of exposure to the two languages, the children demonstrated different patterns of grammatical production. The child with LI demonstrated greater loss of her first language than did her typical language peer, as indicated by changes in mean length utterance (MLU) and grammaticality. In English, she used fewer verb forms, and those that are commonly difficult for children with LI (e.g., past-tense forms, third-person singular present tense) were produced less accurately.

In the area of grammatical morphology, Spanish–English and French–English bilinguals have patterns of error similar to those of monolingual English speakers (Gutiérrez-Clellen & Simon-Cereijido, 2007) when English is their dominant language. For example, Gutiérrez-Clellen et al. (2008) compared bilingual Spanish–English speakers and English-as-a-first-language speakers, with and without LI, on measures of verb marking and subject use. They found that both groups of children with LI scored significantly lower than their typical peers. In this analysis, there were no significant effects associated with bilingual status. Similarly, German monolingual and Turkish–German bilingual children with LI showed similar patterns of error on agreement-marked verb forms (Rothweiler, Chilla, & Clahsen, 2012). A comparison of monolingual Dutch and bilingual Frisian–Dutch children with LI demonstrated more agreement errors and greater omissions with increased complexity in Dutch compared to monolingual Dutch speakers without LI (Spoelman & Bol, 2012). There were no significant differences between monolingual and bilingual children with LI. Together, these studies demonstrate that monolinguals and bilinguals with LI show similar patterns of impairment when compared in their stronger language.

For children who are in the process of learning a second language, findings are not as clear. In a large study of risk for LI in Spanish–English bilingual preschoolers, Gutiérrez-Clellen et al. (2008) found that typically developing children who were ELLs and whose best language was Spanish made errors on finite verb use (consistent with the performance of children with LI) but not on nominative subject use (consistent with the performance of typically developing children). Similarly, Peña, Gillam, Bedore, and Bohman (2011) found that English-dominant bilinguals and monolinguals scored similarly in English. Spanish-dominant bilinguals and monolinguals scored similarly in Spanish on screening measures of morphosyntax and semantics. Bilingual children, however, who were defined as those using and hearing both languages between 40% and 60% on average, demonstrated lower scores compared to both Spanish and English monolinguals. At the individual level, they demonstrated more mixed patterns of performance in each language, so that their scores were below the average range in one but not both of their languages (see also Bedore et al., 2012). Thus, children in the process of learning a second language may present with patterns that are similar to children with LI and to those with typical development when tested in only one language. Similar to the patterns found for English-dominant bilinguals, Spanish-speaking children with LI from bilingual backgrounds present many of the same kinds of errors that are reported for monolingual Spanish-speaking children. Early work with monolingual or functionally monolingual children showed that Spanish learners have the most difficulties with articles and direct-object clitics (Ambert, 1986; Bedore & Leonard, 2001; Bosch & Serra, 1997; Simon-Cereijido & Gutiérrez-Clellen, 2007).

Difficulties involving overregularization of past tense and adjective agreement were also noted. Restrepo and Gutiérrez-Clellen (2001) reported that Spanish-speaking 5- to 7-year-old children with LI who were exposed to English had significant difficulties with definite articles. The most common errors were omissions and gender errors. Jacobson and Schwartz (2002) evaluated clitic production and verb-tense marking in incipient bilingual preschoolers with LI who used Spanish but had passive knowledge of English. These children produced verb-tense markers accurately but produced clitics with 65% accuracy as compared to the 84% accuracy of their typically developing peers. Recent research with Spanish-speaking children with LI indicates that the combination of correct use of articles, verbs, and clitics has fair discrimination accuracy, and that incorporating semantic-syntactic complexity measures, such as MLU, omissions of direct objects, and use of indirect objects, can increase diagnostic accuracy in assessments.

Semantics and Language Impairment in Bilinguals

Children with LI also make errors in the semantic domain. Bilingual children with LI demonstrate delays in early vocabulary in both their languages (Thordardottir, Ellis Weismer, & Evans, 2002; Thordardottir, Ellis Weismer, & Smith, 1997). In addition, they have difficulty organizing and gaining access to the lexical system.

The types of errors seen in monolingual English-speaking children with LI are also observed in other languages as well as in bilinguals. In Ambert's (1986) study of monolingual Spanish speakers with LI, participants' word-use errors suggested poor representation of word meaning and possible word-finding difficulties. Some examples included word substitutions (e.g., música/"music" for película/"movie") and circumlocution (no hace frío y hace calor/"it's not cold and it's hot" for verano/"summer"). Sheng, McGregor, and Marian (2006) explored lexical-semantic organization in Mandarin–English bilingual and English monolingual children. Performance on a repeated associations task in which children responded with a related word, such as "chair" when given a prompt such as "table," indicated that both bilinguals and monolinguals had similar patterns of associations within language. For bilinguals, performance across languages was similar. This work has been extended to Spanish–English bilinguals (Sheng, Bedore, Peña, & Fiestas, 2013) and to Spanish–English bilinguals with LI (Sheng, Bedore, Peña, & Taliancich-Klinger, 2013; Sheng, Peña, Bedore, & Fiestas, 2012). Findings from this work suggest that children with LI have sparse lexical-semantic networks. Specifically, compared to their typically developing peers, they had significant difficulty generating words associated with a given target.

Semantics is one area in which children can mix their two languages. Yet, whereas some children use code-mixing or code-switching, not all bilinguals do. Work by Greene, Peña, and Bedore (2013) demonstrated that on a test of semantics, about 50% of the children code-mixed in Spanish or English, and a small subset code-mixed in both. Mixing was related to language dominance consistent with reports by Gutiérrez-Clellen, Simon-Cereijido, and Leone (2009). Children at risk for LI, however, were more likely to make errors even when they employed code-mixing. These findings are consistent with the notion that children with LI have sparse lexical-semantic networks (McGregor, 2009).

Semantics and Language Impairment in Bilinguals

CHAPTER 2

Preparing to Test

The BESA should be used by bilingual speech-language pathologists who are fluent in Spanish and English. It is designed for use with Latino children between the ages of 4;0 and 6;11.

CHILD ELIGIBILITY

Latino children in the United States, Canada, and other English-speaking countries who speak Spanish or English or both are eligible for assessment using the BESA. Although the test was specifically developed for U.S. bilingual children, a small number of monolingual English-speaking European American and African American children have taken the English version of the test. Thus far, we have found no significant differences across the scores of monolingual English speakers from Latino American, African American, and European American backgrounds.

There are some groups who are using the Spanish version of the BESA in Spanish-speaking countries. As yet, however, we do not know how children from monolingual Spanish backgrounds residing outside the United States would compare to the current sample. A preliminary study of monolingual children in Mexico shows that children with typical development score a little higher than U.S. bilinguals with 80% exposure to Spanish (Jackson-Maldonado et al., 2015). We expect that monolingual children with LI would score significantly below their typical peers, but the cutpoints for determining LI in this population need to be determined. Thus, scores obtained on the Spanish version of the test outside the United States should be interpreted with caution.

EXAMINER QUALIFICATIONS

Examiners who use the BESA should have appropriate training in test administration and interpretation. Typically, such training involves coursework in tests and measurement as well as supervised clinical experience in diagnostics. In addition to these basic competencies, examiners should have knowledge of bilingual language acquisition as well as knowledge of speech and language impairment patterns in Spanish and English. Coursework in this area is available in some graduate programs as part of a bilingual specialization. Other ways that bilingual speech-language pathologists gain training in this area is through independent study and workshops. Bilingual Spanish–English fluency is highly desirable. The examiner should be able to converse with native-like fluency with the child and family and should be able to differentiate dialectical variants from speech and language errors with accuracy.

If the BESA will be used by a trained interpreter, bilingual assistant, or bilingual student, the supervising speech-language pathologist is responsible for interpretation of the test scores and for making the diagnosis. The supervising speech-language pathologist should ensure that the test procedures are carefully followed and that the interpreter, assistant, or student is appropriately trained in administration and scoring of the BESA. Data on the BIOS and ITALK can be successfully collected by a trained interviewer who is a member of the assessment team or by a bilingual assistant; scoring and interpretation of the data from these two questionnaires is the responsibility of the trained examiner.

TRAINING PROCEDURES

It is important for examiners to thoroughly familiarize themselves with the test procedures, possible child responses, and scoring of the individual test items, as described in Chapter 3. Specific examples of correct and incorrect test responses are provided in Chapter 3 and Appendix A and should be reviewed prior to test administration. It is strongly recommended that the Phonology and Morphosyntax subtests be audiorecorded (with permission from all participants) to ensure accurate transcription and scoring of the target items. Before administering the BESA for the first time, examiners should practice the elicitation scripts and feedback so that the instructions and vocabulary are familiar. Note the alternative instructions and possible responses indicated in Chapter 3 before starting the evaluation.

ORDER OF ADMINISTRATION

The order of the tests is somewhat flexible, depending on the presenting assessment questions, the needs of the child, and available time. Generally, it is recommended that the ITALK and BIOS surveys be administered prior to the direct assessment in order to determine the language of testing and to select which tests to administer. For bilingual children, generally the Spanish version should be given first. This is because in previous studies by these authors, it was shown that children are likely to switch to English when being tested in Spanish but are less likely to switch from English to Spanish, even if they know the correct response in Spanish (Bedore, Peña, García, & Cortez, 2005). This pattern of response may occur because bilingual and ELL children in the United States, even from a very young age, recognize that English is the language of schooling (Gutiérrez-Clellen et al., 2009; Huerta, 1977). Beginning the testing in Spanish gives those students every opportunity to demonstrate their knowledge.

It is also recommended that tests for the two languages be given on different days. Thus, Spanish Pragmatics, Phonology, Morphosyntax, and Semantics subtests might be given on one day and the English versions of the same subtests on another day. Because the Spanish and English versions are not direct translations of each other, test responses in one language should not influence responses in the other language.

Finally, for especially young or shy children, we recommend beginning with the Pragmatics activity, which can serve as an exercise that children enjoy doing, while also building rapport with the examiner. Phonology, which requires single-word naming, can also serve as a useful warm-up task prior to Morphosyntax or Semantics subtests.

TESTING TIME

Examiners should allow approximately 1 hour per language to conduct the complete battery of BESA components. If administering all the tests in both languages, allow at least 2 sessions. Experience indicates that most children enjoy taking the test and remain involved for the duration of its administration in each language. If the child, however, has a limited attention span, it is advisable to administer the BESA over more than one testing session for each language. We recommend completing the testing within 2 weeks. The BIOS and ITALK together will take about 20 minutes to complete with the family and about 10 minutes for teachers to complete.

TESTING ENVIRONMENT

The test should occur in a quiet, well-lit, well-ventilated room that is free of distractions. Testing a child while corner-sitting at a child-sized table is the most typical setting. Those administering the test should use their clinical judgment and knowledge of the surroundings to determine the setting that is most conducive to a good testing environment. Examiners also must be responsive to the child's needs.

CHAPTER 3

BESA Administration and Scoring

This chapter describes the procedures used to administer and score the BESA Spanish and English Protocols as well as the instructions for the use of BIOS, ITALK, and the Pragmatics activity. Although they are not scored components of the BESA, the BIOS and the ITALK will help clinicians decide which languages to assess and how to interpret the results of the assessment. BIOS provides the examiner with information about the child's language history over time as well as current use and exposure to each language in the home, school, and other settings. In turn, ITALK provides information about the child's proficiency in both languages. As mentioned previously, it is recommended to administer the BIOS and ITALK questionnaires prior to testing with the BESA. The Pragmatics activity, as a rapport-building exercise, ensures that the child's responses reflect his or her best effort, while also allowing the examiner to observe how the child uses language interactions when engaged in a familiar activity. The three subtests allow in-depth analyses of phonology, morphosyntax, and semantics abilities in both Spanish and English. See Figure 3.1 for a flowchart showing how the questionnaires and protocols work together.

BILINGUAL INPUT-OUTPUT SURVEY (BIOS)

The BIOS addresses the child's language exposure history and current use of Spanish and English in the home (BIOS-Home) and at school (BIOS-School). The BIOS-Home form can be completed over the telephone or in person with the parent. Many parents are able to complete the form accurately on their own, but we have found that completing it in an interview helps to better identify parent concerns. The BIOS-School form can be completed by the examiner via an interview with the teacher.

BIOS-Home: Administration

For the BIOS-Home Form, start by introducing yourself to the parent and explaining its purpose. Ask what language they prefer to be interviewed in. The BIOS survey has two parts. First, the examiner asks questions about the year-by-year exposure to English and Spanish at home and in daycare or school:

We are interested in your child's history of language exposure each year. Let's start with the first year. What language did you and your family use at home since birth: Spanish, English, or both?

Quisiéramos saber el uso de lenguaje en su hogar, empezando desde que su hijo/a nació. Cuando su hijo/a nació ¿qué idioma usaron en casa: español, inglés, o los dos?

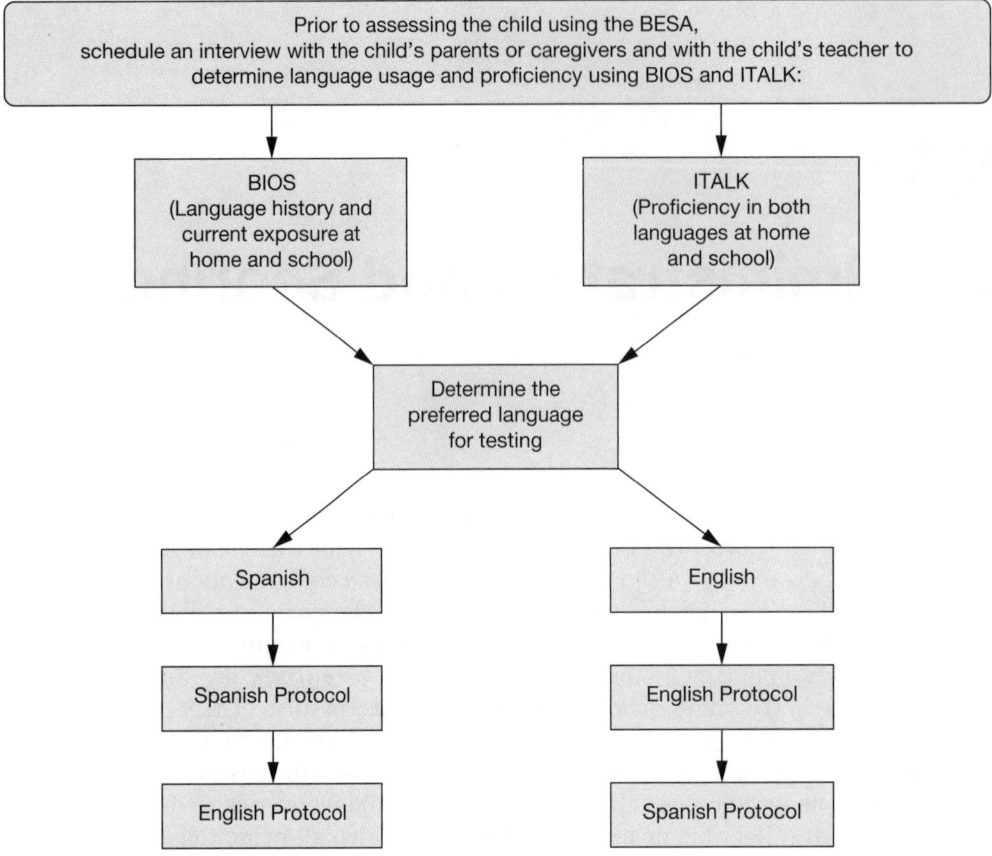

Figure 3.1. BESA forms flow chart.

From 1 to 2 years old, what language did you and your family use at home since birth: Spanish, English, or both? *(Fill out up to child's current age.)*

Y cuando tenía un año, ¿qué idioma usaron en casa: español, inglés, o los dos? *(Complete hasta la edad actual del niño/a).*

Did your child attend day care or preschool? *(If yes, continue.)*

¿Su hijo/a asistía a la guardería infantil o al centro pre-escolar? *(Si contesta sí, continúe.)*

How old was he or she when enrolled in day care? What language did the day care or preschool use: Spanish, English, or both? *(If yes to day care, complete for the ages the child was in day care or preschool.)*

¿Desde qué edad? ¿Qué idioma usaron en la guardería infantil: español, inglés, o los dos? *(Complete las edades en que el niño/a asistió a la guardería infantil o al centro pre-escolar.)*

On the form, check whether the child heard Spanish, English, or both languages at home for each age, through the child's current age. Then, complete the information for the years that the child was at daycare or preschool for the corresponding years. Check *N/A* if the child was not in daycare or preschool for any given year (see Figure 3.2). The summary totals should be entered on the form at the bottom of the table (see Figure 3.2). In the example shown in Figure 3.2, the child had exposure to both languages for

	At Home			At School/Preschool/Day Care			
Ages	Both	Spanish	English	Both	Spanish	English	NA
0-1		✓					✓
1-2		✓				✓	
2-3		✓				✓	
3-4	✓					✓	
4-5	✓					✓	
5-6	✓					✓	
6-7							
7-8							
8-9							

Total # of years in:	Both	Spanish	English	Both	Spanish	English	NA
	3	3	0	0	0	5	1
First year of exposure to English: 1-2							

Figure 3.2. BIOS–Home Form: Language exposure at home versus daycare/preschool.

3 years, Spanish for 3 years, and English at daycare for 5 years. The year of first English exposure was 1–2 years of age.

Next, you'll ask questions about the child's current exposure to Spanish and English. Explain to the parent that you are trying to gain a picture of the child's language use and exposure for a typical day of the week and during the weekend. Use the following script to introduce this section:

During the week: We're interested in what a typical day during the week is like for your child: what activities s/he participates in, who s/he interacts with, and what language(s) s/he uses and hears

Durante la semana: Quisiéramos saber qué hace su hijo/a en un día normal durante la semana. ¿En qué actividades participa, con quién, y qué idiomas usa y escucha?

During the weekend: We're interested in what a typical day during the weekend is like for your child: who s/he interacts with and what language(s) s/he uses and hears

Durante el fin de semana: Quisiéramos saber qué hace su hijo/a en un día normal durante el fin de semana. ¿Con quién participa en actividades, y qué idiomas usa y escucha?

You may need to guide parents through a typical weekday with suggestions as follows:

What time does (child's name) *get up? Who is with him/her and what language is used? In what language does your child respond?*

¿A qué hora se despierta? ¿A esa hora con quién está? ¿Y en qué idioma habla con él/ella? ¿Y en qué idioma contesta?

During what hours is (child's name) *at school?* (BIOS-School will be used to fill in exposure/use for that time.)	*¿A qué hora se va a la escuela y a qué hora sale?* (El cuestionario BIOS-School se usará para completar el uso del idioma durante ese tiempo.)
What does your child do when s/he gets home from school? Who is s/he with? What language do they use? In what language does the child respond?	*¿Qué hace después de la escuela? ¿Y con quién está? ¿Y en qué idioma habla con él/ella? ¿Y en qué idioma contesta?*
If the parent needs examples: *For example, go to the park, go to the store, play with brothers and sisters or friends, do homework.*	Si el padre necesita ejemplos: *¿Por ejemplo se van al parque, a la tienda, juegan con sus hermanos o amigos, o hacen su tarea?*
What time does your child eat dinner? Who is s/he with? What language is used? In what language does the child respond?	*¿A qué hora cena? ¿Y con quién está? ¿Y en qué idioma habla con él/ella? ¿Y en qué idioma contesta?*
What time does s/he go to bed? Who is s/he with? What language is used? In what language does the child respond?	*¿A qué hora se va a dormir? ¿Y con quién está? ¿Y en qué idioma habla con él/ella? ¿Y en qué idioma contesta?*

This script is then repeated for a typical weekend day. On the form, note with whom the child interacts during which hours. Circle each waking hour. For the corresponding waking hour, indicate whether the child is with a person who uses Spanish, English, or both, and whether the child uses Spanish, English, or both. This information will provide a complete language profile of the child, as reported by the parent. The total number of waking hours is summed and entered in the space at the bottom of the column. The participant and child language scores are summed for each language (shown circled in Figure 3.3). These scores are used in combination with the weekend data to calculate the percentage of English and Spanish input and output.

BIOS-Home: Score Calculations

The purpose of the BIOS is to document children's language history of Spanish and English exposure and current Spanish and English exposure. For the BIOS, documenting the number of years of exposure to each language, in conjunction with the child's first year of exposure, can help clinicians interpret the child's test data. Percentages of input and output in Spanish and English are calculated from the hour-by-hour information provided via the Home Language Exposure Profile and School Language Exposure Profile.

On the BIOS-Home Language Exposure Profile Worksheet (see Figure 3.4), enter the total weekday and weekend input scores (Steps A and B). The weekday input is multiplied by 5 to project the total amount of weekday input. The weekend input score is multiplied by 2 to estimate the total weekend input. The two products are added together to estimate the total weekly (7-day) input. Next, enter the weekday and weekend output scores into the worksheet (steps C and D) and multiply those values by 5 (weekday) and 2 (weekend), respectively. These two scores are then added to obtain the total weekly output score.

The next steps (E and F) are to calculate the denominator. The weekday output is multiplied by 10 to project the total amount of weekday output. The weekend input score is multiplied by 4 to estimate the weekend output. The two products are added together to estimate the total weekly (7-day) waking hours. The two products are added together to estimate the number of waking hours during a typical week.

Home Language Profile/Familial Routine: Weekday (Circle hours awake during a typical weekday; circle the number corresponding to Spanish, English, or both; add each at bottom of column.)

	Participants		Language(s)					
	(parent, sibling, peer)	Waking Hours	Participant—Input			Child—Output		
Time			Spanish	Both	English	Spanish	Both	English
7 a.m.		1	2	1	0	2	1	0
8 a.m.	Mom	(1)	(2)	1	0	2	(1)	0
9 a.m.	May substitute school data here	1	2	1	0	2	1	0
10 a.m.		1	2	1	0	2	1	0
11 a.m.		1	2	1	0	2	1	0
12 p.m.		1	2	1	0	2	1	0
1 p.m.		1	2	1	0	2	1	0
2 p.m.		1	2	1	0	2	1	0
3 p.m.		1	2	1	0	2	1	0
4 p.m.		1	2	1	0	2	1	0
5 p.m.		1	2	1	0	2	1	0
6 p.m.		1	2	1	0	2	1	0
7 p.m.		1	2	1	0	2	1	0
8 p.m.	Mom	(1)	(2)	1	0	2	(1)	0
9 p.m.	Mom + brother	(1)	2	(1)	0	2	(1)	0
10 p.m.	Mom + brother	(1)	2	(1)	0	(2)	1	0
11 p.m.		1	2	1	0	2	1	0
		Sum Weekday Hours: 4 (E)	4 + 2 + 0 = 6 (A) Sum Weekday Input Score:			2 + 3 = 5 (C) Sum Weekday Output Score:		

NOTE: Values for E, A, and C should be entered in their corresponding steps on the Home Language Profile Worksheet.

Figure 3.3. BIOS–Home Language Profile: weekday data.

Steps G and H involve calculation of the proportion of input and output. Divide the numerator by the denominator for input and for output and enter the quotient into the appropriate box. This number should be between 0 and 1. Multiply by 100 to convert to a percentage.

The final step (I) is to obtain the percentage of Spanish input (SI) and Spanish output (SO) as well as English input (EI) and English output (EO) by averaging the individual input and output percentages for each language separately. In the example shown in Figure 3.4, Spanish input was 90% and output was 79%; thus, the average input and output for Spanish (SIO) is 84%. For English, input was 10%, and output was 21%, which averages to 16% (EIO). These averages are entered in Step I.

The percentage of English input/output (EIO) and the percentage of Spanish input/output (SIO) are then recorded (shown **underlined in bold**, in Figure 3.5) on the chart on the back cover of the Protocol to determine the language to use for testing.

BIOS-School: Administration and Scoring

The BIOS-School form is similar to the BIOS-Home form. The BIOS-School form can be completed as an interview with the teacher. In the first part of the questionnaire, ask how often the child uses Spanish, English, or both with the teacher, other children, and other adults at school. This information is entered into the BIOS-School form and scored by the examiner. In the example shown in Figure 3.6 (ratings are circled), the

HOME LANGUAGE PROFILE WORKSHEET (to be filled out by the professional)

STEP					
A	Enter total Weekday Input Score	6	Multiply Weekday Input Score by 5 =	30	Add scores = 38 (Input Numerator)
B	Enter total Weekend Input Score	4	Multiply Weekend Input Score by 2 =	8	
C	Enter total Weekday Output Score	5	Multiply Weekday Output Score by 5 =	25	Add scores = 33 (Output Numerator)
D	Enter total Weekend Output Score	4	Multiply Weekend Output Score by 2 =	8	
E	Enter total Weekday Waking Hours	3	Multiply Weekday Waking Hours by 10 =	30	Add scores = 42 (Denominator)
F	Enter total Weekend Waking Hours	3	Multiply Weekend Waking Hours by 4 =	12	

G	Input Numerator (from steps A & B)	38	Divide scores = 0.90	x 100= 90% % **Spanish Input** (SI-Home)	Subtract from 100% = 10% **% English Input** (EI-Home)
	Denominator (from steps E & F)	42			
H	Output numerator (from steps C & D)	33	Divide scores = 0.79	x 100= 79% **% Spanish Output** (SO-Home)	Subtract from 100% = 21% **% English Output** (EO-Home)
	Denominator (from steps E & F)	42			
I				(90% (SI-Home) + 79% (SO-Home)) ÷ 2 = Average % Spanish Input and % Spanish Output	84% **(SIO: Obtained %)**
				(10% (EI-Home) + 21% (EO-Home)) ÷ 2 = Average % English Input and % English Output	16% **(EIO: Obtained %)**

Figure 3.4. BIOS–Home Language Exposure Profile Worksheet.

BIOS-Home Language Profile: Enter and circle Averaged Input/Output to determine testing language(s).										
SPANISH	0%–10%	11%–20%	21%–30%	31%–40%	41%–50%	51%–60%	61%–70%	71%–80%	81%–90%	91%–100%
SIO: Obtained %									84%	
EIO: Obtained %									16%	
ENGLISH	91%–100%	81%–90%	71%–80%	61%–70%	51%–60%	41%–50%	31%–40%	21%–30%	11%–20%	0%–10%
	Test in English			**Test in Both**				**Test in Spanish**		

Figure 3.5. BIOS–Home Language Profile--Recording of Spanish and English input and output on the back cover of the English and Spanish Protocol.

report indicates that the child always uses English and never Spanish with the teacher, uses Spanish more with peers but also uses some English, and uses both often with other adults (Figure 3.6).

The BIOS-School Language Profile is completed and scored just like the BIOS-Home Language Profile. The interviewer first circles the hours spent in the classroom and the activity for each hour (see Figure 3.7). Then, the interviewer circles the score

	Speaks with the teacher in		**Speaks with other children in**		**Speaks with other adults (e.g., classroom assistant) in**	
	Spanish	English	Spanish	English	Spanish	English
Never uses the indicated language	(0)	0	0	0	0	0
Rarely uses the indicated language	1	1	1	1	1	1
Sometimes uses the indicated language	2	2	2	(2)	2	2
Very often uses the indicated language	3	3	3	3	(3)	(3)
Usually uses the indicated language	4	4	(4)	4	4	4
Always uses the indicated language	5	(5)	5	5	5	5
DK—Do not know	DK	DK	DK	DK	DK	DK

Please complete the Relative Use and Classroom Language Profile.

Relative Use refers to how much the child uses each language. Check the appropriate rank for each language and contexts listed in the table below.

RELATIVE USE AND CLASSROOM LANGUAGE PROFILE

Enter summary score.

Classroom form (0–5); leave blank if teacher does not know.
Calculate an average for each language.

Speaks with	Spanish	English
the teacher	0	5
other children	4	2
other adults	3	3
Average Scores	2.3	3.3

Figure 3.6. BIOS–School: Relative use and classroom language profile.

Time	Activity (e.g., reading, math, group)	Hours in School	Language(s)					
			Participant–Input			Child–Output		
			Spanish	Both	English	Spanish	Both	English
7 a.m.		1	2	1	0	2	1	0
8 a.m.	Lang./Read	1	2	1	0	2	1	0
9 a.m.	Music	1	2	1	0	2	1	0
10 a.m.	Writing	1	2	1	0	2	1	0
11 a.m.	Math	1	2	1	0	2	1	0
12 p.m.	Math	1	2	1	0	2	1	0
1 p.m.	Word	1	2	1	0	2	1	0
2 p.m.	Social Science	1	2	1	0	2	1	0
3 p.m.	Lang./Read	1	2	1	0	2	1	0
4 p.m.		1	2	1	0	2	1	0
5 p.m.		1	2	1	0	2	1	0
6 p.m.		1	2	1	0	2	1	0
		Total Weekday Hours: 8 (C)	Total Weekday Input Score: 2 + 2 + 0 = 4 (A)			Total Weekday Output Score: 0 + 2 + 0 = 2 (B)		

Figure 3.7. BIOS–School: Language Profile.

corresponding to the language used in input and the language the child uses in output. The number of hours in school is summed. The total input score and a total output score are calculated by summing the circled scores. In the example shown in Figure 3.7, the child is in school for 8 hours, the input score is 4, and the output score is 2. Those scores are recorded on the back cover of the Protocol and are used to calculate percentage of school input and output (see Figure 3.5).

For the BIOS-School, enter the ratings (which range from 0 to 5) for the three language use conditions (i.e., Spanish, English, or both) on the BIOS-School form. Leave the cells blank if the teacher responded that he or she did not know (DK). Compute the average of the available scores for Spanish and English (Figure 3.7). Compare the average English and Spanish scores to estimate an index of relative use of the two languages at school.

The next step is to obtain the level of exposure to the languages at school to determine the BIOS's School Language Profile. This calculation is the same as for the BIOS's Home Language Profile, but there is no need to estimate weekend language exposure (see steps A through F in Figure 3.8).

Scores from the BIOS's Home Language Profile and School Language Profile should be transferred to the front cover of the BIOS form (see Figure 3.9)

The appropriate ranges for the average Spanish input/output and the average English input/output percentages are circled on the BIOS section of the Protocol, as shown in Figure 3.10. The BIOS-Home and BIOS-School input and output percentages are used together to determine the language of testing. If children use each language 30% or more, they should be tested in both languages. If the home and school profile indicate 70% or more exposure to Spanish or English, then only test that language. If the home profile indicates exposure less than 30% in one language (e.g., Spanish) and the school profile indicates exposure less than 30% in the other language (e.g., English), then both languages should be tested. In the current example, the child uses and hears more Spanish at home but more English at school. Bilingual testing is indicated.

SCHOOL LANGUAGE PROFILE WORKSHEET (to be filled out by the professional)

STEP					
A	Enter total Input Score	4	Multiply Input Score by 5 =	20 (numerator D)	
B	Enter total Output Score	2	Multiply Output Score by 5 =	10 (numerator E)	
C	Enter total school hours	8	Multiply hours by 10 =	80 (denominator D & E)	
D	Input numerator (from step A)	20	Divide scores = 0.25	× 100= 25% **% Spanish Input** (SI-School)	Subtract from 100% = 75% **% English Input** (EI-School)
	Denominator (from step C)	80			
E	Output numerator (from step B)	10	Divide scores = 0.13	× 100= 13% **% Spanish Output** (SO-School)	Subtract from 100% = 87% **% English Output** (EO-School)
	Denominator (from step C)	80			
F				(25% (SI-School) + 13% (SO-School)) ÷ 2 = Average % Spanish Input and % Spanish Output	19% **(SIO: Obtained %)**
				(75% (EI-School) + 87% (EO-School)) ÷ 2 = Average % English Input and % English Output	81% **(EIO: Obtained %)**

Figure 3.8. BIOS–School: Language Exposure Profile Worksheet.

besa BILINGUAL ENGLISH-SPANISH ASSESSMENT™

Bilingual Input-Output Survey (BIOS)

NOTE: This form contains both home and school surveys to be completed by SLP professionals during interviews with parent/s and teacher/s.

Name: Isabel Sex: ☐ M ☑ F Test date: 2017 yr 04 mo 10 days

School: ______ Grade: K Birth date: 2010 yr 10 mo 24 days

Examiner: Ms. Smith Age: 6 yr 5 mo 16 days

Who was interviewed: ☑ **Parent/Guardian** ☑ **Teacher**

BIOS SCORE SUMMARY

ENTER THE PERCENTAGES FOR EACH LANGUAGE

HOME:		
	% SI: 90	% EI: 10
	% SO: 79	% EO: 21
	% SIO: 84	% EIO: 16

SCHOOL:		
	% SI: 25	% EI: 75
	% SO: 13	% EO: 87
	% SIO: 19	% EIO: 81

Figure 3.9. BIOS Score Summary.

INVENTORY TO ASSESS LANGUAGE KNOWLEDGE (ITALK)

The ITALK survey is used as an interview to gather input from the child's family and teacher(s) about the child's speech and language performance in Spanish and English at home and at school. This information is used to guide decision making regarding which language to use for the assessment.

BIOS-School Language Profile: Enter and circle Averaged Input/Output to determine testing language(s).										
SPANISH	0%–10%	11%–20%	21%–30%	31%–40%	41%–50%	51%–60%	61%–70%	71%–80%	81%–90%	91%–100%
SIO: Obtained %		19%								
EIO: Obtained %		81%								
ENGLISH	91%–100%	81%–90%	71%–80%	61%–70%	51%–60%	41%–50%	31%–40%	21%–30%	11%–20%	0%–10%
	Test in English			**Test in Both**				**Test in Spanish**		

Figure 3.10. BIOS–School Language Profile: Recording of Spanish and English Input and Output on back cover of the English and Spanish Protocol.

ITALK-Home

The ITALK-Home Form is designed to obtain information about the child's speech and language skills in each language as used at home. Based on the information obtained in this inventory, clinicians can make decisions about possible risk for speech and language impairment and pinpoint areas of possible difficulty.

The ITALK-Home Form should be completed as an interview by the speech-language pathologist with the parents. It can be completed over the phone or in person in conjunction with the BIOS-Home (discussed earlier in this chapter). The interview can be conducted in Spanish or English and should focus on the child's skills in *both* languages. After determining the parent's preferred language for the interview, introduce the task as follows:

We would like you to rate how well your child uses English and Spanish. Rate the child's proficiency in each language using the following scales.

Nos gustaría que usted indique qué bien usa su hijo/a el inglés y/o el español. Use las siguientes escalas para clasificar sus habilidades en los dos idiomas.

For each domain (e.g., vocabulary, articulation, grammar, and comprehension), read the question in the parents' preferred language. Remind them to select the description that best matches the child's skills in that language. First, identify the domain (e.g., vocabulary, grammar) that is being asked about, using the definitions given on the ITALK-Home Form. Then, ask them to identify the rating that best describes the child's abilities in that domain. Ask the parents to rate the child's English and Spanish. Circle the appropriate rating for each language on the form. If the child does not speak the target language, mark the appropriate place on the form (see Figure 3.11). This process is repeated for each question in the survey, asking the parents to rate both English and Spanish as much as they are able. If they do not know for a given language, circle *DK*

VOCABULARY PROFICIENCY / HABILIDAD DEL VOCABULARIO

Vocabulary Proficiency refers to how often the child uses home vocabulary (e.g., food or clothing names) and academic vocabulary (e.g., science terms) in each language.

Habilidad del Vocabulario se refiere a la frecuencia con que su hijo/a usa el vocabulario del hogar (p.ej., nombres de comidas o ropa) y el vocabulario académico (p.ej.,términos/palabras de la ciencia) en cada idioma.

Circle the appropriate level for each language.

Marque el nivel indicado para cada idioma.

How much **English** vocabulary does your child use from the words s/he learns at home (e.g., food, clothing) or school (e.g., science terms)? Del vocabulario que aprende en el hogar (nombres de comidas o ropa) y en la escuela (p.ej., palabras de la ciencia), ¿cuántas palabras usa su hijo/a en **inglés**?		How much **Spanish** vocabulary does your child use from the words s/he learns at home (e.g., food, clothing) or school (e.g., science terms)? Del vocabulario que aprende en el hogar (nombres de comidas o ropa) y en la escuela (p.ej., palabras de la ciencia), ¿cuántas palabras usa su hijo/a en **español**?	
Does not speak in the indicated language./ No habla el idioma indicado.	–	Does not speak in the indicated language./ No habla el idioma indicado.	–
A few words/unas pocas palabras	1	A few words/unas pocas palabras	1
A limited range of words/poca variedad de palabras	2	A limited range of words/poca variedad de palabras	2
Some words/algunas palabras	3	Some words/algunas palabras	3
Many words/muchas palabras	4	Many words/muchas palabras	4
Extensive vocabulary/vocabulario amplio	5	Extensive vocabulary/vocabulario amplio	5
DK—Do not know/No sé	—	DK—Do not know/No sé	—

Figure 3.11. ITALK–Home Form: Vocabulary Proficiency.

on the form. First explain the area of language targeted, using the definition provided. Then ask the parent to select the best descriptor to rate the child's English and Spanish. If the parent does not know, mark that in the appropriate space.

The ITALK-Home Form starts with vocabulary, as shown in Figure 3.11. In the example shown in Figure 3.11, the parent has indicated that in English the child knows few words, so a *1* is circled. The parent reports that in Spanish, the child knows some words, so a *3* is circled.

PLEASE NOTE
The following excerpts shown in this chapter are for illustration purposes only; examiners should become familiar with and rely on the actual form provided with the BESA kit to learn the scripts to use when interviewing the parents.

Next, the clinician asks questions to obtain information about the child's articulation in each language. As before, first provide the parents with a definition or explanation of articulation, referred to as *speech proficiency* on the form. Then ask them to provide a rating for each language (see Figure 3.12). If the parent doesn't know, mark *DK*, or if the child doesn't speak the language being asked about, mark "does not speak in the indicated language." These answers are excluded from scoring. The next question focuses on the child's sentence length, called *sentence production proficiency.* Here, the goal is to get a sense of the child's typical sentence length in both Spanish and English. The definition and ratings are found in Figure 3.12. In the example shown in the figure, the child uses two- to three-word sentences in English, and three- to four-word sentences in Spanish.

The fourth question focuses on the child's ability to produce grammatical sentences (grammatical proficiency). Provide the parents with examples of grammatical errors common in each language, as given in the examples (see Figure 3.13). The next question focuses on the child's comprehension skills (comprehension proficiency). Here, parents make a judgment about how well the child understands both English and Spanish (see Figure 3.13).

In the final question, the clinician asks the parents whether they have concerns about the child's speech or language. If so, ask the parents to describe their concern (Figure 3.14). This final question can be used to further probe and document possible concerns about speech and language as well as other related concerns.

Scoring the ITALK-Home

To score the ITALK-Home, transfer the individual scores from each section for each language to the ITALK-Home Summary (see Figure 3.14). The scores for the five areas (vocabulary, speech, sentence production, grammar, and comprehension) in each language should be summed and then divided by the number of scored responses. For example, if the parents report that they don't know about the child's English grammar, then divide by 4 instead of by 5.

In Figure 3.14, the total of 11 points for English is divided by 5 responses, yielding an average of 2.2, and the total of 19 points for Spanish is divided by 5 responses, yielding an average of 3.8. The higher score is for Spanish, indicating that Spanish is likely the child's better language at home. As shown on the form, if the highest average is equal to or greater than 4.18, there are no concerns about the child's language development.

SPEECH PROFICIENCY / HABILIDAD DEL HABLA

Speech Proficiency refers to how easily the child can be understood in each language.

Circle the indicated level for each language.

Habilidad del Habla se refiere a la facilidad con que los demás entienden a su hijo/a en cada idioma.

Marque el nivel indicado para cada idioma.

How often can you understand your child's speech in **English**? Difficulties in this area might be noted when a child mispronounces a sound such as /r/ or /s/ or a cluster of sounds (e.g., /sk/), or omits part of a word (e.g., says "evator" for "elevator"). ¿Con qué frecuencia puede Ud. entender el habla de su hijo/a en **inglés**? Las dificultades en esta área se notan cuando el niño/a no pronuncia sonidos como /r/ o /s/, un grupo de sonidos (p.ej., /sk/) u omite parte de una palabra (p.ej., dice "evator" en vez de "elevator").		How often can you understand your child's speech in **Spanish**? Difficulties in this area might be noted when a child mispronounces a sound such as /r/ or /s/ or a cluster of sounds (e.g., /st/), or omits part of a word (e.g., says "maposa" for "mariposa"). ¿Con qué frecuencia puede Ud. entender el habla de su hijo/a en **español**? Las dificultades en este área se notan cuando el niño/a no pronuncia sonidos como /r/ o /s/, un grupo de sonidos (p.ej., /st/) u omite parte de una palabra (p.ej., dice "maposa" en vez de "mariposa").	
Does not speak in the indicated language./ No habla el idioma indicado.	–	Does not speak in the indicated language./ No habla el idioma indicado.	–
Never/Nunca	1	Never/Nunca	1
Rarely/Rara la vez	(2)	Rarely/Rara la vez	2
Sometimes/A veces	3	Sometimes/A veces	3
Very often/Casi siempre	4	Very often/Casi siempre	(4)
Always/Siempre	5	Always/Siempre	5
DK—Do not know/No sé	–	DK—Do not know/No sé	–

SENTENCE PRODUCTION PROFICIENCY / HABILIDAD DE LA PRODUCCIÓN DE ORACIONES

Sentence Production Proficiency refers to the usual length of the child's sentences when he or she is conversing, responding in class, or telling a story.

Circle the indicated level for each language.

Habilidad de la Producción de Oraciones se refiere a qué tan largas son las oraciones de su hijo/a cuando está charlando, respondiendo en clase, o contando un cuento.

Marque el nivel indicado para cada idioma.

How long are your child's sentences in **English** typically? (Remember that children commonly use sentences of a certain length but when answering a question such as "Would you like a cookie?" may use sentences that are shorter or longer than the usual length.) ¿Qué tan largas son las oraciones de su hijo/a en **inglés** típicamente? (Recuerde que los niños usan oraciones cortas y largas. Usan oraciones cortas cuando están contestando una pregunta por ejemplo, "Would you like a cookie?")		How long are your child's sentences in **Spanish** typically? (Remember that children commonly use sentences of a certain length but when answering a question such as "¿Quieres una galleta?" may use sentences that are shorter or longer than the usual length.) ¿Qué tan largas son las oraciones de su hijo/a en **español** típicamente? (Recuerde que los niños usan oraciones cortas y largas. Usan oraciones cortas cuando están contestando una pregunta por ejemplo, "¿Quieres una galleta?")	
Does not speak in the indicated language./ No habla el idioma indicado.	–	Does not speak in the indicated language./ No habla el idioma indicado.	–
1–2 words/palabras	1	1–2 words/palabras	1
2–3 words/palabras	(2)	2–3 words/palabras	2
3–4 words/palabras	3	3–4 words/palabras	(3)
4–5 words/palabras	4	4–5 words/palabras	4
5 or more words/5 o más palabras	5	5 or more words/5 o más palabras	5
DK—Do not know/No sabe	–	DK—Do not know/No sabe	–

Figure 3.12. ITALK–Home Form: Speech Profiency and Sentence Production Proficiency.

If the highest average score is lower than 4.18, further speech-language assessment is indicated. In this example, a highest average score of 3.8 indicates that a speech-language assessment is needed. Transfer this score to the front page of the ITALK Form, as shown in Figure 3.15, and also to the back page of the Protocol, as shown in Figure 3.16. Examination of the specific areas of concern can be used to guide which subtests of the BESA to administer. The BESA will be able to provide more specific information about performance in that area to delineate any specific difficulty.

GRAMMATICAL PROFICIENCY / HABILIDAD GRAMATICAL

Grammatical Proficiency refers to the grammatical acceptability.

Circle the indicated level for each language.

Habilidad Gramatical se refiere a la frecuencia del uso de oraciones correctas.

Marque el nivel indicado para cada idioma.

How often does your child produce well-formed sentences in **English** when conversing or telling stories? Some forms that may be difficult in English are past-tense forms (e.g., *walked*) or present-tense forms (e.g., *walks*). ¿Con qué frecuencia produce su hijo/a oraciones bien formadas en **inglés** cuando está conversado o contando cuentos? Entre las formas difíciles en inglés son el tiempo pasado (p.ej., *walked*) y el presente (p.ej., *walks*).		How often does your child produce well-formed sentences in **Spanish** when conversing or telling stories? In Spanish, children might have trouble with articles (el *naranja* instead of la *naranja*) or pronouns such as lo *comió* (referring to the orange) instead of la *comió*. ¿Con qué frecuencia produce su hijo/a oraciones bien formadas en **español** cuando está conversado o contando cuentos? En español, los niños pueden tener dificultad con los artículos (el *naranja* en vez de la *naranja*) o pronombres (por ejemplo, lo *comió* en vez de la *comió*).	
Does not speak in the indicated language./ No habla el idioma indicado.	–	Does not speak in the indicated language./ No habla el idioma indicado.	–
Never/Nunca	1	Never/Nunca	1
Rarely/Rara la vez	(2)	Rarely/Rara la vez	2
Sometimes/A veces	3	Sometimes/A veces	3
Very often/Casi siempre	4	Very often/Casi siempre	(4)
Always/Siempre	5	Always/Siempre	5
DK—Do not know/No sé	–	DK—Do not know/No sé	–

COMPREHENSION PROFICIENCY / HABILIDAD DE LA COMPRENSIÓN

Comprehension Proficiency refers to how easily the child understands each language.

Circle the indicated level for each language.

Habilidad de la Comprensión se refiere a la facilidad con que su hijo/a entiende cada idioma.

Marque el nivel indicado para cada idioma.

How often does your child understand what is said in **English**? Difficulties in this area might be noted when s/he frequently asks for repetition or only attends to part of what you say (e.g., last part of a story, one part of a series of instructions). ¿Con qué frecuencia entiende su hijo/a lo que se dice en **inglés**? Por ejemplo, si Ud. nota que pide con frecuencia que Ud. repita o si atiende solamente parte de lo que Ud. dice (p.ej., la parte final de un cuento, parte de una serie de instrucciones).		How often does your child understand what is said in **Spanish**? Difficulties in this area might be noted when s/he frequently asks for repetition or only attends to part of what you say (e.g., last part of a story, one part of a series of instructions). ¿Con qué frecuencia entiende su hijo/a lo que se dice en **español**? Por ejemplo, si Ud. nota que pide con frecuencia que Ud. repita o si atiende solamente parte de lo que Ud. dice (p.ej., la parte final de un cuento, parte de una serie de instrucciones).	
Does not understand the indicated language./ No entiende el idioma indicado.	–	Does not understand the indicated language./ No entiende el idioma indicado.	–
Never/Nunca	1	Never/Nunca	1
Rarely/Rara la vez	2	Rarely/Rara la vez	2
Sometimes/A veces	3	Sometimes/A veces	3
Very often/Casi siempre	(4)	Very often/Casi siempre	4
Always/Siempre	5	Always/Siempre	(5)
DK—Do not know/No sé	–	DK—Do not know/No sé	–

Figure 3.13. ITALK–Home Form: Grammatical Proficiency and Comprehension Proficiency.

ITALK-School

The ITALK-School Form should be completed as an interview with the child's teacher and should be completed in conjunction with the BIOS-School. The ITALK-School focuses on the child's skills in both Spanish and English at school, as reported by the teacher. The questions are the same as in the ITALK-Home and they are scored in the same way. As the survey is completed, enter the scores on the ITALK Clinical Summary. Calculate the average score for English and for Spanish. The higher average score

OVERALL LANGUAGE PERFORMANCE

Are you concerned about the way your child talks? ¿Se preocupa por la manera en que habla su hijo/a?

❒ Yes/Sí ❒ No

If yes, please describe your concern. Si se preocupa, explique porque se preocupa.

ITALK-HOME SUMMARY:

Enter and average scores from the ITALK-Home Form.

English	Score	Spanish	Score
Vocabulary	1	Vocabulary	3
Speech	2	Speech	4
Sentence Production	2	Sentence Production	3
Grammar	2	Grammar	4
Comprehension	4	Comprehension	5
TOTAL	11	**TOTAL**	19
Divide total by number of completed indicators **AVERAGE**	22	Divide total by number of completed indicators **AVERAGE**	38

Enter Highest Average Here

3.8

Scoring Interpretation: **If highest average ≥4.18, no concerns**
If highest average < 4.18, speech-language assessment is indicated

Figure 3.14. ITALK–Home: Overall language performance.

should be determined and entered into the BESA Score Summary on the Protocol back cover page for each language. Again, if the higher average score is below 4.18, a speech and/or language concern is indicated. Examine the patterns of concern to guide which subtests of the BESA to use in assessment.

Using the ITALK-Home and ITALK-School Together

The most complete information about the child's speech and language will come from using both the home and school versions of the ITALK. Surveying performance at both school and home will help the examiner to better understand communication demands in these settings and document how the two languages are used.

A score below the cut-off point of 4.18 on either the ITALK-Home <u>or</u> ITALK-School is indicative of a speech or language concern (see Figure 3.16). Evidence of speech or language concern should be followed up with the administration of the BESA. A possible exception is if the concern is related only to the nondominant language. For example, a child might speak mainly Spanish at home, as indicated by the BIOS-Home and ITALK-Home scores. However, the teacher might be able to report only on the child's English usage at school. It is important to use clinical judgment and to take into consideration besa™ BILINGUAL ENGLISH-SPANISH ASSESSMENT™

Inventory to Assess Language Knowledge (ITALK)

NOTE: This form contains both home and school surveys to be completed by SLP professionals during interviews with parent/s and teacher/s.

Name: Isabel Sex: ☐ M ☑ F Test date: 2017 yr 04 mo 10 days

School: ______ Grade: K Birth date: 2010 yr 10 mo 24 days

Examiner: Ms. Smith Age: 6 yr 5 mo 16 days

Who was interviewed: ☑ **Parent/Guardian** ☐ **Teacher**

ITALK SCORE SUMMARY

ENTER THE HIGHEST AVERAGE AND CIRCLE THE LANGUAGE

SCHOOL FORM: 2.2 **(ENGLISH)** **SPANISH**

HOME FORM: 3.8 **ENGLISH** **(SPANISH)**

Score Interpretation: **If highest average score ≥4.18, no concerns**
If highest average score <4.18, speech-language assessment is indicated

Figure 3.15. ITALK–Home Summary.

the input from both the family and school personnel. The ITALK and BIOS can help guide clinical decisions to assess or monitor the child's Spanish and English development so that normal second-language acquisition differences are not confused with speech or language disorders.

THE BESA PROTOCOLS PRAGMATICS ACTIVITY

The Pragmatics activity is based on Fey's model of assertiveness and responsiveness in children (Fey, 1986) and consists of a short task that elicits a series of interactions while wrapping a gift to be given to a third party (Diego). Appendix A: Acceptable and Unacceptable Responses contains lists of acceptable and unacceptable responses for Spanish (Table A.1) and English (Table A.2). The context necessary to elicit target communicative acts is provided on the English Protocol and Spanish Protocol. The Pragmatics activity should be used in conjunction with the three subtests to make diagnostic decisions. For some children, especially those who are reticent, this activity serves as a good warm-up task for the rest of the assessment. This activity is used for *descriptive purposes only;* there are *no* standardized scores associated with the child's performance.

ITALK: Indicate higher (Span./Eng.) home and school scores below.																	
						Needs Assessment											
Home	5	4.8	4.6	4.4	4.2	4	(3.8)	3.6	3.4	3.2	3	2.8	2.6	2.4	2.2	2	1.8	1.6
School	5	4.8	4.6	4.4	4.2	4	3.8	3.6	3.4	3.2	3	2.8	2.6	2.4	(2.2)	2	1.8	1.6

Figure 3.16. Comparison of ITALK–Home and ITALK–School ratings.

Encouragement/Reinforcement

The reinforcement provided here should be general social reinforcement. Responses to the child's communicative acts are provided. Our experience is that children enjoy the idea of helping the examiner to wrap a gift and do not need much encouragement to participate.

Repetition

Repetition is not typically necessary, but questions or cues can be repeated once. The examiner should interact with the child in as natural a way as possible.

Item Types

The tasks focus on assertive acts, with some responsive acts, within the context of wrapping a gift for Diego. The context is set up so that the child may request clarification or information, make statements, disagree, or request actions. Responsive acts are the child's responses to requests for information.

Language to Use

The Pragmatics activity should be conducted in the language the child knows better or feels more comfortable using. Because the focus is on communicative acts, code-switching is allowed. It is also acceptable to use only one language. Depending on the child's preferred language, you could begin in one language but switch to the other language during the activity. Child responses should be written out verbatim as you move through the task, for later reference. Please note that, in some cases, the child might produce an assertive act different from the expected—this is not unusual. Additionally, some children may be quiet but still provide appropriate nonverbal responses. The Protocol lists typical and expected responses.

Alternate Administration Using a Puppet

During the Pragmatics activity, children must sometimes "correct" the examiner, pointing out, for example, that the item that was given to them was not the one they selected. We have found that some children are reluctant to overtly disagree with the examiner. One alternative is to engage a puppet, "Timmy," who is introduced as a friend who sometimes can be silly. Focusing on the puppet helps children to overcome their reluctance to correct an adult, and they seem to enjoy "catching" Timmy when he does something silly. We find that younger children, and those who are newer immigrants, do better when they correct Timmy instead of directing comments to the adult examiner. Use this approach as you deem necessary to facilitate the child's participation.

Pragmatics Activity: Administration

Before starting these tasks, familiarize yourself with the Protocol, materials, and the script for the directions to the child (see Figures 3.17 and 3.18). It is important that you have all the materials gathered before beginning. You will need the following:

- One small box
- Wrapping paper cut to size
- Three short colored sample ribbons attached to an index card for the child to identy color by pointing (red, blue, green)
- Three long colored ribbons (red, blue, green) that will not quite fit around the box
- Two tape dispensers (one empty)
- One mushki (nondescript hard object that will loosely fit in your box and has a bell or ringer to make noise)
- One hand puppet (optional).

All the materials except the mushki in the small box should be in an opaque bag or box so that the child cannot see them. It is important not to show the child all the materials in the bag in order to set up an authentic, believable situation. Start by showing the child the small box containing the mushki and shaking the box so that the child can hear the object moving inside the box.

The task begins with the examiner explaining that they are going to wrap a gift for Diego. It is important to adhere as closely as possible to the script provided on each

Figure 3.17. Materials used in the BESA Pragmatics activity.

ENGLISH PRAGMATICS ACTIVITY: A Present for Diego

NOTE: This is an optional activity that can be used to establish rapport with the child as well as to observe how the child uses/understands pragmatic language. This activity is to be used for descriptive purposes only and does NOT contribute to any score.

MATERIALS: 1 small box, wrapping paper cut to size, 3 short colored sample ribbons attached to an index card for the child to identify color by pointing (red, blue, green), 3 long colored ribbons (red, blue, green) that will not quite fit around the box, 2 tape dispensers (one empty), 1 mushki (nondescript object that makes noise), 1 hand puppet

Context		Expected Child's Response (Verbal/Nonverbal)	Can Do Task (Y, N)	
Keep all materials in bag. Only bring out the closed box containing the mushki.				
E-PR1: **Alt:**	Let's wrap Diego's present. I bought Diego a great gift. It's in the box *(shake box)*. What do you think it is? Let's wrap Diego's present. This is my friend Timmy. He's going to help us wrap Diego's present. Sometimes he can be silly, but don't let him fool you. I bought Diego a great gift. It's in the box *(Timmy shakes box)*. Tell Timmy what you think it is.	**Response to request for information** ❒ **Ball** ❒ **Bracelet** ❒ **Bell** ❒ **[Gestures ringing]** ❒ **Coins (quarters)** ❒ I don't know/NR ❒ [Shrug]	Y	N
E-PR2:	It's a mushki. *(mumbled)*	**Request clarification or information** ❒ **Oh!?** ❒ **[Purses lips, questioning look]** ❒ **What is that?** ❒ **What's a mushki?** ❒ **[Tilts head, questioning look]** ❒ **Hmmm?** ❒ NR ❒ [Shrug]	Y	N
E-PR3:	A mushki, see *(open box)*. We use mushkis to bingle the waddles.	**Request for clarification** ❒ **Mushki?** ❒ **Hmmm?** ❒ **Bingle?** ❒ **[Confusion/ questioning look]** ❒ **Waddle?** ❒ **To do what?** ❒ NR ❒ I like that.	Y	N
E-PR4: **Alt:**	Let's see. To wrap the present, we need wrapping paper, tape, and ribbon. *(Do not take out materials).* What do I do next? Let's see. To wrap the present we need wrapping paper, tape, and ribbon. *(Do not take out materials).* Do you know how to wrap a present? Tell Timmy how to wrap a present.	**Statement** ❒ **Get paper, then tape, then ribbon.** ❒ **Cut the paper, wrap gift** ❒ **[Other 2-part wrapping sequence]** ❒ NR ❒ I don't know.	Y	N
E-PR5:	*(Examiner starts wrapping.)* Let me have the ribbon. *(Not on table.)*	**Comment or Disagreement** ❒ **I don't know where it is.** ❒ **There's no ribbon.** ❒ **They're in there.** ❒ **[Looks around and shrugs to indicate it's not there]** ❒ NR ❒ [Opens box and closes it]	Y	N

Context		Expected Child's Response (Verbal/Nonverbal)	Can Do Task (Y, N)	
E-PR6: **Alt:**	Oh, I forgot. It's in the bag. *(Pull out the **short** red, green, and blue ribbons.)* I have a red ribbon, a blue ribbon, and a green ribbon. Which one should we use? *(Pause for reply.)* Here's the ______. *(Give child the **wrong** ribbon.)* Oh, I forgot. It's in the bag. *(Pull out the **short** red, green, and blue ribbons.)* We have a red ribbon, a blue ribbon, and a green ribbon. Tell Timmy which one you want. Here's the ______. *(Puppet gives child the **wrong** color ribbon.)*	**Disagreement** ❒ **[Comments about wrong color]** ❒ **I want(ed) the *xx* one.** ❒ **[Gives ribbon back and indicates no]** ❒ **[Looks at wrong color and pauses, or looks at examiner]** ❒ NR ❒ [Continues to wrap present]	Y	N
E-PR7: **Alt:**	Oh, I'm sorry. *(Give child correct color ribbon and begin wrapping gift.)* Please give me some tape. *(Tape dispenser has no tape.)* Oh, Timmy is being silly again. *(Give child correct color ribbon. Child and puppet begin wrapping present.)* Please give Timmy some tape. *(Tape dispenser has no tape.)*	**Comment** ❒ **There's no tape/where's the tape?** ❒ **Did you take the tape?** ❒ **[Gestures that there's no tape]** ❒ **[Shows examiner empty dispenser]** ❒ NR ❒ [Continues to try getting tape]	Y	N
E-PR8:	I'd better get another one. *(Get dispenser with tape.)* Okay, now we have to put the ribbon on. Go ahead, put the ribbon on.	**Request for Action** ❒ **Give me the *xx* ribbon.** ❒ **[Looks for ribbon actively]** ❒ **[Gestures for ribbon]** ❒ NR	Y	N
E-PR9: **Alt:**	*(Give short ribbon.)* *(Puppet gives child too-short ribbon.)*	**Comment** ❒ **It's too short/small.** ❒ **[Gestures too small]** ❒ NR ❒ [Continues to try tying ribbon]	Y	N
E-PR10: **Alt:**	What should we do? *(Attempt to finish wrapping the gift.)* Tell Timmy what you think we should do. *(Attempt to finish wrapping the gift.)*	**Statement** ❒ **Tape two together.** ❒ **Get a longer one.** ❒ **Tape it on.** ❒ **[Gestures taping or longer ribbon]** ❒ NR ❒ I don't know.	Y	N
E-PR11: **Alt:**	Great idea. I think Diego is going to love his present. What do you think Diego is going to say? Great idea. I think Diego is going to love his present. Tell Timmy what you think Diego is going to say.	**Comment** ❒ **Thank you.** ❒ **He'll be surprised.** ❒ **He will like it.** ❒ **He'll want to play with it.** ❒ **[Gestures thank you]** ❒ NR ❒ I don't know.	Y	N

TOTAL ______ /11

END OF PRAGMATICS ACTIVITY

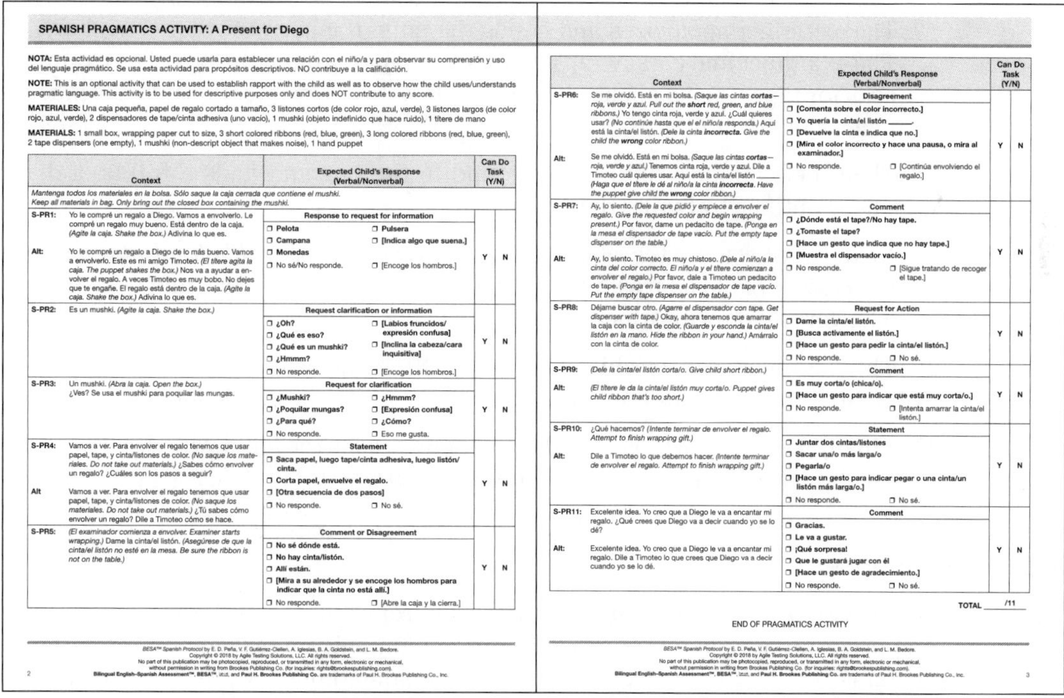

SPANISH PRAGMATICS ACTIVITY: A Present for Diego

NOTA: Esta actividad es opcional. Usted puede usarla para establecer una relación con el niño/a y para observar su comprensión y uso del lenguaje pragmático. Se usa esta actividad para propósitos descriptivos. NO contribuye a la calificación.

NOTE: This is an optional activity that can be used to establish rapport with the child as well as to observe how the child uses/understands pragmatic language. This activity is to be used for descriptive purposes only and does NOT contribute to any score.

MATERIALES: Una caja pequeña, papel de regalo cortado a tamaño, 3 listones cortos (de color rojo, azul, verde), 3 listones largos (de color rojo, azul, verde), 2 dispensadores de tape/cinta adhesiva (uno vacío), 1 mushki (objeto indefinido que hace ruido), 1 títere de mano

MATERIALS: 1 small box, wrapping paper cut to size, 3 short colored ribbons (red, blue, green), 3 long colored ribbons (red, blue, green), 2 tape dispensers (one empty), 1 mushki (non-descript object that makes noise), 1 hand puppet

Context		Expected Child's Response (Verbal/Nonverbal)	Can Do Task (Y/N)	
Mantenga todos los materiales en la bolsa. Sólo saque la caja cerrada que contiene el mushki. *Keep all materials in bag. Only bring out the closed box containing the mushki.*				
S-PR1: **Alt:**	Yo le compré un regalo a Diego. Vamos a envolverlo. Le compré un regalo muy bueno. Está dentro de la caja. *(Agite la caja. Shake the box.)* Adivina lo que es. Yo le compré un regalo a Diego de lo más bueno. Vamos a envolverlo. Este es mi amigo Timoteo. *(El títere agita la caja. The puppet shakes the box.)* Nos va a ayudar a envolver el regalo. A veces Timoteo es muy bobo. No dejes que te engañe. El regalo está dentro de la caja. *(Agite la caja. Shake the box.)* Adivina lo que es.	**Response to request for information** ❒ **Pelota** ❒ **Pulsera** ❒ **Campana** ❒ **[Indica algo que suena.]** ❒ **Monedas** ❒ No sé/No responde. ❒ [Encoge los hombros.]	Y	N
S-PR2:	Es un mushki. *(Agite la caja. Shake the box.)*	**Request clarification or information** ❒ **¿Oh?** ❒ **[Labios fruncidos/ expresión confusa]** ❒ **¿Qué es eso?** ❒ **¿Qué es un mushki?** ❒ **[Inclina la cabeza/cara inquisitiva]** ❒ **¿Hmmm?** ❒ No responde. ❒ [Encoge los hombros.]	Y	N
S-PR3:	Un mushki. *(Abra la caja. Open the box.)* ¿Ves? Se usa el mushki para poquilar las mungas.	**Request for clarification** ❒ **¿Mushki?** ❒ **¿Hmmm?** ❒ **¿Poquilar mungas?** ❒ **[Expresión confusa]** ❒ **¿Para qué?** ❒ **¿Cómo?** ❒ No responde. ❒ Eso me gusta.	Y	N
S-PR4: **Alt**	Vamos a ver. Para envolver el regalo tenemos que usar papel, tape, y cinta/listones de color. *(No saque los materiales. Do not take out materials.)* ¿Sabes cómo envolver un regalo? ¿Cuáles son los pasos a seguir? Vamos a ver. Para envolver el regalo tenemos que usar papel, tape, y cinta/listones de color. *(No saque los materiales. Do not take out materials.)* ¿Tú sabes cómo envolver un regalo? Dile a Timoteo cómo se hace.	**Statement** ❒ **Saca papel, luego tape/cinta adhesiva, luego listón/ cinta.** ❒ **Corta papel, envuelve el regalo.** ❒ **[Otra secuencia de dos pasos]** ❒ No responde. ❒ No sé.	Y	N
S-PR5:	*(El examinador comienza a envolver. Examiner starts wrapping.)* Dame la cinta/el listón. *(Asegúrese de que la cinta/el listón no esté en la mesa. Be sure the ribbon is not on the table.)*	**Comment or Disagreement** ❒ **No sé dónde está.** ❒ **No hay cinta/listón.** ❒ **Allí están.** ❒ **[Mira a su alrededor y se encoge los hombros para indicar que la cinta no está allí.]** ❒ No responde. ❒ [Abre la caja y la cierra.]	Y	N

Context		Expected Child's Response (Verbal/Nonverbal)	Can Do Task (Y/N)	
S-PR6: **Alt:**	Se me olvidó. Está en mi bolsa. *(Saque las cintas **cortas**—roja, verde y azul. Pull out the **short** red, green, and blue ribbons.)* Yo tengo cinta roja, verde y azul. ¿Cuál quieres usar? *(No continúe hasta que el el niño/a responda.)* Aquí está la cinta/el listón. *(Dele la cinta **incorrecta.** Give the child the **wrong** color ribbon.)* Se me olvidó. Está en mi bolsa. *(Saque las cintas **cortas**—roja, verde y azul.)* Tenemos cinta roja, verde y azul. Dile a Timoteo cuál quieres usar. Aquí está la cinta/el listón ______ *(Haga que el títere le dé al niño/a la cinta **incorrecta**. Have the puppet give child the **wrong** color ribbon.)*	**Disagreement** ❒ **[Comenta sobre el color incorrecto.]** ❒ **Yo quería la cinta/el listón ______.** ❒ **[Devuelve la cinta e indica que no.]** ❒ **[Mira el color incorrecto y hace una pausa, o mira al examinador.]** ❒ No responde. ❒ [Continúa envolviendo el regalo.]	Y	N
S-PR7: **Alt:**	Ay, lo siento. *(Dele la que pidió y empiece a envolver el regalo. Give the requested color and begin wrapping present.)* Por favor, dame un pedacito de tape. *(Ponga en la mesa el dispensador de tape vacío. Put the empty tape dispenser on the table.)* Ay, lo siento. Timoteo es muy chistoso. *(Dele al niño/a la cinta del color correcto. El niño/a y el títere comienzan a envolver el regalo.)* Por favor, dale a Timoteo un pedacito de tape. *(Ponga en la mesa el dispensador de tape vacío. Put the empty tape dispenser on the table.)*	**Comment** ❒ **¿Dónde está el tape?/No hay tape.** ❒ **¿Tomaste el tape?** ❒ **[Hace un gesto que indica que no hay tape.]** ❒ **[Muestra el dispensador vacío.]** ❒ No responde. ❒ [Sigue tratando de recoger el tape.]	Y	N
S-PR8:	Déjame buscar otro. *(Agarre el dispensador con tape. Get dispenser with tape.)* Okay, ahora tenemos que amarrar la caja con la cinta de color. *(Guarde y esconda la cinta/el listón en la mano. Hide the ribbon in your hand.)* Amárralo con la cinta de color.	**Request for Action** ❒ **Dame la cinta/el listón.** ❒ **[Busca activamente el listón.]** ❒ **[Hace un gesto para pedir la cinta/el listón.]** ❒ No responde. ❒ No sé.	Y	N
S-PR9: **Alt:**	*(Dele la cinta/el listón corta/o. Give child short ribbon.)* *(El títere le da la cinta/el listón muy corta/o. Puppet gives child ribbon that's too short.)*	**Comment** ❒ **Es muy corta/o (chica/o).** ❒ **[Hace un gesto para indicar que está muy corta/o.]** ❒ No responde. ❒ [Intenta amarrar la cinta/el listón.]	Y	N
S-PR10: **Alt:**	¿Qué hacemos? *(Intente terminar de envolver el regalo. Attempt to finish wrapping gift.)* Dile a Timoteo lo que debemos hacer. *(Intente terminar de envolver el regalo. Attempt to finish wrapping gift.)*	**Statement** ❒ **Juntar dos cintas/listones** ❒ **Sacar una/o más larga/o** ❒ **Pegarla/o** ❒ **[Hace un gesto para indicar pegar o una cinta/un listón más larga/o.]** ❒ No responde. ❒ No sé.	Y	N
S-PR11: **Alt:**	Excelente idea. Yo creo que a Diego le va a encantar mi regalo. ¿Qué crees que Diego va a decir cuando yo se lo dé? Excelente idea. Yo creo que a Diego le va a encantar mi regalo. Dile a Timoteo lo que crees que Diego va a decir cuando yo se lo dé.	**Comment** ❒ **Gracias.** ❒ **Le va a gustar.** ❒ **¡Qué sorpresa!** ❒ **Que le gustará jugar con él** ❒ **[Hace un gesto de agradecimiento.]** ❒ No responde. ❒ No sé.	Y	N

TOTAL ______ /11

END OF PRAGMATICS ACTIVITY

Figure 3.18. BESA Protocol Pragmatics Activity.

Protocol when giving directions to the child; minor variations are permitted, if needed. The administration instructions provided here are numbered (in **bold**) to match the Protocol. Placed on the table where testing occurs are the box with the mushki inside, wrapping paper, an empty tape dispenser, and an opaque bag or box containing the ribbons and the filled tape dispenser (see Figure 3.17).

1. The examiner shakes the box and asks the child to guess what is inside. *(Child is expected to make a statement.)*
2. Then the examiner shows the child the mushki, mumbling while naming it. *(Child is expected to ask for clarification.)*
3. Once the examiner clarifies the name, the examiner explains what it is used for, using nonsense words. *(Child is again expected to ask for clarification.)*
4. Next, the examiner asks the child to explain how to wrap a gift. *(Child is expected to provide two-step statements.)* After the child explains, the examiner brings out the empty tape dispenser and the wrapping paper.
5. Then the examiner asks the child to hand him or her the ribbon, which is not on the table. *(Child is expected to make a statement indicating that there is no ribbon.)*
6. The examiner then brings out three ribbons, all of which are too short to go around the package. The examiner asks the child to indicate the color of the one he or she wants. The examiner then gives the child the incorrect one. *(Child is expected to make a statement or complain that the wrong ribbon was given.)*
7. The examiner apologizes and hands the child the correct color (but short) ribbon. The examiner and child wrap and fold the paper around the box. The examiner then asks for tape (tape dispenser is empty). *(Child is expected to indicate that the dispenser is out of tape.)*
8. Then the examiner rummages around in the bag and finds a full tape dispenser. They continue by taping the paper.
9. Next, they try to tie the ribbon around the package. *(Child should then assert that the ribbon is too short.)* The examiner then looks in the bag and does not take out a longer ribbon with which to tie the package.
10. The examiner asks the child what to do. Often, the examiner and child come up with creative solutions for how to tie the package with the short ribbons.
11. Finally, the gift is wrapped and the examiner asks the child what Diego will think of the gift. *(Child is expected to provide a statement.)*

Acceptable Responses

Any assertive act that is communicatively appropriate is considered correct. Generally, responses are considered correct if 1) they communicate that something in the conversation is wrong and the examiner should do something else, or 2) the child notes an error and proposes a solution. While this activity is not scored, the number of accepted "yes" responses (out of a possible 11) is noted as an important clinical observation. Both verbal and nonverbal responses are acceptable; the Protocol lists some of the most common responses; Appendix A lists acceptable and unacceptable responses. The list of tasks that the child was able or not able to do successfully can be used descriptively when reporting results of testing.

Encouragement/Reinforcement

It is important to establish rapport at the outset of the testing session and to maintain it by praising the child's effort from time to time, without indicating whether the child's answers are right or wrong. For example, you may say, "That's very good answering," or "You are doing just fine." If the child appears reluctant to answer an item, offer encouragement by saying, "Give it a try" or "It's all right, keep on going." Interacting with the child in an open and friendly manner helps make the testing experience pleasant for both you and the child.

Sample reinforcement statements, in both English and Spanish, are provided throughout the practice items for every subtest. Read the instructions carefully. Encourage the child to guess if he or she does not know the correct answer.

Repetition of Stimuli

Repeat the directions and/or the practice items according to the instructions in each part of the subtest. Provide additional explanation, if needed, until the child knows what to do. Model the correct answer on the practice items so that he or she hears the correct response. It is not necessary that the child produce the correct response after the model, but that he or she understands the task.

GENERAL INSTRUCTIONS FOR SUBTESTS

The Phonology, Morphosyntax, and Semantics subtests are standardized subtests utilizing picture plates from the BESA Stimulus Book. Note that the Stimulus Book is comprehensive, including sets for both the Spanish and English versions of the subtests. Tabbed dividers indicate the subtest and language. The examiner should sit next to the child so that both can view the test stimuli. Each version of the Protocol should be within reach of the examiner so that she or he can write down the child's responses to the items. It is recommended that testing be conducted in one language in one session and the other language during another session. The usual order of subtest administration (after the Pragmatics activity) is Phonology, Morphosyntax, and then Semantics. However, the subtest order can be varied depending on the diagnostic question and individual child's needs.

> REMINDER
> Appendix A contains lists of acceptable and unacceptable responses for all subtests, derived from the normative sample. Although it is intended to guide the practitioner, it is not, nor can it be, an exhaustive list of all possible responses.

> REMINDER
> This chapter contains figures showing scripts and expected responses for the demonstration items for all subtests. Those figures are for illustration purposes; examiners are expected to become familiar with the instructions and scripts shown on the protocols.

PHONOLOGY SUBTESTS—OVERVIEW

The Phonology subtests are single-word phonological assessments designed primarily to identify phonological delays in each language. Analyses are also included that allow the examiner to profile the phonological skills of the child in each language. The assessment includes two measures—one in Spanish and one in English to capture the unique phonology of each language. The Spanish measure assesses phonological production using 28 Spanish words depicting objects and attributes that are familiar to children. Twenty-six of the 28 words included in the assessment are nouns, and two are adjectives. The English measure assesses phonological production using 31 English words depicting objects and attributes familiar to children. All words included on the English measure are nouns.

Item Types

All singleton consonants in Spanish and English are targeted (with the exception of /ʒ/ in English because that phoneme has a low occurrence in the language and is difficult to picture). Each sound is targeted at least one time. Most sounds are targeted at least one time in syllable initial and syllable final positions each, if appropriate (e.g., /ʧ/ was not targeted in syllable final position because it can occur only in syllable initial position in Spanish). Commonly occurring initial consonant clusters (e.g., /**pl**ato/) and commonly occurring abutting consonant pairs (e.g., /elefa**nt**e/) are targeted. All vowels are targeted at least once (with the exception of /ɑɪ/ and /ɑʊ/ in English). These do not add unique information for classifying phonological impairment. Words of varying length and stress patterns are included. The measures provide for the testing of 1-, 2-, 3-, 4-, and 5-syllable words in Spanish and 1-, 2-, 3-, and 4-syllable words in English. The words are stressed on antepenultimate, penultimate, and final syllables.

SPANISH PHONOLOGY SUBTEST—ADMINISTRATION AND SCORING

This subtest should take 5–10 minutes to administer. The clinician elicits a spontaneous production of the target word using picture stimuli from the BESA Stimulus Book (see Figure 3.19) under the tab for Spanish Phonology. There are two demonstration items for the Spanish measure, labeled as "Demo-A" and "Demo-B." Figure 3.20 shows the examiner scripts used to introduce the demonstration items and the expected responses from the child. This subtest requires the use of the *Stimulus Book.*

To elicit the target items, the examiner prompts a response by asking, "Qué es ésto?"/"What is this?" If this does not elicit the target word, the examiner describes the function of the object ("Se usa para . . ."). If the child does not produce the target word, the examiner should use a fill-in-the-blank (cloze) sentence in order to elicit it (e.g., for the target word *doctor*, the sentence is "Cuando estaba enfermo/a, vi al. . .______."). The functions and fill-in-the-blank sentences are provided on the scoring form. If the child still does not name the object, the examiner can use delayed imitation, naming the object followed by a wh- question (e.g., "Es un vagón/carro; que es esto?") to elicit the child's response. Follow the same sequence of prompts to elicit the target word: first with a cue (F1), then with a cloze phrase (F2), and then with a model for imitation any time the child does not spontaneously name the target. Once the child has named the item, go on to the next item. You may need to repeat this procedure more than once. It is not necessary to use any additional prompts once the picture has been named. Circle the type of prompt used to elicit the target word. This procedure is followed until the child has produced all target words.

Figure 3.19. Example of BESA stimulus plates.

Spanish Phonology—Transcribing

As the child produces the target word, the examiner should transcribe the child's production in the space provided, using International Phonetic Alphabet (IPA) symbols. Do not use standard orthography. If the production matches the target exactly, then place a check mark above the horizontal line in the production box. If there is an error in the production, transcribe the entire production, not just the sound in error. Using IPA, distinguish between the Spanish trill (transcribed as /r/), the Spanish flap (transcribed as /ɾ/), and the English "r" (transcribed as /ɹ/—it's a backward, upside down "r").

Figure 3.21 shows a sample item. The stimulus, *tren*, is written in standard orthography (see A); below it, the item is transcribed using IPA symbols, [tɾen] (see B). The child's production in this example is [tet] (see C). In the elicitation box (see D), the

BESA SPANISH PHONOLOGY

Pida al niño/a que nombre los dibujos. Empiece por decir, **Vamos a ver unos dibujos. Quiero que me digas el nombre de cada uno.** Provoque una respuesta preguntando, **¿Qué es esto?** Si el niño/a no responde con la respuesta apropiada, se le dará una pista, [F1 y F2]. Si el niño/a no nombra el objeto después de la pista final, se dirá el nombre correcto y se le pedirá que lo repita. Transcriba la respuesta del niño/a, marcándola como correcta (1) o incorrecta (0) en la columna "Whole-Word Production". En la columna "Elicitation" marque con un círculo la pista a la que el niño/a responde. La codificación del fonema es opcional. Otras variantes dialécticas aparecen en la última columna.

Ask the child to name each picture. Use elicitation cues and imitation if the child does not name the picture spontaneously. Transcribe the child's response, coding each response as correct (1) or incorrect (0) in the Whole-Word Production column. Circle the cue to which the child responded in the Elicitation column. Coding at the phoneme level is optional. Alternate, correct dialectal variants are listed in the last column.

Empiece con ***S-P Demo A:*** **botella** y ***S-P Demo B:*** **silla** antes de continuar con la prueba. Estos no contribuyen a la calificacion. Introduzca la prueba diciendo **Vamos a ver unos dibujos. Quiero que me digas el nombre de cada uno.** Provoque una respuesta preguntando, **¿Qué es esto?**

S-P Demo A: **botella**

Muestre el dibujo de una botella y pregunte: **¿Qué es esto?**

C: ________________________ ***(botella)***

Si el niño/a responde con la respuesta apropiada, diga: **¡Muy bien!**

Si el niño/a no responde con la respuesta apropiada, se le dará una pista: **Para agua.**

Si el niño/a todavía no responde con la respuesta apropiada, se le dará una frase para completar: **Hay líquido en la . . .**

Si el niño/a no nombra el objeto después de las pistas, se le pedirá que lo repita: **Es una botella. ¿Qué es esto?**

C: ________________________ ***(botella)***

Después diga: **¡Muy bien!** Continúe con el siguiente dibujo.

S-P Demo B: **silla**

Muestre el dibujo de una silla y pregunte: **¿Qué es esto?**

Si el niño/a responde con la respuesta apropiada, diga: **¡Muy bien!**

Si el niño/a no responde con la respuesta apropiada, se le dará una pista: **Para sentarse.**

Si el niño/a todavía no responde con la respuesta apropiada, se le dará una frase para completar: **Yo me siento en una . . .**

Si el niño/a no nombra el objeto después de las pistas, se le pedirá que lo repita: **Es una silla. ¿Qué es esto?**

C: ________________________ ***(silla)***

Después diga: **¡Muy bien!**

Después de asegurar que el niño/a entiende cómo responder a los dibujos, prosiga con la prueba.

Figure 3.20. Spanish Phonology demonstration items scripts and responses.

examiner should note the method used to elicit the child's response. The child may respond as a spontaneous elicitation, as a result of a functional or fill-in-the-blank cue (F1 and F2, respectively), or as an imitation. In this example, the child's production was a spontaneous elicitation, so "Spontaneous" should be circled. (*Note*: In Figure 3.25, the elicitation method is underlined.) Mark each item by transcribing words, noting where the child makes any errors, and noting the elicitation method. We recommend audio recording the subtest administration (with permission) to check for transcription accuracy. The pattern of elicitation information is used to provide clinical information that can be incorporated into a clincal report.

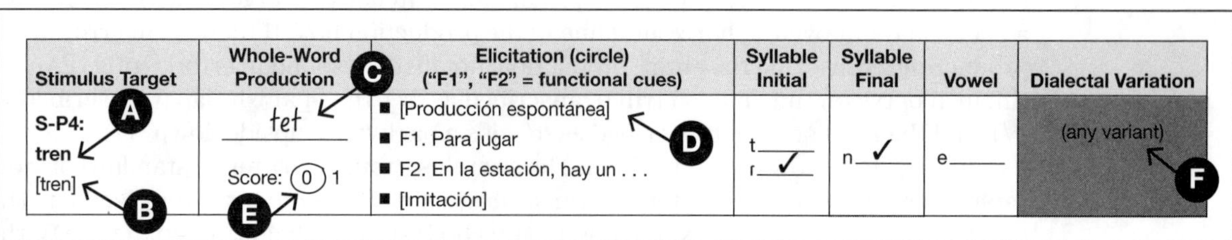

Stimulus Target	Whole-Word Production	Elicitation (circle) ("F1", "F2" = functional cues)	Syllable Initial	Syllable Final	Vowel	Dialectal Variation
S-P4: tren [tren]	tet Score: (0) 1	■ [Producción espontánea] ■ F1. Para jugar ■ F2. En la estación, hay un . . . ■ [Imitación]	t___ r ✓	n ✓	e___	(any variant)

Figure 3.21. Transcription and scoring sample for Spanish Phonology.

Spanish Phonology—Word-Level Scoring

The first level of scoring for the phonology test is word-level scoring (Whole Word Production), which is used to derive the standard score for this measure. Figure 3.21 also shows how the sample item tren is scored. If there are no errors, circle the 1 next to "Score." The child's actual response [tet] is incorrect and should be scored as a 0 (see E). Note that if the word-level production matched an expected dialectal variation, it would be recorded (see F) and considered correct. The total from the Whole-Word Production column is then entered as the *Spanish Phonology Raw Score* on the *Scoring Summary* shown on the front page of the Protocol and is converted to a standard score (Appendix B: Raw Score to Scaled Score Conversions—Spanish Subtests).

Scoring Considerations for Dialectal Variations

Given that there are a number of dialectal differences across the varieties of Spanish, the data obtained on the assessment must be analyzed taking the child's dialect into account. That is, if a child uses any of the dialect features of Spanish, it should not be scored as an error. For example, in the Puerto Rican dialect of Spanish, there is a rule that deletes word-final /s/ and /n/. Thus, /dos/ (two) is produced as [do:] (the vowel is generally lengthened). The Puerto Rican child's production of [do:] should not be counted as an instance of final consonant deletion. However, if that same child produced /floɾ/ (flower) as [flo], then the production would be scored as an instance of final consonant deletion because the deletion of word-final /ɾ/ is not a feature of the dialect. Table 3.1 lists common dialect variations for Spanish dialects (spoken in the United States) observed on the Phonology test. Appendix A: Acceptable and Unacceptable Responses provides a list of acceptable answers for the Spanish Phonology subtest (Table A.3).

Descriptive Analysis

The Protocol also allows for a more in-depth analysis of the child's production patterns to assess whether there is a phonological impairment. For each incorrect word, the examiner checks the line next to the incorrect sound(s), indicating if the error occurred in the initial/final position or on the vowel. To complete this analysis, first place a "✓" next to the sound(s) that is (are) in error (see G, H, and I in Figure 3.22). "✓" should be used to indicate deletions, substitutions, additions, or distortions. In the example in Figures 3.22, [tɾ] is marked in the Spanish measure because the child pronounced it as [t]. The [n] is marked because the child produced it as [t]. Dialectal variations should <u>not</u> be marked in these boxes because dialectal differences are not true errors. In this example, there was no vowel error, so the line was left blank. The Protocol includes acceptable dialectal variations for each item (see F in Figure 3.21); however in this example, there is no acceptable dialectical variation, so that column is grayed out on the Protocol.

Features of the major Spanish dialects used in the United States (i.e., Cuban, Dominican, Mexican, and Puerto Rican) are included in Table 3.1. Remember that these variations are likely to be the *most common* variants of the target but may *not* be the only possibilities.

In the descriptive analysis, found at the end of the Phonology subtest, a chart is provided in which the examiner records the total number of errors and correct occurrences of whole words produced, syllable-initial consonants, syllable-final consonants, total consonants, and total vowels. Across the top two rows, the values are summed to derive the total number of segments correct and total number of segment errors. Remember that some final consonant deletions that are dialect features should not

Table 3.1. Features of Spanish dialects

Pattern	Example	Spanish word	English translation	Dialect
Stops				
/b/ → [v]	/boka/ → [voka]	boca	mouth	M
/b/ → Ø	/klabo/ → [klao]	clavo	nail	PR
/d/ → Ø	/sed/ → [se]	sed	thirsty	C, D
/d/ → Ø	/dedo/ → [deo]	dedo	finger	M, C, PR, D
/k/ → Ø	/doktoɾ/ → [dotoɾ]	doctor	doctor	M, D
/g/ → Ø	/ignacio/ → [inacio]	Ignacio	Ignatius	M, D
	/xugo/ → [xuo]	jugo	juice	PR
/g/ → [ɣ]	/goma/ → [ɣoma]	goma	tire	D
Nasals				
/n/ → [ŋ]	/jamon/ → [jamoŋ]	jamón	ham	C, PR, D
/n/ → Ø	/jamon/ → [jamo]/[jamõ]	jamón	ham	C, PR
Fricatives				
/f/ → [Φ]	/kafe/ → [kaΦe]	café	coffee	PR, D
/s/ → Ø	/dos/ → [do]	dos	two	M, C, PR, D
/s/ → Vʰ	/dos/ → [doʰ]	dos	two	M, C, PR, D
/x/ → [h]	/xamon/ → [hamon]	jamón	ham	M, C, PR, D
Liquids				
/ɾ/ (flap) → [l]	/koɾtaɾ/ → [koltaɾ]	cortar	to cut	PR, C, D
/ɾ/ (flap) → [i]	/koɾtaɾ/ → [koitaɾ]	cortar	to cut	PR, D
/r/ (trill) → [ʀ]/[x]	/pero/ → [peʀo/pexo]	perro	dog	PR, D, (M; rare)
/l/ → [ɾ]	/papel/ → papeɾ]	papel	paper	PR
Glides				
/j/ → [dʒ]/[ʒ]	/jo/ → [dʒo/ ʒo]	yo	I	C, M, PR, D
/w/ → [gw]/[ɣ]	/weso/ → [gweso]/[ɣueso]	hueso	bone	C, M, PR, D
Affricate				
/tʃ/ → [t tʃ]	/mutʃo/ → [muʃo]	mucho	a lot	D

Sources: Canfield, 1981; Goldstein, 2001; Greet Cotton and Sharp, 1988; Guitart, 1976; Lombardi and de Peters, 1981; Navarro Tomás, 1966.
Key: Ø, deleted; C, Cuban; D, Dominican; h, aspirated; M, Mexican; PR, Puerto Rican.

Stimulus Target	Whole-Word Production	Elicitation (circle) ("F1", "F2" = functional cues)	Syllable Initial	Syllable Final	Vowel	Dialectal Variation
S-P4: **tren** [tren]	tet Score: (0) 1	■ [Producción espontánea] ■ F1. Para jugar ■ F2. En la estación, hay un . . . ■ [Imitación]	t____ r ✓ G	n ✓ H	e____ I	

Figure 3.22. Production patterns for Spanish Phonology.

	Whole-Word Production	Syllable Initial	Syllable Final	Total Consonants	Total Vowels	Total Segments
Total Number of Errors		2	1	3	1	4
Total Correct (Raw Score)	*25	68	11	79	69	148
Total Possible	28	70	12	82	70	152
Percent Correct	89.2%	97.1%	91.6%	96.3%	98.6%	95.4%

**Transfer whole word raw score to the BESA score summary on the front page of this Protocol.*

Figure 3.23. Descriptive analysis for Spanish Phonology.

count as errors. Divide the number of correct responses by the total possible responses (shown on the chart) to obtain the percentage correct values for all columns.

Two additional worksheets are included in the Supplemental Analyses Section at the back of the Protocol: Phonological Process Analysis and Segmental Inventory Analysis worksheets. These worksheets provide further description of the child's patterns of speech. The Phonological Process Analysis will help identify processes used by the child during the test. The Segmental Inventory Analysis can be used to identify the specific segments the child produces.

The percentage correct values can be interpreted in light of "percent consonants correct" (PCC) and "percent vowels correct" (PVC) and "total segments correct" as discussed in Shriberg, Austin, Lewis, McSweeny, and Wilson (1997) and Shriberg and Kwiatkowski (1982) (see Figure 3.23). These scores can be used in the description of your findings when drafting a clinical report. Descriptive findings for the normative group and a group of children with phonological impairment by age are included in Appendix H: Percentage of Consonants, Vowels, and Segments Correct. Comparison to the normative and phonologically impaired groups can be used to further interpret and describe your findings.

ENGLISH PHONOLOGY SUBTEST—ADMINISTRATION AND SCORING

The administration procedure for the English Phonology subtest is the same as for the Spanish Phonology test. First, introduce the practice items of the test, using the script shown in Figure 3.24. These items require the use of the *Stimulus Book* under the tab for English Phonology.

To elicit the target items, the examiner prompts a response by asking, "What is this?" If this does not elicit the target word, the examiner describes the function of the object ("It is used for . . ."). If the child does not produce the target word, the examiner should use a fill-in-the-blank (cloze) sentence in order to elicit it (e.g., for the target word *pencil*, the sentence is "The girl drew a picture with the_______."). A list of the functions and fill-in-the-blank sentences is provided on the scoring form. If the child still does not name the object, the examiner can use delayed imitation, naming the object, followed by a *Wh* question (e.g., "It is a wagon; what is this?") to elicit the child's response.

Follow the same sequence of prompts to elicit the target word: first with a cue (F1), then a cloze phrase (F2), and then an imitation any time the child does not spontaneously name the target. Once the child has named the item, go on to the next item. You may have to repeat this process more than once. It is not necessary to use any additional

BESA ENGLISH PHONOLOGY

Ask the child to name each picture. Use elicitation cues and imitation if the child does not name the picture spontaneously. Transcribe the child's response, coding each response as correct (1) or incorrect (0) in the Whole-Word Production column. Circle the cue to which the child responded in the Elicitation column. Coding at the phoneme level is optional. Alternate, correct dialectal variants are listed in the last column.

Administer **E-P Demo A: pencil** and **E-P Demo B: telephone** prior to the remaining test items.

E-P Demo A: Say, **We are going to look at some pictures. I want you to tell me the name of each one.**

Prompt a response by asking, **What is this?**

C: ______________________ (***pencil***)

Then say, **Great job!**

If the child does not respond with the target answer, use an elicitation cue: **It is used for writing.**

If the child does not name the item, give a cloze sentence, **The girl drew a picture with the . . .**

If the child does not name the item after the two cues, have him/her repeat it. **It is a pencil. What is it?**

C: ______________________ (***pencil***)

Then say, **Great job!** Proceed to next picture.

E-P Demo B: Ask, **What is it?**

C: ______________________ (***telephone***)

If the child does not respond with the target answer, use an elicitation cue: **It is used to talk to someone.**

If the child does not name the item, give a cloze sentence: **I'm going to call my friend on the . . .**

If the child does not name the item after the two cues, have him/her repeat it. **It is a telephone. What is it?**

C: ______________________ (***telephone***)

After establishing that the child knows how to respond to the items, begin testing. Do not model the correct targets after testing has started.

Figure 3.24. English Phonology demonstration items scripts and responses.

prompts once the picture has been named. Circle the type of prompt used to elicit the item. This procedure is followed until the child has produced all the target words.

English Phonology—Transcribing

Transcribe the production in the space provided at the time of the production using IPA symbols. As in the Spanish Phonology subtest, do *not* use standard orthography. If the production matches the target *exactly*, then place a check mark in the production box. If there is an error in the production, transcribe the entire production, not just the error. Using IPA, distinguish between the Spanish /r/ (transcribed as /r/), the Spanish flap /r/ (transcribed as /ɾ/), and the English "r" (transcribed as /ɹ/—it's a backward, upside down "r").

Figure 3.25 contains an example item from the Protocol. The stimulus item, *frog*, is written in standard orthography (see A in the sample); below it, the item is transcribed

Stimulus Target	Whole-Word Production (C)	Elicitation (circle) ("F1", "F2" = functional cues)	Syllable Initial	Syllable Final	Vowel	Dialectal Variation
(A) **E-P18:** **frog** [fɹɑg] (B)	[fag] Score: 0 1	■ Spontaneous (D) ■ F1. It jumps, is green, and says "ribbit." ■ F2. We heard the croak of a . . . ■ Imitation	f__ɹ__	g_____	ɑ_____	

Figure 3.25. Transcription and scoring sample for English Phonology.

using IPA symbols, [fɹɑg] (see B). The child's production (in this example [fɑg]) should be transcribed during administration of the subtest (see C). In the elicitation box (see D), the examiner should note the elicitation method. In the example, because the target was elicited spontaneously, "Spontaneous" should be circled or underlined. Complete each item this way by transcribing words where the child makes any errors and noting the elicitation method. We suggest audio recording the testing (with permission) to check transcription accuracy. After completion of the Phonology subtest, continue on to scoring and analysis of the child's productions.

English Phonology Subtest Word-Level Scoring

The first level of scoring for the Phonology subtest is word-level scoring, which is used to derive the standard score. Figure 3.26 continues the item shown in Figure 3.25.

If there are no errors, simply circle the 1 next to "score." Since the child produced the wrong word, it should be scored as a 0 (see E); this is the "whole word" score. Dialectal variations should *not* be scored as errors. Acceptable dialectal variants are recorded in the last column (F). The total from the production column is then entered as the English Phonology Raw Score on the Scoring Summary shown on the front page of the Protocol.

Scoring Considerations for Dialect

Dialectal variants also influence the production of English targets. Children produce Spanish-influenced English targets such as final devoicing of phonemes such as /z/ in /noz/ or stopping of fricatives such as /v/, resulting in /b/. In addition, in some communities, children's English speech production may be influenced by African American English. These variants would be considered correct. Common variants are listed in Table 3.2. Remember that these variations are likely to be the *most common* variants of the target but may *not* be the only possibilities. Appendix A: Acceptable and Unacceptable Responses provides a list of acceptable answers for the English Phonology subtest (see Table A.4).

Descriptive Analysis

For each incorrect word, the examiner checks the line next to the sound(s) in error, indicating if the error occurred in the initial/final position or on the vowel. To complete this analysis, **first place a ✓ next to the sound(s) that is (are) in error** (see G, H, and I in Figure 3.27). ✓ should be used to indicate deletions, substitutions, additions, or distortions. In the example shown in Figure 3.27, [fɹ] is marked because it was omitted. Dialectal variations should *not* be marked in these boxes because dialectal differences are not true errors. In this example, there was no vowel error, so the line was left blank. The Protocol includes acceptable dialectal variations for each item, as

Stimulus Target	Whole-Word Production	Elicitation (circle) ("F1", "F2" = functional cues)	Syllable Initial	Syllable Final	Vowel	Dialectal Variation
E-P18: frog [fɹɑg]	[fag] Score: (0) 1 ↑ E	■ Spontaneous ■ F1. It jumps, is green, and says "ribbit." ■ F2. We heard the croak of a . . . ■ Imitation	f✓ɹ__	g____	ɑ____	(any variant here) ↖ F

Figure 3.26. Word-level scoring sample for English Phonology.

Table 3.2. Features of Spanish-Influenced English and African American English

Pattern	Example	Word	Dialect
Stops			
/t/ → [t̪]	/plate/ → [pleɪt̪]	plate	SIE
/d/ →[d̪]	/daktɚ/→ [d̪aktɚ]	doctor	SIE
Nasals			
/n/ → [ŋ]	/wægʌn/ → [wægʌŋ]	wagon	SIE
[ŋ] → [n]	/ɹɪŋ/ → [ɹɪn]	ring	AAE
Fricatives			
/s/ → [es]	/stop/ → [estap]	stop	SIE
/s/ → Ø	/pænts/ → [pænt]	pants	SIE, AAE
/z/ → [s]	/noz/ → [nos]	nose	SIE
/ʃ/ → [tʃ]	/ʃʌvəl / → [tʃʌvəl]	shovel	SIE
/v/ → [b]	/ʃʌvəl/ → /ʃʌbəl/	shovel	SIE, AAE
/θ/ → [t]	/θʌm/ → [tʌm]	thumb	SIE, AAE
/ð/ → [d]	/fɛðɚ/ → [fɛdɚ]	feather	SIE, AAE
Final consonants			
Final consonant deletion	/bʊk/ → [bʊ]	book	AAE
Final consonant devoicing	/frag/ → [frag]	frog	AAE
Clusters			
Final cluster reduction	/tost/ → [tos]	toast	AAE
Liquids			
/ɹ/ → [r]	/ɹɪŋ / → [rɪŋ]	ring	SIE
/ɹ / → [ɾ] (flap)	/tɹeɪn / → [tɾeɪn]	train	SIE
/ɹ/ → [Ø]	/fɛðɚ/ → [fɛðə]	feather	AAE
/l/ → [Ø]	/skul/ → [sku]	school	AAE
Glides			
/j/ → [dʒ]	/jɛlo/ → [dʒɛlo]	yellow	SIE
Vowels			
tense → lax	/kwin/ → [kwɪn]	queen	SIE
lax → tense	/bɹɪdʒ/ → [bɹidʒ]	bridge	SIE
diphthongs → monophthongs	/pleɪt/ → [plet]	plate	SIE, AAE
Central → [ɑ]	θɚmamədɚ→ θɚmamɑdɚ	thermometer	SIE
/ɚ/ → [ɛɾ]	/fɛðɚ/ → [fɛðɛɾ]	feather	SIE

Key: SIE, Spanish-Influenced English; AAE, African American English.

well as differences related to the influence of Spanish on English (see Figure 3.27). Two additional worksheets are included in the Supplemental Analyses Section at the back to the Protocol: Phonological Process Analysis and Segmental Inventory Analysis worksheets. These worksheets provide further description of the child's patterns of speech (see Figure 3.28). The Phonological Process Analysis will help identify processes used by the child during the test. The Segmental Inventory can be used to identify the specific segments the child produced.

The same descriptive analysis as described earlier for the Spanish Phonology subtest is found at the end of the English Phonology subtest, with a chart provided

Stimulus Target	Whole-Word Production	Elicitation (circle) ("F1", "F2" = functional cues)	Syllable Initial	Syllable Final	Vowel	Dialectal Variation
E-P18: **frog** [fɹɑg]	[fag] Score: (0) 1	■ Spontaneous ■ F1. It jumps, is green, and says "ribbit." ■ F2. We heard the croak of a . . . ■ Imitation	f ✓ɹ__ G	g____ H	ɑ____ I	(any variant here) F

Figure 3.27. Sample from English Phonology Protocol sheet.

in which the examiner records the total number of errors and correct occurrences of whole words produced, syllable-initial consonants, syllable-final consonants, total consonants, and total vowels. Across the top two rows, the values are summed to derive the total number of segments correct and total number of segment errors. Remember that some final consonant deletions that are dialect features should not count as errors. Divide the number correct by the total possible (shown on the chart) to obtain the percentage correct values for all columns. A sample analysis is shown in Figure 3.29 (it is similar to Figure 3.23 for Spanish).

The percentage correct values can be interpreted in light of "percent consonants correct" (PCC) and "percent vowels correct" (PVC) and "total segments correct" as discussed in Shriberg, Austin, Lewis, McSweeny, and Wilson (1997) and in Shriberg and Kwiatkowski(1982). These scores can be used in the description of your findings when drafting a clinical report. Descriptive findings for the normative group and a group of children with phonological impairment by age are included in Appendix H: Percentage of Consonants, Vowels, and Segments Correct. Comparison to the normative and

SUPPLEMENTAL ANALYSES

PHONOLOGICAL PROCESS ANALYSIS WORKSHEET

Target	Number of Occurrences	Number of Possible Occurrences	Percentage of Occurrence
Syllabic Processes			
Initial Consonant Deletion		/17	
Final Consonant Deletion		/18	
Cluster Deletion		/15	
Cluster Reduction		/16	
Syllable Reduction		/19	
Substitution Processes			
Liquid Simplification		/17	
Fronting		/19	
Backing		/81	
Stopping		/21	
Affrication		/18	
Deaffrication		/3	

Count the number of occurrences of each process and divide by the number of possible occurrences to determine the percentage of occurrence.

SEGMENTAL INVENTORY ANALYSIS WORKSHEET

Syllable Initial								
Stops	p	b	t	d	k	g		
Nasals	m	n						
Fricatives	f	v	s	z	ʃ	ʒ	θ	ð
Glides	w	j						
Affricates	tʃ	dʒ						
Liquids	l	r						
Syllable Final								
Stops	p	t	k	g				
Nasals	m	n						
Fricatives	f	v	s	z	ʃ	ʒ	θ	ð
Glides	w	j						
Affricates	tʃ	dʒ						
Liquids	l	r						
Vowels	i	e	u	o	a			

Circle the segments that appear in the child's inventory.

SUPPLEMENTAL ANALYSES *(continued)*

MORPHOSYNTAX ANALYSIS WORKSHEET

Form	Correct Times Produced	Number of Possible Occurrences
Possessive		/3
Third person singular		/3
Regular past		/3
Plural –s		/3
Present progressive		/3
Copula		/3
Negative		/3
Passive		/3

Use this worksheet to mark subtotals by morphological form from the cloze items.

SEMANTICS ANALYSIS WORKSHEET

	Receptive Items	Expressive Items
AN (analogies)	E-S14	
CP (characteristic properties)	E-S18	E-S12
CT (categorization)	E-S6B E-S19	E-S3 E-S5B E-S9 E-S10 E-S13 E-S20 E-S23 E-24B
FN (functions)	E-S4B E-S21 E-S7	
LC (linguistic concepts)	E-S17B	E-S2 E-S22
SD (similarities and differences)	E-S1 E-S15	E-S8 E-S11 E-S16 E-S25

Use this worksheet to identify child response patterns.

Figure 3.28. Sample Phonological Process Analysis and Segmental Inventory Analysis worksheets.

	Whole-Word Production	Syllable Initial	Syllable Final	Total Consonants	Total Vowels	Total Segments
Total Number of Errors	3	2	1	3	1	4
Total Number Correct	*28	62	22	84	49	133
Total Possible	31	64	33	97	51	148
Percentage Correct	90.3%	96.8%	66.7%	86.6%	96.1%	89.9%

Transfer whole-word raw score to the BESA score summary on the front page of this Protocol.

Figure 3.29. Descriptive analysis, English Phonology.

phonologically impaired groups can be used to further interpret and describe your findings.

MORPHOSYNTAX SUBTESTS—OVERVIEW

Both the Spanish and English Morphosyntax subtests consist of two parts. The first part, the cloze task, requires the child to complete the sentence with the grammatically appropriate word or words. The second part, the sentence repetition task, requires the child to repeat a sentence verbatim. Both the cloze and sentence repetition sections must be administered to obtain a Total Morphosyntax score. The cloze task should be administered first, followed by the sentence repetition task.

If the child shows fatigue, the cloze and sentence repetition tasks can be administered on different days.

Cloze Task Description

In both languages, the cloze task targets the ability to complete sentences with the appropriate grammatical forms. The targeted morphosyntactic constructions include articles, present progressive verb forms, direct object clitics, and subjunctive verb forms in Spanish; and possessives, third-person singular present-tense verbs, regular past-tense verbs, plural nouns, present/past auxiliary verbs plus progressive *-ing*, copula verbs, negations with auxiliaries, and passive-voice constructions in English (see Table 3.3).

Every construction section consists of a set of one or two demonstration items and another set of three to four test items. For each grammatical target, first work through the demonstration items. If the child has difficulty with the demonstration items, encourage the child to answer by completing the sentence. You may provide a model using the demonstration item. Apply the same format with the second demonstration item if the child does not respond correctly or does not respond at all. The demonstration items serve as models of the target and may be repeated to ensure the child knows how to do the task. These items require the use of the stimulus for Spanish and English Morphosyntax.

When administering the cloze task, it is very important to encourage the child to complete the phrase, rather than to comment. Read the complete prompt. When presenting demonstration items, always stress the targets that you are trying to elicit. For example, when training for Spanish articles, accentuate the appropriate grammatical

Table 3.3. Morphosyntax constructions of Cloze task in Spanish and English

Spanish	English
Articles	Possessives
Present progressive verbs	Present and past auxilliary + -ing
Direct object clitics	Third-person singular present verbs
Subjunctive verbs	Copula verbs
	Regular past verbs
	Negatives
	Plural nouns
	Passives

feature (i.e., gender, number, person) and point to the picture as you read the prompt and test items. If the child does not respond, use the provided prompts to encourage the child to repeat and complete the phrases. It is not necessary for the child to correctly imitate the target during testing but instead to demonstrate that he or she understands the task. Provide models so that he or she hears the target during demonstration. Once testing has begun, do not provide additional models other than those in the prompt. During testing, repetitions of the prompt on test items are allowed *only* if, on the first presentation of the stimulus, the examiner knows that the child did not hear the stimulus or was not paying attention at the time of the stimulus's presentation. This may occur if 1) the child interrupts the examiner before he or she has finished presenting the stimulus or 2) the examiner is interrupted by an external source (e.g., someone walking into the room, a class bell). If the child interrupts you while you are reading the prompt or test items, stop testing and remind the child that he or she must wait for his or her turn.

SPANISH MORPHOSYNTAX SUBTEST—ADMINISTRATION AND SCORING

Part 1: Spanish Cloze Items

In this section, the cloze items are presented by type in the order in which they are presented. Only the target forms (in **bold**) are scored. If the child code-switches on the target, it is marked as incorrect. However, do not penalize the child for code-switching on nontarget words and forms. There are four target forms included on the Spanish cloze subtest.

Introduce the test items by saying "Vamos a hacer otro." For each item, turn to the appropriate *Stimulus Book* page and read the sentence shown on the Protocol. You are allowed to repeat the item once *only if* the conditions explained earlier in this section are met. Record responses to this section verbatim in the spaces provided on the Protocol page. Correct responses and common alternatives are indicated on the Protocol. Circle 1 if the response is correct or 0 if the response is incorrect. Appendix A: Acceptable and Unacceptable Responses provides a list of acceptable and unacceptable answers for the Spanish Morphosyntax cloze items (Table A.5).

Articles

This section elicits the use of definite and indefinite articles in noun phrases. The article and the noun should agree in gender and number. Table 3.4 includes a list of Spanish articles. Note that if the child speaks Caribbean Spanish, he or she should *not* be penalized for the omission of plural *-s*.

Table 3.4. Definite and indefinite Spanish articles

	Feminine		Masculine	
Article type	Singular	Plural	Singular	Plural
Definite	La	Las	El	Los
Indefinite	Una	Unas	Un	Unos

There are two demonstration items for the section on articles. First, administer the stimulus plates marked "Demo A" and "Demo B"; the examiner's script and expected responses from the child are shown in Figure 3.30 and are also provided on the Protocol pages.

Correct responses and common alternatives are indicated on the Protocol. Incorrect responses might include errors such as omission of the article (e.g., "carros"), lack of gender or number agreement (e.g., "*la* pan"), and production of a quantitative adjective (e.g., "*dos* gatos"), among other errors. Code-switching on the target (e.g., "*the carros*") or with unintelligible utterances (e.g., "*XXXtos*") are also marked as errors. Administer all items. If the child speaks Caribbean Spanish, do not penalize omission of plural *-s* on the article *unos.*

Present Progressive

This section elicits the use of verbs in the present progressive or present tense. Verbs should agree in person and number with the subject. Any verb appropriately conjugated in the present progressive is marked as correct. If the child responds with a verb the examiner is unfamiliar with, the examiner should consult a Spanish dictionary and textbook. If the verb agrees in number and person with the subject but is in a different verb form, it is scored as 0.

There are two demonstration items for present progressive. Begin with demonstration items to ensure that the child knows how to respond (see Figure 3.31). Record responses to this section verbatim in the spaces provided on the Protocol page. Administer all items.

ARTICLES

Si cuenta los objetos, responda diciendo, **No digas cuántos. Fíjate en lo que yo digo** y repita la primera oración.

Demonstration Items: Articles

S-M Demo A: Diga, **Mira aquí.** Lea la primera oración y apunte al primer dibujo. **María tiene *una* flor.** Apunte al segundo dibujo y pregunte **Y aquí, ¿qué tiene María?** Espere que responda el niño/a.

C: ______________________ ***(unas/las** flores)*

Después diga, **¡Muy bien!**

Si el niño/a no responde, repita la primera oración y diga, **Fíjate en lo que yo digo . . . María . . . tiene . . . unas . . . flores. Ahora lo dices tú solito/a. María . . . tiene . . .**

C: ______________________ ***(unas/las** flores) "María tiene **tres** flores" (incorrecto)*

Note que el niño/a sólo necesita utilizar el artículo designado **en negrita**, p. ej., ***unas***.

Repita el proceso con el segundo objeto si es necesario. Provea un modelo para el niño/a por si no logra responder con la respuesta apropiada durante la demostración. No utilice los artículos designados como ejemplos después de que comience la prueba.

S-M Demo B: **El gato tiró los platos al suelo. Y aquí, ¿qué tiró el gato? El gato tiró . . .**

C: ______________________ ***(unas/las** manzanas)*

Figure 3.30. Definite Spanish articles: demonstration items scripts and responses.

PRESENT PROGRESSIVE

Demonstration Items: Present Progressive

S-M Demo C: Diga, **Mira aquí.** Lea la primera oración y apunte al primer dibujo. **Los niños van a nadar. Lo están haciendo ahora. Aquí, ¿qué están haciendo? Los niños . . .** Apunte al segundo dibujo y espere que el niño/a responda.

C: ______________________ ***(están nadando/nadan)***

Después diga, **¡Muy bien!**

Si el niño/a no responde, repita la primera oración y diga, **Los niños van a nadar. Lo están haciendo ahora. Aquí, ¿qué están haciendo? Los niños están nadando . . . Ahora lo dices tú solito/a.**

Los niños . . .

C: ______________________ ***(están nadando/nadan)***

Después diga, **¡Muy bien! Vamos a hacer otro** y siga con la siguiente pregunta.

Si el niño/a responde con un verbo, aunque sea con la conjugación correcta (p. ej., *están haciendo eso*), pregúntele, **Dime qué hacen. Fíjate en lo que yo digo e imita la primera oración. Los niños están nadando. Ahora lo dices tú solito/a.**

C: ______________________ ***(están nadando/nadan)*** *están haciendo eso (incorrecto)* o *hacen eso (incorrecto)*

Si es necesario, repita este proceso con la siguiente pregunta de demostración. Si el niño/a no responde con la palabra o frase apropiada, provea un modelo. Una vez que empiece la prueba no provea ningún modelo que no esté en el libro de estímulo.

S-M Demo D: **María y su perro van a caminar. Lo están haciendo ahora. Aquí, ¿qué están haciendo? María y su perro . . .**

C: ______________________ ***(están caminando/caminan)***

Figure 3.31. Present progressive Spanish verbs: demonstration items scripts and responses.

Correct responses should be in the present progressive or present tense. Common alternatives are indicated on the Protocol. Incorrect responses might include agreement errors (e.g., "*está leyendo*" for a plural item) or use of the incorrect tense (e.g., *caminaron*). Code-switching on the target (e.g., "*están walking*") or with unintelligible utterances (e.g., "*XXXan*") is also marked as an error. Circle the score in the space next to the item.

Direct Object Clitic

This section elicits the use of clitic pronouns functioning as direct or indirect objects. Clitics should agree in case (direct or indirect object), person, gender, and number with the object. For example, if the child is referring to "*las rosas,*" he or she would be expected to produce a feminine plural direct object clitic (e.g., "*las cortó*") that agrees in number and gender with the direct object. The direct object clitics elicited here are *las* and *los*. *Note:* if the child speaks Caribbean Spanish, do *not* penalize omission of plural *-s* in any of the items.

This section starts with two demonstration items. Begin with the demonstration items to ensure that the child knows how to respond (see Figure 3.32).

Correct responses are indicated on the Protocol. Incorrect responses include errors such as omission of the clitic (e.g., "___ *besó*" for "*los besó*"), lack of gender agreement (e.g., "*los agarra*" for "*las agarra,*" referring to a feminine object), and lack of number agreement (e.g., "*lo abren*" for "*los abren*" referring to a plural object), among other errors. If the child responds with code-switching on the target (e.g., "*abre books*") or with unintelligible utterances (e.g., "*XXXen*"), score as incorrect (0). Administer all items. Notice that clitics may replace or double the object of the verb (e.g., "*le* dio un beso a la niña"). In addition, the position of the clitic may be preverbal (before a finite verb) as in "*la* pinta," or postverbal (after a nonfinite verb) as in "está pintándo*la*." Both placements are correct.

DIRECT OBJECT CLITICS

Demonstration Items: Direct Object Clitics

S-M Demo E: Diga, **Mira aquí.** Lea la primera oración y apunte al primer dibujo. **Aquí la mamá va a regañar a la niña.** Apunte al segundo dibujo y diga, **Y aquí, ¿qué hace la mamá con ella?** Espere que el niño/a responda.

C: ______________________ *(**la** regaña/**la** está regañando/está regañándo**la**)*

Después diga, **¡Muy bien!**

Si el niño/a no responde, repita la primera oración y diga, **Fíjate en lo que yo digo . . . La . . . regaña. Ahora lo dices tú solito/a.**

C: ______________________ *(**la** regaña/**la** está regañando/está regañándo**la**)*

Después diga, **¡Muy bien! Vamos a hacer otro** y siga con el segundo dibujo. Si responde con una frase en vez de usar el clítico, provoque con las frases de ejemplo (p. ej., **regaña** a la niña). El niño/a necesita comprender que debe usar el clítico.

Note que algunas de las pistas se utilizarán con menos frecuencia en la segunda demostración para reducir la repetición excesiva y enfocar la atención del niño/a en la tarea.

No es necesario que el niño/a utilice el objetivo designado sino que él/ella entienda lo que debe hacer. Si no produce el objetivo designado, pero responde apropiadamente, provea un ejemplo y siga con la siguiente demostración.

S-M Demo F: **Aquí el papá va a abrazar a los niños. Y aquí, ¿qué hace el papá con los niños?**

C: ______________________ *(**los** abraza/**los** está abrazando/está abrazándo**los**)*

Figure 3.32. Direct object clitic Spanish pronouns: demonstration items scripts and responses.

All items elicit direct object clitics. Of note, some Spanish dialects exhibit "leísmo," the use of the indirect object "le" as direct object (e.g., "*le* mira" for "*lo* mira"). If the child exhibits these dialect-based case substitutions, the use of "le" as a direct object is considered correct. Consult with a family member close to the child to decide on the appropriate usage.

Subjunctive

This section elicits the child's ability to use the subjunctive mood. In these cases, the verb must agree with the subject in terms of person and number. Two items request the subjunctive third-person singular and two items the subjunctive third-person plural. *The child may use any verb.*

Some of the most common alternatives are shown on the Protocol. Verbs in other moods are scored as errors (0). Use of a general verb such as "hacer" (e.g., *hagan* eso) or repetition of the verb from the carrier phrase is also scored as 0. There are two subjunctive demonstration items. Begin with demonstration items to ensure that the child knows how to respond (see Figure 3.33).

The correct responses and common answers are listed on the Protocol. However, any verb in the subjunctive mood, in the present tense, and with the appropriate person and number is deemed to be correct. This is done to address potential dialectal differences. If the verb is in the indicative mood (e.g., "que *come*"), in the wrong tense (e.g., "que *comiera*"), or in the wrong person and/or number (e.g., "que *comamos*"), the score is 0. If the child responds with a code-switching utterance (e.g., "quiere que ***wash***") or with unintelligible utterances (e.g., "*XXXgan*"), the score is 0. Circle the score in the space next to the item. Administer all items.

When finished, count the number of correct test items and enter the raw score at the end of the cloze task section and transfer it to BESA Score Summary on the front cover of the Spanish Protocol. You will use this score to derive the scaled score in the norms tables in Appendix B: Raw Score to Scaled Score Conversions—Spanish Subtests. The scaled scores for the cloze and sentence repetition tasks will be combined after they both have been administered and converted to scaled scores to derive a Spanish Morphosyntax standard score in Appendix D: Converting Sum of Scaled Scores to Standard Scores and Percentile Ranks.

SUBJUNCTIVE

Demonstration Items: Subjunctive

S-M Demo G: Diga, **Mira aquí.** Lea la primera oración y apunte al primer dibujo. **La mamá quiere que entren.** Apunte al segundo dibujo y pregunte, **Y aquí, ¿qué quiere? La mamá quiere que . . .** Espere que el niño/a responda.

C: ______________________ *(quiere que . . . **salgan**)*

Después diga, **¡Muy bien!**

Si el niño/a no responde, repita la primera oración y diga, **Fíjate en lo que yo digo . . . La mamá . . . quiere . . . que . . . salgan. Ahora lo dices tú solito/a.** Espere que el niño/a le imite.

C: ______________________ *(quiere que . . . **salgan**)*

Después diga, **¡Muy bien! Vamos a hacer otro** y siga con la siguiente pregunta.

Algunas de las pistas se utilizarán con menos frecuencia en la segunda demostración para reducir la repetición excesiva y enfocar la atención del niño/a en la tarea.

No es necesario que el niño/a utilice el objetivo designado sino que él/ella entienda lo que debe hacer. Si el niño/a no produce el objetivo designado, pero responde apropiadamente, provea un ejemplo y siga con la siguiente demostración.

S-M Demo H: **La mamá quiere que tomen la leche. ¿Y aquí, qué quiere la mamá? La mamá quiere que . . .**

C: ______________________ *(quiere que . . . **coman** la ensalada)*

Figure 3.33. Subjunctive Spanish verbs: demonstration items scripts and responses.

Part 2: Spanish Sentence Repetition Items

No stimuli are needed for these items. The goal of this task is for the child to repeat sentences verbatim, word by word. The target words and phrases are **shown in bold** on the Protocol. Not every word in the sentence is used for scoring. However, the child must be encouraged to repeat the full sentence without substitutions or comments. Sometimes, tapping on the table will help to signal that it is time for the child to repeat the sentence.

The test items are presented only once. No repetitions are allowed unless interruptions occur, as described previously. If the child makes comments about the sentences rather than repeat them, stop the child and repeat the instructions. The child must produce the word or phrase to receive credit for that item. Scripts and responses for demonstration items are shown in Figure 3.34.

It is recommended that this section of the test be audio recorded (with permission). Introduce the test items by saying, "Mira, voy a decir una oración. Cuando yo termine, tú me copias. Di exactamente lo que yo digo. Pero no hables hasta que yo termine. ¿Listo/a? Escucha." Read the test items at a normal, conversational rate. You are

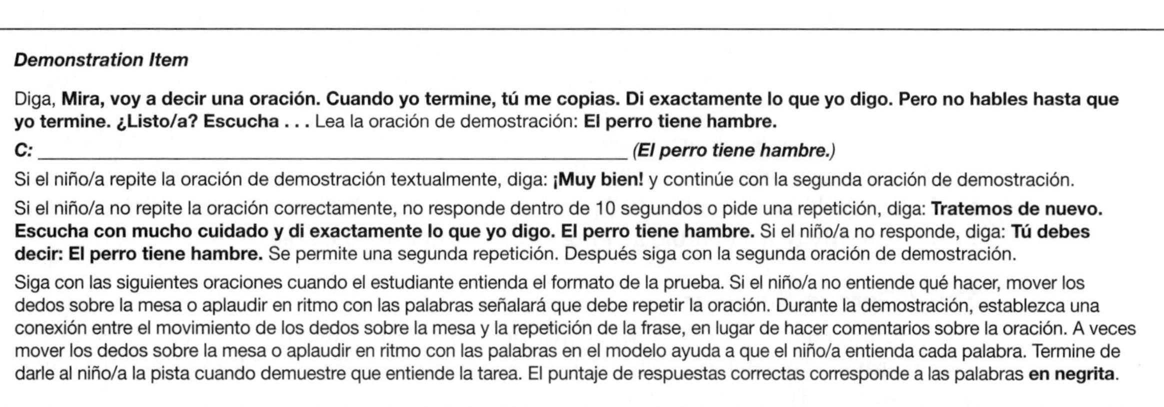

Demonstration Item

Diga, **Mira, voy a decir una oración. Cuando yo termine, tú me copias. Di exactamente lo que yo digo. Pero no hables hasta que yo termine. ¿Listo/a? Escucha . . .** Lea la oración de demostración: **El perro tiene hambre.**

C: ______________________ ***(El perro tiene hambre.)***

Si el niño/a repite la oración de demostración textualmente, diga: **¡Muy bien!** y continúe con la segunda oración de demostración.

Si el niño/a no repite la oración correctamente, no responde dentro de 10 segundos o pide una repetición, diga: **Tratemos de nuevo. Escucha con mucho cuidado y di exactamente lo que yo digo. El perro tiene hambre.** Si el niño/a no responde, diga: **Tú debes decir: El perro tiene hambre.** Se permite una segunda repetición. Después siga con la segunda oración de demostración.

Siga con las siguientes oraciones cuando el estudiante entienda el formato de la prueba. Si el niño/a no entiende qué hacer, mover los dedos sobre la mesa o aplaudir en ritmo con las palabras señalará que debe repetir la oración. Durante la demostración, establezca una conexión entre el movimiento de los dedos sobre la mesa y la repetición de la frase, en lugar de hacer comentarios sobre la oración. A veces mover los dedos sobre la mesa o aplaudir en ritmo con las palabras en el modelo ayuda a que el niño/a entienda cada palabra. Termine de darle al niño/a la pista cuando demuestre que entiende la tarea. El puntaje de respuestas correctas corresponde a las palabras **en negrita**.

Figure 3.34. Spanish Sentence Repetition Items – Demonstration Items Scripts and Responses.

allowed to repeat the item *only* if there is an interruption or a misreading of the item. Write responses to this section verbatim on the line below the test item on the Protocol, even if you are audio-recording the child's responses. Complete responses may provide additional information to the evaluator. Also, noting the nature of the errors will provide important descriptive information about the child's performance.

The word or set of words that must be scored are in **bold** and written out item by item on the Protocol. Score each item by comparing the response to the stimulus sentence. Score 1 if the response is repeated verbatim, or 0 if the response is omitted or substituted. Do not penalize additions or repetitions of words.

When all Morphosyntax sentence repetition items have been administered, record the raw score at the end of the sentence repetition section and transfer it to the BESA Score Summary on the cover page of the Spanish Protocol. Look up the scaled score in Appendix B: Raw Score to Scaled Score Conversions—Spanish Subtests. Add the cloze and sentence repetition scaled scores, record that sum, and then look up the corresponding Morphosyntax standard score in Appendix D: Converting Sum of Scaled Scores to Standard Scores and Percentile Ranks and record it on the cover page of the Spanish Protocol.

ENGLISH MORPHOSYNTAX SUBTEST—ADMINISTRATION AND SCORING

Part 1: English Cloze Items

The cloze items are grouped by type in the order in which they are presented in the *Stimulus Book* and on the English Protocol. Administration of these items requires the use of illustrations in the *Stimulus Book* under the tab labeled English Morphosyntax.

Always begin with the two demonstration items to ensure that the child knows how to respond. Introduce the test items by saying, "Let's do another one." For each item, turn to the appropriate stimulus page and read the sentence. You are allowed to repeat the item once. Record responses for the items verbatim on the Protocol. The correct responses are indicated in **bold type** on the Protocol. Appendix A: Acceptable and Unacceptable Responses provides a list of acceptable and unacceptable answers for the English Morphosyntax cloze items (Table A.6). Score 1 if the response is correct for the target item, or 0 if the response is incorrect. If the child code-switches on the target, it is marked as incorrect.However, the child may code-switch on nontarget words and forms. There are seven target forms included in the English cloze task.

Possessive 's

This section elicits the use of the possessive *'s*. Always begin with the two demonstration items to ensure that the child knows how to respond (see Figure 3.35). Once you have established that the child can respond by completing the sentence, introduce the test items.

The possessive *'s* morpheme should be produced in the correct word order. If the child omits the morpheme, uses a different morpheme, or uses an incorrect word order, the item should be scored as 0. Appropriate lexical substitutions (e.g., **girl's** watch for **lady's** watch) are acceptable as long as the child uses the possessive correctly.

Third-Person Singular

This section elicits the use of the third-person singular morpheme *s* as in "he drink**s.**" Begin with the two demonstration items to ensure that the child knows how to respond (see Figure 3.36).

Score 1 if the response is correct, or 0 if the response is incorrect or substituted or if the morpheme is omitted. If the child responds by code-switching on the target item

POSSESSIVE '*S*

Demonstration Items: Possessive 's

E-M Demo A: Say, **Look. What's happening in this picture?** Read the first sentence while pointing to the first picture. **This is a doctor, and this is the doctor's watch.** Point to the second picture and say, **This is a lady, and this is the** . . . Wait for the child to respond.

C: ______________________ (***lady's*** *watch.*)

Then say, **Great job!**

If the child does not respond, repeat the stimulus sentence and say, **Listen to how I say it. This . . . is . . . the . . . *lady's* . . . watch. Now you say it by yourself.** Say the sentence deliberately and wait for the child to complete the sentence. Here, you may provide a model of the target for the child to imitate.

C: ______________________ (***lady's*** *watch.*)

Then say, **Great job! Let's do another one. I'll help you.** Then proceed to the next item.

E-M Demo B: Say, **Look, this is a chicken, and these are the chicken's eggs. This is a duck, and these are the . . .**

C: ______________________ (***duck's*** *eggs.*)

Do not model the correct targets after testing has started.

Figure 3.35. English possessive *'s*: demonstration items scripts and responses.

(e.g., *"**va** school"*), or with unintelligible utterances (e.g., *"XXXing"*), score as incorrect. It is permissible to substitute the verb as long as the target third-person singular form is produced correctly (e.g., *"sips water"* substituted for *"drink**s** water"*). Here, acceptable code-switching would be a response that does not change the target (e.g., *"drink**s** agua"*). The child's response should always be entered in the space provided to serve as a description of errors and substitutions.

Regular Past Tense

This section elicits the child's use of the past-tense morpheme *-ed* in target regular verbs. Always begin with the two demonstration items to ensure that the child knows how to respond (see Figure 3.37). The goal with the demonstration items is to help the child know that they need to complete the sentence. It is not necessary that the child produce the correct target for the demonstration items, but if he or she uses the wrong form, provide the correct model before moving on to testing.

THIRD PERSON SINGULAR

Demonstration Items: Third Person Singular

E-M Demo C: Say, **Look. What's happening in this picture?** Read the first sentence while pointing to the first picture. **Every day these dogs drink water. And here, this dog does it, too.** Point to the second picture and say, **What does he do every day? Every day the dog . . .** Wait for the child to respond.

C: ______________________ (***drinks*** *or* ***drinks*** **water.**)

Then say, **Great job!**

If the child does not respond, repeat the stimulus sentence and say, **Listen to how I say it. Every . . . day . . . the . . . dog . . . *drinks*. Now you say it by yourself.** Say the sentence deliberately and wait for the child to complete the sentence.

C: ______________________ (***drinks*** *or* ***drinks*** **water.**)

If the child does not complete the sentence, provide the model, "drinks," and go on to the next demonstration item.

Say, **Let's do another one. I'll help you.**

E-M Demo D: Say, **Every day they play with the ball. And here, this cat does it, too. What does she do every day? Every day the cat . . .**

C: ______________________ (***plays*** *with the ball.*)

Do not model the correct targets after testing has started.

Figure 3.36. English third-person singular: demonstration items scripts and responses.

REGULAR PAST

Demonstration Items: Regular Past

E-M Demo E: Say, **Look. What's happening in this picture?** Read the first sentence while pointing to the first picture. **Today, the boy is going to wash his dog. And yesterday, he did it, too.** Point to the second picture and say, **What did the boy do yesterday? Yesterday he** . . . Wait for the child to respond.

C: ______________________ (***washed*** *his dog.*)

Then say, **Great job!**

If the child does not respond, repeat the stimulus sentence and say, **Listen to how I say it. Yesterday . . . he . . . *washed* . . . his . . . dog. Now you say it by yourself.** Repeat the carrier phrase and wait for the child to complete the sentence. You can provide a model here if needed.

C: ______________________ (***washed*** *his dog.*)

Then say, **Great job! Let's do another one.** Proceed to next item.

E-M Demo F: Say, **Today, he is walking his dog. And yesterday, he did it, too. What did he do yesterday? Yesterday he . . .**

C: ______________________ (***walked*** *his dog.*)

Do not model the correct targets after testing has started.

Figure 3.37. English regular and irregular past tense: demonstration items scripts and responses.

Correct responses are verbs in the simple past tense. If the child responds by mixing the two languages (e.g., "***dropped*** bola") without switching the target, and uses the correct past tense, score the item as correct. Ungrammatical elements that are *not* part of the target form are not counted against the child's score. Thus, in the example above, the missing article would not count as an error. Unintelligible utterances (e.g., *"dropXX"*) *are* scored as errors.

Plural Nouns

This section elicits the child's use of plural morphemes. Always begin with the two demonstration items to ensure that the child knows how to respond. Once the child understands the task, proceed to the test items. It is not necessary that the child produce the target correctly during the demonstration tasks (see Figure 3.38). However, if the child does not produce it, provide a correct model of the response so that he or she

PLURAL NOUNS

Demonstration Items: Plural Nouns

E-M Demo G: Say, **Look. What's happening in this picture?** Read the first sentence while pointing to the first picture. **This girl has an apple.** Point to the second picture and say, **And here, what does she have?** Wait for the child to respond.

C: ______________________ (*The girl/she has many* ***apples***.)

Then say, **Great job!**

If the child does not respond, repeat the stimulus sentence and say, **Listen to how I say it. Yesterday . . . she . . . had . . . many . . . *apples*. Now you say it by yourself.** Say the sentence word by word and wait for the child to produce the target.

C: ______________________ (*The girl/she has many* ***apples***.)

Then say, **Great job! Let's do another one. I'll help you.** Proceed to the next item.

E-M Demo H: Say, **She has a flower. And here, what does she have?**

C: ______________________ (*She has many* ***flowers***.)

Do not model the correct targets after testing has started.

Figure 3.38. English plural nouns: demonstration items scripts and responses.

hears it. Once testing has started, *do not* model the correct response other than with those included in the stimulus item. If the child code-switches (e.g., "*manzanas*") or responds with unintelligible utterances (e.g., "*appleXX*"), score as incorrect (0). Omission or substitution of the morpheme /s/ is scored as 0. If the child changes the noun, mark it as correct if the alternative is plausible and if he or she produces the plural /s/ (e.g., pear**s** instead of apple**s**).

Present/Past Auxiliary + Progressive -ing

This section elicits the child's use of present and past forms of the progressive. Always begin with the two demonstration items to ensure that the child knows how to respond (see Figure 3.39).

Do not model the correct targets after testing has started; only read the stimulus item and wait for the child to respond. In order to be scored as correct, the child must produce both the past or present auxiliary as indicated and the verb + *-ing.* If the child responds by mixing the two languages in production of the target (e.g., "***was manejado*** *su bicicleta*") or with unintelligible utterances (e.g., "*was XX*"), score the item as incorrect (0). Substitutions of the verb by another equivalent verb (e.g., *gnawing* instead of *eating* the bone) are acceptable, but a general *do* verb (e.g., *are doing* it) is scored as incorrect. An acceptable code-switched response is one in which the child does not switch on the target (e.g., "***was riding*** *su bicicleta*").

Copula

This section elicits the child's use of the copula verb *to be.* Always begin with the two demonstration items to ensure that the child knows how to respond (see Figure 3.40). Provide models for the child if he or she does not understand how to respond. It is not necessary that the child imitate you as long as he or she hears the model. Do not model the correct targets after testing has started.

If the child responds by mixing the two languages (e.g., "***está*** *sick*") or with unintelligible utterances (e.g., "*XXXck*"), score as 0. Omission of the morpheme is scored as 0. If a copula verb is used with the incorrect tense, person, or number, it should be scored as 0.

PRESENT/PAST AUXILIARY + PROGRESSIVE *-ING*

Demonstration Items: Present/Past Auxiliary + Progressive –ing

E-M Demo I: Say, **Look. What's happening in this picture?** Read the first sentence while pointing to the first picture. **Maria and Juan want to watch TV. They are doing it now.** Point to the picture on the right. **What are they doing here? They . . .** Wait for the child to respond.

C: ______________________________ (***are watching*** *TV.*)

Then say, **Great job!**

If the child does not respond, repeat the stimulus sentence and say, **Listen to how I say it. They . . . *are watching* . . . TV. Now you say it by yourself.** Say the sentence deliberately and wait for the child to complete the sentence. Here, you may provide a model of the target for the child to imitate.

C: ______________________________ (***are watching*** *TV.*)

Then say, **Great job! Let's do another one. I'll help you.** Proceed to the next item.

E-M Demo J: Say, **Yesterday, Juan wanted to ride his bicycle. Yesterday he was doing it. What was he doing yesterday? Yesterday he . . .**

C: ______________________________ (***was riding*** *his bicycle.*)

Do not model the correct targets after testing has started.

Figure 3.39. Present/past auxiliary + progressive *–ing*: demonstration items scripts and responses.

COPULA

Demonstration Items: Copula

E-M Demo K: Say, **Look. What's happening in this picture?** Read the first sentence while pointing to the first picture. **In this pond, there is one fish in the water.** Point to the second picture and say, **And in this pond?** Wait for the child to respond.

C: ____________________ (*There* ***are*** *two fish in the water.*)

Then say, **Great job!**

If the child does not respond, repeat the stimulus sentence and say, **Listen to how I say it. There . . .** ***are*** **. . . two . . . fish. Now you say it by yourself.** Wait for the child to respond.

C: ____________________ (*There* ***are*** *two fish in the water.*)

Then say, **Great job! Let's do another one. I'll help you.** Proceed to the next item.

E-M Demo L: Say, **There was a big party yesterday. At the party, there were two balloons. And here?**

C: ____________________ (*There* ***was*** *one balloon.*)

Do not model the correct targets after testing has started.

Figure 3.40. English copula: demonstration items scripts and responses.

Negatives

This section elicits the child's use of the negative forms *do not* and *are not.* Always begin with the two demonstration items to ensure that the child knows how to respond (see Figure 3.41). Do not model the correct targets after testing has started.

Contracted forms ("don't," "aren't") are scored as correct. Score only production of the target as indicated by the **bold type**.

Passives

This section elicits the child's use of the passive voice. Multiple correct forms are shown on the Protocol. All answers should be in the third-person singular form. The prepositional phrase *"by + noun"* is not required. Do not model the correct targets after testing has started (see Figure 3.42).

If the child responds by mixing the two languages in production of the target (e.g., *"****está*** *chased by the cat"*) or with unintelligible utterances (e.g., *"XXX cat"*), score the

NEGATIVES

Demonstration Items: Negatives

E-M Demo M: Say, **Look. What's happening in this picture?** Read the first sentence while pointing to the first picture. **These men have mustaches.** Point to the second picture and say, **And these men?** Wait for the child to respond.

C: ____________________ (*These men* ***don't*** *have mustaches.*)

Then say, **Great job!**

If the child does not respond, repeat the stimulus sentence and say, **Listen to how I say it. These . . . men . . .** ***don't*** **. . . have . . . mustaches. Now you say it by yourself.**

C: ____________________ (*These men* ***don't*** *have mustaches.*)

Then say, **Great job! Let's do another one. I'll help you.** Proceed to the next item.

E-M Demo N: Say, **She likes pizza. And what about her?**

C: ____________________ (*She* ***doesn't*** *like it/pizza.*)

Do not model the correct targets after testing has started.

Figure 3.41. English negatives: demonstration items scripts and responses.

PASSIVES

Demonstration Items: Passives

E-M Demo O: Say, **Look. What's happening in this picture?** Read the first sentence while pointing to the first picture. **The cat is chased by the dog.** Point to the second picture and say, **But here the *dog* . . .** [stress the word *dog*]. **What happened to the dog here?** Wait for the child to respond.

C: ______________________________ (*The dog **is/was/got chased** by the cat.*)

Then say, **Great job! The dog is/was/got chased by the cat.** [Repeat the form that the child used.]

If the child does not respond, repeat the stimulus sentence and say, **The cat is chased by the dog.** Point to the second picture and say, **But here the *dog* was chased by the cat. Now you say it by yourself.**

C: ______________________________ (*The dog **was chased** by the cat.*)

Then say, **Great job! Let's do another one. I'll help you.** Proceed to the next item.

E-M Demo P: Say, **The truck is hit by the car. What happened to the car here?**

C: ______________________________ (*The car **is/was hit** by the truck.*)

Do not model the correct targets after testing has started.

Figure 3.42. English passives: demonstration items scripts and responses.

item as incorrect (0). An acceptable use of code-switching is when the child uses Spanish in production of words other than the target (e.g., "***was** chased by el gato*").

When finished, count the number of correct test items and enter the raw score at the end of the cloze task section and transfer it to BESA Score Summary on the front cover of the English Protocol. You will use this score to derive the scaled score in the norms tables in Appendix C: Raw Score to Scaled Score Conversions—English Subtests. The scaled scores for the cloze and sentence repetition tasks will be combined after they both have been administered and converted to scaled scores to derive an English Morphosyntax standard score in Appendix D: Converting Sum of Scaled Scores to Standard Scores and Percentile Ranks.

Part 2: English Sentence Repetition Items

In this part of the test, children listen to a sentence and repeat it verbatim. No stimuli are needed for these tasks. First begin with the demonstration item to ensure that the child knows how to respond (see Figure 3.43). Proceed to the test items once the child understands the task format. If the child does not understand what to do, tapping on the table or clapping will help to signal that it is time to repeat the sentence. During the demonstration item, establish the association between tapping and remembering to repeat the statement rather than making comments about the sentence in question. Sometimes tapping or clapping in time to the words in the model helps the child to attend to the words in the sentence. Fade out the cue once the child demonstrates that the task is understood.

Introduce the test items by saying, *"Let's do another one. Remember to listen carefully. Say exactly what I say."* Read the test items at a normal conversational rate. The test items are presented only once. No repetitions are allowed unless interruptions occur, as described earlier. If the child makes comments about the sentences rather than repeating them, stop the child and repeat the instructions. It is recommended to write down the child's responses verbatim on the Protocol while the child is speaking, even if the examiner is audio-recording the child's responses. Information about complete responses provides the examiner with additional information for interpretation of results.

To score the items, in the lines next to the target, mark out the words omitted and write in the words substituted. Only the responses indicated in **bold** are scored.

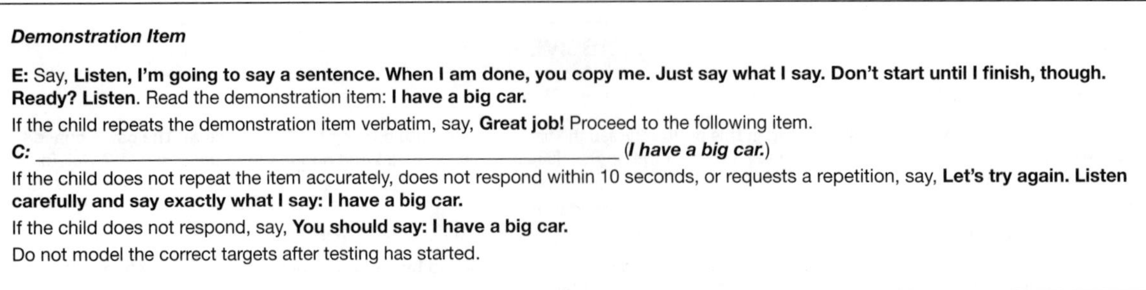

Demonstration Item

E: Say, **Listen, I'm going to say a sentence. When I am done, you copy me. Just say what I say. Don't start until I finish, though. Ready? Listen**. Read the demonstration item: **I have a big car.**

If the child repeats the demonstration item verbatim, say, **Great job!** Proceed to the following item.

C: ______________________________ ***(I have a big car.)***

If the child does not repeat the item accurately, does not respond within 10 seconds, or requests a repetition, say, **Let's try again. Listen carefully and say exactly what I say: I have a big car.**

If the child does not respond, say, **You should say: I have a big car.**

Do not model the correct targets after testing has started.

Figure 3.43. English sentence repetition task: demonstration items scripts and responses.

The child must produce the word or phrase to receive credit for that item. Note that the Protocol shows acceptable substitutions. If the item is a phrase or clause (e.g., "to open"), all the words need to be repeated for credit. There is no partial credit. Score each item by comparing the response to the stimulus sentence. Score 1 if the response is repeated verbatim, or 0 if the response is omitted or substituted. Do not penalize additions or repetitions of words. Word order changes across targets should not be penalized. For example, in "**Does she have** the key **to open** the door?" if the child says, "**She does . . . ?**" it would be scored as correct because "she" and "does" are scored as separate targets. However, if the child says, ". . . **open to** . . .," the item would be marked as incorrect because "to open" is scored as one target.

In the space provided, write in the total correct targets produced on the sentence repetition task. This is the raw score. In Appendix C: Raw Score to Scaled Score Conversions—English Subtests, find the scaled score corresponding to the raw score for the child's age and enter it in the space provided on the front cover of the English Protocol.

Subscores

Two raw scores will be recorded for the morphosyntax test in each language: a **cloze score** and a **sentence repetition score**. Scaled scores will be derived for each raw score using tables in Appendix C: Raw Score to Scaled Score Conversions—English Subtests. Add the cloze and sentence repetition scaled scores together, then look up the resulting Morphosynax standard score in Appendix D: Converting Sum of Scaled Scores to Standard Scores and Percentile Ranks.

SEMANTICS SUBTESTS—OVERVIEW

The Semantics subtests consist of expressive and receptive tasks. For each language, the test yields expressive and receptive scaled scores, which, when combined, yield a total Semantics standard score. All items should be given in one session.

Encouragement/Reinforcement

It is important to establish rapport at the outset of the testing session and to maintain it by praising the child from time to time, without indicating whether the child's answers are right or wrong. For example, you may say "That's very good answering," or "You are doing just fine," or "Qué bien trabajas." Encourage the child to look at all the options, saying "Look at all the pictures," or "Mira todos los dibujos." If the child appears reluctant to answer an item, offer encouragement by saying "Give it a try," or "It's all right, keep on going," or "Trata de hacerlo." On items that require more than one response (e.g., category generation), encourage the child to keep going. Although these items are not timed, we have found that most children can generate a list within 30 to 60 seconds.

Repetition of Stimuli

During the practice items, provide additional explanations, if needed, until the child understands the instructions. Repeat the directions and/or the practice items according to the instructions in the subtest. Once the test begins, questions should be repeated once only if the child did not hear the question, there was an interruption, or the child was not paying attention. Additional cues should not be given. The Semantics subtest is given conversationally so that expressive and receptive items are intermixed. On receptive items, it is not required that the child provide a verbal response, but it is acceptable if he or she does. Some items require that the child point to or generate more than one response. In these cases, *all* responses must be correct in order to give credit for the item. There is no partial credit. However, errors and partial answers should be noted because these are useful for interpreting the child's performance when reporting the results.

Note that some items do not have a corresponding picture; in such cases, the picture plate is blank but is labeled with the corresponding item number. Some picture plates have more than one corresponding item and are labeled with each of the items that correspond to the picture. Some items start with a background story or short scenario corresponding to one picture plate, and the question is asked on the following plate. These two-part picture plates are labeled A and B.

Item Types

There are six types of items. Linguistic concepts (LC) items focus on classroom concepts such as color, number, and shape. Similarities and differences (SD) items ask children to observe and make comparisons among objects. Categorization (CT) items require the child to name or identify items in a given category. Characteristic property (CP) items elicit descriptions of objects. Function (FN) items require that the child name or point to how a named object is used. Analogies (AN) require that the child understand the relationship between pairs of objects and respond verbally or by pointing. Comprehension of passages requires that the child pay attention to and respond to *wh-* questions about objects or actions taken by the characters given in a short passage. The Supplemental Analyses section on the Protocol allows for summarizing observations of how the child responded by item type. Although there are not sufficient items of any one type to conduct an item analysis, observation of children's response patterns can help guide follow-up probes to be used in determining intervention goals.

Language of Testing

The Spanish subtest should be administered only in Spanish, and the English subtest only in English. The examiner should not provide on-line translation of test questions for the child. The child is allowed to respond in the nontarget language. Correct responses given in the other language are scored as correct. Responding in the other language can be noted on the Protocol by circling the abbreviation for "other language," *OL*, for a given item. If the child responds in Spanish, check off the Spanish response; if he or she responds in English, check off the English response. The Protocol allows ample space to record and summarize observations about the language of testing. Appendix A: Acceptable and Unacceptable Responses provides a list of acceptable and unacceptable answers for the Spanish Semantics (Table A.7) and English Semantics (Table A.8) subtests.

SPANISH SEMANTICS SUBTEST—ADMINISTRATION AND SCORING

First, introduce the practice section of the test. Always begin with the demonstration items to ensure that the child knows how to respond (see Figure 3.44). These items require the use of the *Stimulus Book*.

INTRODUCCIÓN: Te voy a contar unos cuentos. Vamos a mirar los dibujos y te voy a hacer unas preguntas mientras te cuento el cuento. ¿Estás listo/a?

S-S Demo A: **Estos cuentos se tratan de Miguel** *(niño con camisa azul, boy in blue shirt),* **María** *(niña con vestido azul, girl in blue dress),* **Ana** *(niña con vestido rosa, girl in pink dress)* **y Diego** *(niño hincado, boy who is kneeling).* **Aquí están sus familias. Vamos a empezar con "El cuento de Miguel y su mamá".**

S-S Demo B: "¡Miguel!", gritó mamá, "¡Ven aquí y recoge tus juguetes!" **Enséñame todos los juguetes.**

Señala los siguientes dibujos.

- ❐ **carro** ❐ **trocas**
- ❐ **bate de béisbol**
- ❐ **pelota**
- ❐ **aspiradora**

S-S Demo C: **Y esto, ¿qué es?** *(Señale la aspiradora; si no sabe dígale,* ***Es una aspiradora****. Point to vacuum, if child doesn't know, say,* ***Es una aspiradora****.)*

S-S Demo D: **¿Cómo es la aspiradora?** *(Si el niño/a no responde, hágale las siguientes preguntas y provea comentarios. If child doesn't respond, ask the following questions and provide feedback.)*

¿De qué color es?	❐ **azul y roja**
¿Qué ruido (sonido) hace?	❐ **hace ruido**
¿De qué tamaño es?	❐ **es mediana**

S-S Demo E: **¿Qué es esto?** *(Apunte a las tijeras; ayude al niño/a o haga que el niño/a repita si no responde. Point to the scissors; cue the child or have child repeat if they do not respond.)* ❐ **tijera(s)**

S-S Demo F: **¿Para qué se usan las tijeras?** *(Ayude al niño/a o haga que el niño/a repita si no responde. Cue the child or have child repeat if no response.)* ❐ **para cortar (papel)**

LC: linguistic concept	**SC:** similarities and differences
CT: categorization	**CP:** characteristic property
FN: function items	**AN:** analogies

Do not model the correct targets after testing has started.

SUBTOTAL __________

Figure 3.44. Spanish Semantics–Demonstration Items Scripts and Responses.

To continue testing, introduce the next item by saying "ahora vamos hacer más." For each item, turn to the appropriate stimulus and read the sentence provided on the Protocol. You are allowed to repeat the item once. However, you cannot give the child feedback about his or her response. You may provide general feedback, such as "me gusta como contestas" or "qué bien te fijas en los dibujos." Record responses on the Protocol. Write down or check the response in the language the child used to answer. Do not translate the stimulus items. The Protocol supplies some of the most common correct items, indicated in **bold**; you can use this list to check off the child's response, or else write in what he or she says. For items that require pointing or naming more than one thing, you can encourage the child to continue, using general feedback such as "¿alguno/a más?" or "¿otra cosa?". All items should be administered.

Mark each response as 1 if correct or 0 if incorrect. As indicated previously, acceptable responses are credited in either Spanish or English. For responses that require a list or array, the item is scored as correct if the child provides the given number of expected items with no errors. The Semantics subtest uses conceptual scoring. Children can respond in either Spanish or English to any of the items. On the Spanish subtest, English responses are counted toward the total expected items if they are correct and unique. For example, if a child says, "dog, gato, perro," the translated pair "dog/perro" would count as one instance. If the item requires three items to be scored as correct, this response array of two unique items would be scored as 0. On the other hand, if the child responds, "dog, gato, pajaro," then this would count as three unique items and would be scored as 1.

The last column on the Protocol indicates expressive (E) and receptive (R) items. When all items have been administered, count the number of expressive (E) items the child responded to correctly and the number of receptive (R) items the child responded to correctly. These are the expressive and receptive raw scores. Each raw score is converted to a scaled score using the tables in Appendix B: Raw Score to Scaled Score Conversions—Spanish Subtests. The two scaled scores are then summed, and one corresponding standard score is derived (using Appendix D: Converting Sum of Scaled Scores to Standard Scores and Percentile Ranks) for the Semantics subtest.

Use the Semantic Analysis Worksheet in the back of the Protocol under Supplemental Analyses to check the items the child responded to correctly and incorrectly. This information can be used to describe the child's pattern of performance.

ENGLISH SEMANTICS SUBTEST—ADMINISTRATION AND SCORING

First, introduce the practice section of the test. Always begin with the demonstration items to ensure that the child knows how to respond (see Figure 3.45). The English subtest is administered and scored exactly the same as is the Spanish subtest. These items require the use of the *Stimulus Book*. To continue testing, introduce the next item by saying "Now listen to this story about Diego's party. Diego's birthday is coming. He and his mom made invitations for Diego to take to school. Here are some invitations." For each item, turn to the appropriate *Stimulus Book* page and read the sentence provided on the Protocol. You are allowed to repeat the item once. Refrain from giving the child feedback about his or her response accuracy. You may provide general feedback such as "I like how you're answering questions," or "Good job looking at the pictures." For this subtest, we have found that, given its interactional nature, children often require minimal encouragement to continue. All responses should be recorded on the Protocol in the language the child used to answer. Thus, check off (or write) the Spanish item if the child responds in Spanish and the English item if the child responds in English. Although it is permissible for the child to respond in Spanish, do not translate the questions; administer them in English as written. The Protocol contains some of the most common correct items indicated in **bold**; you can use this list to check off the child's response or write in what is said. For items that require pointing to or naming more than one thing, you can encourage the child to continue, using general feedback such as "Can you think of any more?" or "Is that it?" All items should be administered.

Read each of the prompts to the child starting from the introduction below. Check child's response or write in answer. **Bolded responses** are correct. Mark all responses as correct (1) or incorrect (0) and circle OL (other language) if the child responds in Spanish. Additional scoring criteria are listed below the prompts.

E-S Demo A: **We are going to look at some pictures and I will ask you questions about them. Are you ready? Let's begin.** *(Turn to the picture and say)* **These stories are about Diego and his family. Here's Diego** *(point to boy squatting down)* **and this is his family** *(point to family).* **Diego's sister is the girl wearing the blue dress. Can you find her?**

E-S Demo B: **Here are some things you can do at a birthday party.** *(Gesture to the different parts of the picture.)* **Show me the picture with the ball.** — ❒ **ball**

E-S Demo C: **What are they doing here?** *(Point to picture of two girls with bowls.)* **I think they are eating ice cream.** — ❒ **eating**

E-S Demo D: **Tell me what kinds of ice cream you like. Tell me as many as you can think of.** *(Encourage the child to say as many as possible in about 60 seconds.)* — ❒ **chocolate** ❒ **vanilla** ❒ **strawberry** ❒ **other**

E-S Demo E: **What is he doing in this picture?** *(Point to the picture of the boy with presents.)* — ❒ **unwrapping gifts**

E-S Demo F: **Tell me what a present is for.** — ❒ **for birthdays or holidays** [acceptable to name the specific holiday]

E-S Demo G: **What color are the packages?** — ❒ **purple and red** ❒ **yellow bow**

LC: linguistic concept	**SD:** similarities and differences
CT: categorization	**CP:** characteristic property
FN: function items	**AN:** analogies

Do not model the correct targets after testing has started.

Figure 3.45. English Semantics–Demonstration Items Scripts and Responses.

Mark items as 0 if incorrect and 1 if correct in either Spanish or English. For responses that require a list or array, the item is scored as correct if the child provides the given number of unique expected items with no errors. Spanish responses are counted toward the total expected items if they are correct and unique. For example, if a child says, "dog, cat, perro," the translated pair "dog/perro" would count as one instance. If the item requires three items to be scored as correct, this response array of two unique items would be scored as 0. On the other hand, if the child responds, "dog, cat, pajaro," then this would count as three unique items and would be scored as 1.

Total the number of expressive (E) items and the number of receptive (R) items that the child responded to correctly. These are the expressive and receptive raw scores. Each raw score is converted to a scaled score using the tables in Appendix C: Raw Score to Scaled Score Conversions—English Subtests. These two scaled scores are then summed and one corresponding standard score is derived (using Appendix D: Converting Sum of Scaled Scores to Standard Scores and Percentile Ranks) for the Semantics subtest.

Use the Semantics Analysis Worksheet at the end of the Protocol under Supplemental Analyses to check the items the child responded to correctly and incorrectly. This information can be used to describe the child's pattern of performance.

BESA SCORE SUMMARY

After you complete both the Spanish and English Semantics subtests, transfer the raw scores and scaled scores for receptive and expressive items to the cover page of each Protocol (see Figure 3.46). Then enter the sum of the scaled scores (from Appendix D: Converting Sum of Scaled Scores to Standard Scores and Percentile Ranks) and the standard score and percentile rank (from Appendix E: Converting Scaled Scores to Standard Scores and Percentile Ranks). Appendix G: Age-Equivalents for Raw Scores shows the age-equivalent for raw scores: add those to the Protocol for each subtest and language. Compare the English and Spanish standard scores for each subtest and record the higher number under Best Standard and circle *S* for Spanish or *E* for English below. Finally, to compare the child's performance on the Morphosyntax and Semantics subtests, use Appendix F: Language Index Composite Scores to determine the composite standard score for those two subtests.

besa BILINGUAL ENGLISH-SPANISH ASSESSMENT™

Spanish Protocol

Name: Isabel

Sex: ☐ M ☑ F

Test date: 2017 yr 05 mo 10 days

School:

Birth date: 2010 yr 10 mo 24 days

Examiner: Ms. Smith

Age: 6 yr 6 mo 16 days

Reason for testing:

Circle language/s used to test: Spanish English (Both) (From BIOS and ITALK results; see back cover.)

BESA SCORE SUMMARY

	PHONOLOGY		MORPHOSYNTAX				SEMANTICS			
			SPANISH		ENGLISH		SPANISH		ENGLISH	
	SPANISH	ENGLISH	Cloze	Sentence Repetition	Cloze	Sentence Repetition	Receptive	Expressive	Receptive	Expressive
RAW SCORE			11	23	7	12	8	12	10	9
SCALED SCORE			10	8	5	3	8	14	9	11
SUM OF SCALED			18		8		22		20	
STANDARD SCORE			95		70		105		100	
PERCENTILE RANK										
AGE EQUIVALENT										
BEST STANDARD (circle language)			95				105			
	S	E	(S)		E		(S)		E	

LANGUAGE INDEX (See Appendix F)	

Figure 3.46. Example of BESA Score Summary.

CHAPTER 4

Interpreting the BESA Results

The cover pages of the BESA English and Spanish Protocols show the child's identifying information (name, school, child's sex, birth date), date of testing, age at testing, the reason for testing, the language/s used, and the name of the examiner. The BESA Score Summary shows results obtained for both languages, reported as raw scores, scaled scores, sum of scaled scores, standard scores, percentile ranks, age equivalents, and best standard score for each subtest.

The ITALK and BIOS survey results, which determine the testing language, are summarized on the back cover of both Protocols. The survey information is used to assist the examiner when making decisions about a child's language development.

AGE CALCULATION

It is imperative to determine the child's age (years, months, and days) accurately. This is done by subtracting the test date from the child's date of birth. In Figure 4.1A, the calculation is simple—no borrowing is required when subtracting the birth date (February 11, 2008) from the test date (May 12, 2013); the child's age is 5 years 3 months and 1 day. In Figure 4.1B, borrowing was required when subtracting. The date of testing was May 12, 2017 and the child's birthday was August 15, 2012.

Figure 4.1B demonstrates the process of using borrowing to figure age in years, months, and days. First, start with the "Days" column; because 15 (date of birth) cannot be subtracted from 12 (the day of testing), borrow 1 month from the "Months" column and add 30 days to 12. Now subtract 15 from 42 to obtain **27 days**.

Next, in the "Months" column, subtract 1 month (it was used for the "Days" calculation) from 5 to obtain a difference of 4. Because the child's birth month (8) cannot be subtracted from 4, borrow one year (12 months) from the "Years" column and add those 12 months to the 4 to obtain 16 months. Now subtract 8 (month of birth) from 16 (month of testing plus 12) to obtain **8 months**.

Then, in the "Years" column, subtract 2012 (year of birth) from 2017 (year of testing minus the 1 year borrowed for the "Months" column) to obtain **4 years**. The child's age is 4 years, 8 months, 27 days. The 27 days are rounded to the nearest month so that the child's age is 4 years, 9 months.

ITALK SCORES

The back cover of the Protocol provides a comparison of the ITALK-Home and ITALK-School survey scores (Figure 4.2). Enter only the higher score (between Spanish

A

Date of Testing:	Yr. 2017	Mo. 5	Day 12
Date of Birth:	Yr. 2012	Mo. 2	Day 11
Child's Age:	Yrs. 5	Mos. 3	Days 1

B

		16	
	2016	~~*4*~~	*42*
Date of Testing:	Yr. 2017	~~Mo~~. 5	~~Day~~ 12
Date of Birth:	~~Yr. 2012~~	~~Mo~~. 8	Day 15
Child's Age:	Yrs. 4	Mos. 8	Days 27

Figure 4.1. Calculating chronological age: A) simple calculation B) calculation using borrowing.

and English) for each form. Note that there may be inconsistencies between which language teachers and parents identify as the better language. This inconsistency could arise from differences in parent or teacher proficiency in each language; it could also be because parents and teachers do not hear the child speaking one or the other language very much or because the language demands are different between school and home. These inconsistencies are normal. If either the Home or School ITALK score is below 4.2, a complete language assessment is indicated. Look at particular areas of concern on the ITALK to determine what domains of speech and language should be tested.

BIOS SCORES

Results from the BIOS are used to determine the language(s) of testing. The back cover of the Protocol provides a comparison of the BIOS-Home and BIOS-School survey scores. On the BIOS Language Profiles, circle the percentages of input and output that were calculated for each language (those calculations are made on the BIOS forms). If a child's profile shows Spanish input/output (SIO) between 71% and 100% and English input/output (EIO) between 0% and 30%, then test only in Spanish. If the profile shows SIO between 0% and 30% and EIO between 71% and 100%, test only in English. If each language is used at least 31% of the time (i.e., both SIO and EIO are between 31% and 70%), the child should be tested in both languages.

Previous studies show that at this level of exposure and use, children are very likely to have "mixed dominance" (Bedore et al., 2010; Bedore, Peña, Griffin, & Hixon, 2016; Paradis et al., 2003). *Mixed dominance* means that they may score higher on one subtest in one language but higher on another subtest in the other language. It is best to test bilinguals with 30% or more exposure to English and Spanish in both languages to determine whether a child has a true speech or language impairment.

ITALK: Indicate higher (Span./Eng.) home and school scores below.																		
						Needs Assessment												
Home	5	4.8	4.6	4.4	4.2	4	3.8	3.6	3.4	3.2	3	2.8	2.6	2.4	2.2	2	1.8	1.6
School	5	4.8	4.6	4.4	4.2	4	3.8	3.6	3.4	3.2	3	2.8	2.6	2.4	2.2	2	1.8	1.6

Figure 4.2. ITALK Scores.

BIOS-Home Language Profile: Enter and circle Averaged Input/Output to determine testing language(s).										
SPANISH	0%–10%	11%–20%	21%–30%	31%–40%	41%–50%	51%–60%	61%–70%	71%–80%	81%–90%	91%–100%
SIO: Obtained %							65			
EIO: Obtained %							35			
ENGLISH	91%–100%	81%–90%	71%–80%	61%–70%	51%–60%	41%–50%	31%–40%	21%–30%	11%–20%	0%–10%
	Test in English			**Test in Both**				**Test in Spanish**		

BIOS-School Language Profile: Enter and circle Averaged Input/Output to determine testing language(s).										
SPANISH	0%–10%	11%–20%	21%–30%	31%–40%	41%–50%	51%–60%	61%–70%	71%–80%	81%–90%	91%–100%
SIO: Obtained %				38						
EIO: Obtained %				62						
ENGLISH	91%–100%	81%–90%	71%–80%	61%–70%	51%–60%	41%–50%	31%–40%	21%–30%	11%–20%	0%–10%
	Test in English			**Test in Both**				**Test in Spanish**		

Figure 4.3. BIOS-Home and BIOS-School profiles.

In Figure 4.3, the child's BIOS-Home language profile indicates exposure to English between 31% and 40%, and 61%–70% exposure to Spanish. The opposite is true on the BIOS-School language profile, which indicates 61%–70% exposure to English and 31%–40% exposure to Spanish. This result indicates that the child should be tested in both Spanish and English.

In cases where there are discrepant results between the Home and School profiles (e.g., 31%–40% English and 61%–70% Spanish at home; 81%–90% English and 11%–20% Spanish at school), children should also be tested in both languages. It is not uncommon for children to have more exposure to Spanish at home and more exposure to English at school. Thus, to best capture the child's language abilities, it is recommended that both languages be tested.

SUBTEST SCORES

Completion of all the BESA subtests yields up to six sets of scaled and standard scores depending on whether the child is tested in English, Spanish, or both languages (three sets of scores in Spanish: Phonology, Morphosyntax, and Semantics; and three sets of scores in English: Phonology, Morphosyntax, and Semantics). In addition, a Language Index standard score is derived from a weighted combination of Morphosyntax and Semantics standard scores. All individual subtests were normed independently, so each may stand alone in the case that only selected subtests were administered.

Raw score to scaled score and standard score conversion charts are provided in Appendix B: Raw Score to Scaled Score Conversions—Spanish Subtests, Appendix C: Raw Score to Scaled Score Conversions—English Subtests, and Appendix D: Converting Sum of Scaled Scores to Standard Scores and Percentile Ranks. These scores are recorded on the BESA Score Summary on the front pages of the English Protocol and Spanish Protocol (see Figure 4.4; note: the values shown are for illustration only).

In addition, the BESA yields descriptive information from the Pragmatics activity, which can be completed using either or both languages. The Pragmatics activity is used to give practical context to Phonology, Morphosyntax, and Semantics scores.

BESA SCORE SUMMARY

	PHONOLOGY		MORPHOSYNTAX				SEMANTICS			
			SPANISH		ENGLISH		SPANISH		ENGLISH	
	SPANISH	ENGLISH	Cloze	Sentence Repetition	Cloze	Sentence Repetition	Receptive	Expressive	Receptive	Expressive
RAW SCORE	12	13	4	12	7	8	2	3	7	5
SCALED SCORE	6	5	5	7	6	4	4	6	10	6
SUM OF SCALED			12		10		10		16	
STANDARD SCORE	80	75	80		75		75		90	
PERCENTILE RANK	9	5	9		5		5		27	
AGE EQUIVALENT										
BEST STANDARD (circle language)	80		80				90			
	(S)	E	(S)		E		S		(E)	

LANGUAGE INDEX (See Appendix F)	85

Figure 4.4. BESA score summary.

The **Phonology subtest** yields a standard score for each language based on the whole word score. On the Protocol, enter the total word score and look up the corresponding scaled and standard scores. If the child was tested in both languages, compare the English and Spanish scores. The higher standard score of the two should be entered into the box labeled Best Standard in the Phonology column (see Figure 4.4) on the BESA Score Summary. If the scores are the same, then enter either one.

Percentile scores and age-equivalent scores can also be reported. Look up the corresponding percentile ranks (using Appendix E: Converting Scaled Scores to Standard Scores and Percentile Ranks) and age-equivalent scores (using Appendix G: Age Equivalents for Raw Scores). These data are then recorded on the BESA Score Summary. Finally, Appendix H: Percentage of Consonants, Vowels, and Segments Correct has comparison data on percentage of consonants correct, percentage of vowels correct, and percentage of segments correct.

Note that the Phonology subtest can be used alone to determine whether a child has a phonological disorder, or it can be used as part of the battery of speech and language testing.

The **Morphosyntax subtest** yields scaled scores for the cloze and sentence repetition tasks in each language, for a possible total of four scaled scores. For each language, look up the cloze raw score in Appendices B and C to find the scaled score for the child's age. Write the scaled score in the space provided. Next, look up the sentence repetition raw score in Appendices B and C to determine the scaled score corresponding to the child's age. Write the scaled score in the space provided. Now, add the two scaled scores for each language and, using Appendix D, convert the sum of scores to the child's standard score. If the child was tested in both languages, there will be one standard score for Morphosyntax Spanish and one for Morphosyntax English. These scores should be entered on the BESA Score Summary and the English and Spanish scores compared.

In the box below those columns (Best Standard), enter the higher standard score, and indicate which language received the higher score. If the standard scores are the same, you may enter either score. In Figure 4.4, the English Morphosyntax standard score is 75 and the Spanish Morphosyntax standard score is 80. The higher of the two, 80, is then entered as the Best Standard Morphosyntax score. *Note*: If the BIOS results indicated that testing should be completed using only one language, then use the score from subtests administered in that language as the Best Standard score.

In addition to the standard scores, percentile ranks and age-equivalent scores can be determined. Look up the percentile ranks and age-equivalent scores corresponding to the standard scores using the tables in Appendix E: Converting Scaled Scores to Standard Scores and Percentile Ranks and Appendix G: Age Equivalents for Raw Scores. These data are then recorded in the appropriate spaces on the BESA Score Summary.

The **Semantics subtest** also yields two scaled scores: expressive and receptive. Each receptive and expressive raw score should be converted to a scaled score by looking up the scores in the Appendix B and Appendix C. The scaled scores for each language are then added to yield sums of scaled scores in English and/or Spanish Semantics. These scores are then converted to standard scores: one for English and one for Spanish. The scaled scores, sums, and standard scores are recorded on the BESA Score Summary. If the child was tested in both languages, compare the two test scores and, for the Best Standard Semantics score, record the higher of the two. In the example in Figure 4.4, the English Semantics standard score is 90 and the Spanish Semantics standard score is 75, so 90 is entered as the Best Semantics standard score. If the BIOS indicated that only English or only Spanish testing should be completed, then enter that score as the Best Standard Semantics score.

In addition to the standard scores, percentile scores and age-equivalent scores can be determined. Look up the corresponding percentile scores and age-equivalent scores from the standard scores using the tables in Appendix E: Converting Scaled Scores to Standard Scores and Percentile Ranks and Appendix G: Age Equivalents for Raw Scores, and record them on the BESA Score Summary. Compare the two standard scores; the higher score is entered into the space labeled Best Standard.

The **Language Composite** is a weighted average of the best Morphosyntax and best Semantics Standard Scores. Look up the composite in Appendix F: Language Index Composite Scores using the Morphosyntax and Semantics standard scores. Find the row (left side of the tables) that corresponds to the child's Best Semantics Score. Next, find the column that corresponds to the Best Morphosyntax Score. Find the box where the two scores intersect. This is the Language Composite, and it should be entered into the corresponding box on the BESA Score Summary. The Language Composite is used to describe oral language ability. Oral language ability can be used in conjunction with other assessment results to determine whether a child has LI.

In the example given (Figure 4.4), the child scored similarly in both languages on Phonology and Morphosyntax, but markedly better on English Semantics.

TYPES OF SCORES

Raw scores reflect the number of items a child answered correctly. By themselves, these scores have no value, and because the numbers of items are different across subtests, they cannot be used to make comparisons between them. Note that there are small raw score differences between Spanish and English for each domain. These differences occurred because the structure of each language is different. Thus, raw score differences cannot be used to compare between languages.

Age-equivalent scores are derived from the average raw score at the center of each six-month interval in each language (4;0–6;11). These average scores are used to associate an age-equivalent score for each possible raw score through extrapolation and smoothing. Because the scores are based on group medians and extrapolation, they are considered to be imprecise for clinical decision making (Bracken, 1988; Friberg, 2010; McCauley & Swisher, 1984b). However, these scores are sometimes required for administrative purposes by educational institutions, so they are provided here. *Use these scores with a high degree of caution.* Raw to age-equivalent score conversion tables are found in Appendix G: Age Equivalents for Raw Scores.

Percentile ranks represent a ranked comparison of performance based on a child's age. The ranking ranges from 1 to 99, with a mean of 50. A percentile rank of 75 indicates that the child scored as well as or better than 75% of the normative population; conversely, 25% of the normative sample scored better than that. A percentile of 99 indicates that the child scored as well as or better than 99% of the normative population; conversely, only 1% scored better than that. Remember, however, that percentile ranks do not represent equal intervals. So, direct comparisons between scores cannot be made. The rank differences near a percentile rank of 50 (the midpoint of the distribution) are very small; the percentile differences near 1 or 99 (the extremes of the distribution) are much larger. A percentile rank range from 25 to 75 (the two middle quartiles surrounding the median) is often considered, in educational settings, to be in the "average range." Scaled score to percentile rank conversion tables are found in Appendix E: Converting Scaled Scores to Standard Scores and Percentile Ranks.

A *scaled score* is a type of standardized score that is transformed from raw scores and transformed on the basis of a child's age. These scores can be directly compared to each other because they are transformed to the same scale. They have a mean of 10 and a standard deviation of 3, and range from 1 to 19. The BESA provides scaled scores for all subtests. The Semantics and Morphosyntax subtests each utilize two sub-scores (Morphosyntax has cloze and sentence repetition items, and Semantics has receptive and expressive items), and the summed scaled scores for each subtest are transformed to subtest standard scores. Raw score to scaled score conversion tables are found in Appendix B: Raw Score to Scaled Score Conversions—Spanish Subtests and Appendix C: Raw Score to Scaled Score Conversions—English Subtests.

Standard scores are also types of transformed scores and reported for the child's age. Standard scores can be directly compared to each other and have a mean of 100 with a standard deviation of 15. The range on the BESA subtests is 55 to 145. These represent ±3 standard deviations from the mean. Scaled score to standard score conversion tables are found in Appendix E: Converting Scaled Scores to Standard Scores and Percentile Ranks.

Composite scores, such as the Language Index, combine two or more standard scores. The BESA uses a weighted average; the weights are based on results of discriminant function analyses indicating the best combination of factors that differentiated children with and without LI. For the BESA subtests, one composite score is provided: The Language Index (which is based on standard scores from the Semantics and Morphosyntax subtests). This score has excellent classification accuracy. The weighted average conversion tables can be found in Appendix F: Language Index Composite Scores (see also Chapter 5, Tables 5.32, 5.33, and 5.34, for more information about best cutoff scores by language and by age).

CAUTIONS WHEN INTERPRETING TEST SCORES

Interpretation of test scores is always subject to error. Error limits interpretability of test results and should always be considered in making clinical diagnostic decisions. Test reliability can be affected by error associated with differences in child performance, examiner error, and sampling of the test content. Thus, it is important to recognize that test scores represent an **estimate** of a child's performance. Child performance should be confirmed by additional observations across different contexts and should be informed by people familiar with the child. The Individuals with Disabilities Education Improvement (IDEA) Act of 2004 (PL 108–446) requires that multiple sources of information be considered in assessment of language.

For bilingual children, sources of error can be associated with either of their two languages and may affect test performance differentially. We selected and tested the content for the Spanish and English versions of the BESA subtests very carefully to reflect children's experiences in each of their two languages. But their degree of fluency in each language and their perception of which language they should use, and with whom, may also affect their performance. Clinician fluency in the language could also affect how a child performs. We allow child code-switching on the Semantics subtest to account for children's divided knowledge in the lexical-semantic domain. But, the examiner should stay in the language of the test and should not translate the items. Practice items in the Morphosyntax subtest will also help the child to know how they should respond.

Children often demonstrate "mixed dominance," which makes it important to test children in both languages and compare the scores to determine which language should be used for determining the composite score. If bilingual children are tested in only one language, this may limit interpretability of the test scores obtained. If only one language is selected for assessment and the child uses each language more than 30% of the time, it is likely that he or she will demonstrate mixed dominance. If this is the case, a low score in one domain and a high score in another domain (in the same language) may not indicate a language disorder. That child should be tested in the other language in order to make the most accurate diagnostic decision.

Another important caution is in use of the test scores. Alternative means to further analyze children's performance are provided. For example, the Phonology subtest can be analyzed at the segment level to determine the degree to which the child is accurate. Patterns of performance in the Morphosyntax subtest can help generate hypotheses about which forms the child finds difficult to produce. An analysis of item types on the Semantics subtest can lead to ideas about which aspects of semantics are difficult for the child. At the same time, remember that there are very few of any one type of item represented on the test; that will make it difficult to draw firm conclusions about appropriate targets for intervention. Rather, use these descriptive findings to generate hypotheses about children's pattern of difficulties, and confirm these through further observations, interviews with the family and teachers, and ecologically valid assessment such as language sampling. Together with these observations and data, the BESA can provide important information about intervention approaches and targets.

CHAPTER 5

Technical Information

This chapter presents the normative data and selection, reliability, and validity. We describe the procedures used to collect the sample and norm the BESA. Specifically, we discuss how we selected the sample and the demographic characteristics of the BESA normative sample. Next, we present studies of reliability followed by studies of validity.

PROCEDURES FOR SAMPLE SELECTION

The BESA was developed after testing a total of 1,112 children, with and without LI. A total of 420 children were tested in both languages; 739 were tested in Spanish and 632 children in English. The norms are based on a sample of 756 children, ages 4;0 through 6;11, who had complete test data; in addition, data from a sample of 198 children who had previously been diagnosed as having LI were used for validity studies.

The data collection for norming was completed after developing and trying out a large set of items in each of the four domains (i.e., the Pragmatics Activity and three subtests: Phonology, Morphosyntax, and Semantics). Testing was conducted by the authors of the BESA and by trained bilingual speech-language pathologists and graduate students under their supervision. Approximately 100 assessors tested children for this project.

Data were collected in five states where there are large numbers of Latino children and where there were bilingual testers who could be supervised by certified speech-language pathologists. Most of the data came from California, Texas, and Pennsylvania, representing the Northeast, South, and West regions of the United States. Colleagues also contributed data from Georgia and New Jersey, broadening the representation of the sample. (*Note:* Future editions of the BESA will encompass all geographic regions.)

An important consideration in the normative sample is the dialect of Spanish heard and spoken by the child. For the current sample, children with exposure to speakers from several Spanish-speaking countries are included. Specifically, parents' countries of origin included Argentina, Colombia, Costa Rica, Cuba, Dominican Republic, Ecuador, El Salvador, Guatemala, Honduras, Panama, Puerto Rico, Mexico, Nicaragua, Spain, and the United States.

DEMOGRAPHIC CHARACTERISTICS

The data collection and sampling procedure used for the development and norming of the BESA resulted in a sample that includes three of the four regions of the United States, varying degrees of bilingualism, and 17 dialects. Inclusion of children who were

Table 5.1. Sample distribution by age and geographic region

Age	West	South	East	Total
4	5.30%	15.40%	11.00%	32%
5	9.30%	17.00%	11.00%	37%
6	9.30%	14.40%	7.40%	31%
Sample total	24%	47%	29%	100%
U.S. Census Hispanic percentage	41%	36%	14%	

exposed to the major dialects of Spanish helped us to examine whether items worked equally well across these different groups. We provide information on the characteristics of the normative sample by age, geographic region, language exposure, dialect, sex, parental level of education, and economic status.

Table 5.1 displays the sample distribution by age and region, and then as compared to 2010 U.S. Census data for the Hispanic population (Ennis, Ríos-Vargas, & Albert, 2011). Distribution by region is similar across the three ages. Most of the sample was obtained in the West and South, and the remainder in the Northeast. (*Note:* the sample reflects the participants available to the authors during the development of the test.)

Table 5.2 displays the distribution by age and language exposure. We identified five groups of children consistent with our previous work (Bedore et al., 2012; Peña et al., 2011). Functional Monolingual English and Functional Monolingual Spanish children (FME and FMS, respectively) are those who use one of their two languages exclusively or almost exclusively. These children have very little contact with another language and perform as though they were monolingual. In analyses, the children who had limited or no exposure to another language (i.e., monolingual children who had 1% to 19% exposure to another language) performed on par with monolinguals. Bilingual Dominant English and Bilingual Dominant Spanish (BDE and BDS) children have had more exposure either to English or to Spanish. Generally, these children have 60%–80% exposure to the stronger language and 20%–40% exposure to the weaker language. Children can often converse in their weaker language and show emerging skills in that language but will generally perform best in the language to which the exposure is greater. Some of these BDE and BDS children will demonstrate "mixed dominance," wherein performance is stronger in one domain (e.g., semantics) within one language but stronger in a different domain (e.g., morphosyntax) within the other language. Balanced Bilingual (BB) children are those who have fairly balanced exposure to Spanish and English (between 40% and 60%). Children with "mixed dominance" or those with "balanced dominance" should be tested in *both* languages. Observation of the language distribution of the normative sample (see Table 5.2) shows that at younger ages, children were more likely to be monolingual, whereas at the oldest age, children were more likely to be bilingual.

Table 5.2. Sample distribution by age and language exposure

	Language group					
Age	Functional Monolingual English	Bilingual Dominant English	Balanced Bilingual	Bilingual Dominant Spanish	Functional Monolingual Spanish	Total
4	7.80%	2.90%	3.20%	3.80%	12.80%	31%
5	9.20%	3.90%	6.70%	6.40%	12.00%	38%
6	6.70%	3.80%	7.00%	4.90%	8.90%	31%
Total	24%	11%	17%	15%	34%	100%

Table 5.3. Spanish dialects in the normative sample

Dialect	Sample %	Dialect	Sample %
Mexican	69.84%	Castillian	0.45%
Puerto Rican	19.61%	Cuban	0.30%
Tex-Mex	3.42%	Costa Rican	0.30%
Dominican	2.82%	Ecuadorian	0.30%
Salvadorian	0.59%	Chicano	0.15%
Argentine	0.45%	Chilean	0.15%
Central American	0.45%	Guatemalan	0.15%
Honduran	0.45%	Panamanian	0.15%
Nicaraguan	0.45%		

Children in the normative sample were all residing in the United States. They were exposed to Spanish, English, or both languages in the home, as indicated by parent report. Parents were asked to report the dialect or type of Spanish and English to which their children were exposed. Table 5.3 displays the Spanish dialects reported. Most of the parents reported using Mexican Spanish (approximately 70%), and approximately 20% reported using Puerto Rican Spanish. The remaining 10% of the normative sample spoke other Spanish dialects.

American Spanish dialects can be grouped into two types: conservative and radical dialects, although there are further variations within these (Hammond, 2001). Conservative dialects are generally spoken as they are written. Key features are that the /s/ is produced and that syllable final consonants are retained. Speakers can be expected to produce the final /n/ to mark plurality on verb forms and to produce the final /s/ used to indicate plural agreement in noun phrases. Conservative dialects include those spoken in central Mexico, Colombia, Ecuador, and Argentina.

Radical dialects are spoken in the Caribbean region and the Canary Islands. In radical dialects, syllable final consonants are deleted in most cases. As a result, syllable final /s/ may be aspirated or deleted, and there may be nasalization of vowels preceding syllable final nasals. An exception to this pattern is that the syllable final flap /ɾ/ is not deleted. In addition, the /r/ and /l/ may be neutralized, yielding the interchangeable productions of /ɾ/ and /l/. The changes associated with these dialects primarily affect the expected responses on the Phonology subtest. In the Morphosyntax subtest, it may be difficult to determine whether a speaker of a radical dialect is producing a plural noun form marked with a final /s/, a clitic, or an article plural form, or with a /n/ in the case of third-person plural forms, because final consonants may be deleted. Test items were selected to maximize the likelihood that children from all dialect groups would produce the target forms. When scoring the test, focus attention on the *presence of the form* rather than on the precise production of the agreement marking.

In addition to the dialectal differences associated specifically with the phonology of conservative and radical dialects, vocabulary varies with country of origin. For receptive items, dialectal variants are supplied so that the examiner can be sure to employ familiar vocabulary when asking the questions. Any regionally acceptable response can be credited when scoring. Common responses are listed on the Protocol, and additional responses are listed in Appendix A: Acceptable and Unacceptable Responses.

Information about the English dialect used by the child was also collected (see Table 5.4). Most of the families who reported that they used English at home reported use of general American English. There were other varieties of English also reported, representing many of the dialects of English spoken in the United States. Similar to item

Table 5.4. English dialects in the normative sample

English dialect	Sample %
General American English	88.58%
Texas English	6.13%
Philadelphia English	2.23%
California English	1.11%
African American English	0.84%
Puerto Rican English	0.84%
Virgin Islands English	0.28%

selection for the Spanish version of the test, English items were selected that were likely to be informative for speakers of all dialects of English spoken in the United States.

With respect to the distribution of the sample by sex, there were similar proportions of boys and girls at each age and across the entire sample. Table 5.5 displays the percentages for each group.

Parent level of education was reported for fathers and mothers separately. These data are displayed in Table 5.6. Level of education spanned all ranges. For level of education reported, approximately half of the sample included parents who had not completed high school. About a third of parents had completed high school, and a little more than one tenth completed some college. College or graduate school completion was 7%–8%.

Eligibility for free or reduced school lunch is an index of economic status. Children are eligible for reduced-price lunch if the family income is 185% of the poverty level or below. They are eligible for free lunch if their family income is 130% of the poverty level or below. In the BESA sample, almost one-third of the sample participated in the lunch program (see Table 5.7).

The distribution of dialects of Spanish and English as well as indicators of socioeconomic status of the sample included on the BESA are a good representation of the Hispanic population in the United States. Representation in the normative sample is indicative of the appropriateness of a given test. Once a representative sample is established, it is important to determine reliability and validity.

RELIABILITY

Test reliability refers to the consistency of a measure or test. Tests with high reliability should produce similar results from one administration to another, assuming the test conditions are similar. There are many potential measures of reliability. Hutchinson (1996) proposes four measures of reliability critical for evaluating a test: internal consistency, test–retest reliability, interrater reliability, and standard error of measure.

Table 5.5. Sample distribution by age and sex

	Age group							
Sex	4	4.5	5	5.5	6	6.5	Sample total	Sample %
Female	33	92	74	53	46	60	358	47.35
Male	30	73	62	59	49	43	316	41.80
Not reported	7	9	15	19	17	15	82	10.85
Age group N	70	174	151	131	112	118	756	
Age group %	9.26	23.02	19.97	17.33	14.81	15.61	100.00	100

Table 5.6. Parent level of education of the normative sample

Education level	Father	Mother
Less than high school	47.90%	48.10%
High school	33.10%	32.50%
Some college	11.30%	12.20%
College graduate or graduate school	7.70%	7.20%

Internal Consistency

Coefficient alpha is a measure of internal consistency. Alpha is calculated from the pairwise correlations among the items of the test or subtests. A high alpha coefficient indicates that the items together measure the same construct. Coefficient alpha is presented for each of the subtests at each age in Tables 5.8 and 5.9 for Spanish and English, respectively. Alpha coefficients above 0.7 are considered acceptable and above 0.9 are considered excellent. Here, most of the coefficient alphas by age and for all data are above 0.8. English semantics coefficient alphas for age 6 (Table 5.9) is just under 0.8 and is in the acceptable range.

Split-half reliability is another test of internal consistency. For this analysis, data were analyzed across all ages of children in the normative sample. Results are displayed in the final columns of Tables 5.8 and 5.9. These results are consistent with the coefficient alpha results and are indicative of generally high internal consistency for each of the subtests.

Consistency Over Time

Stability over time provides additional evidence of test reliability. It would be expected that results from a test given to the same person on separate occasions within a short time would be highly correlated. This kind of stability is referred to as test–retest reliability.

Over a longer period of time (i.e., more than 1 to 4 weeks), we would expect some changes as a result of maturation and schooling. Here, we would expect stability of construct measurement through significant correlations between two time points. However, the correlations would not necessarily be expected to be high.

Here, data are presented from a study by Peña, Bedore, Gillam, and Bohman (2006–2011) during BESA development. In that study, 167 Spanish–English bilingual children were followed from kindergarten to first grade. Both raw scores and standardized scores (from the longer experimental version of the BESA Morphosyntax and Semantics) are compared. Results indicate significant correlations between results in kindergarten and first grade, indicating stability of the measure across this time period (see Table 5.10). During this time, individual children showed developmental changes (seen in raw score increases) and also shifted in their use of each of their two languages. Phonology scores are based on individual sound production of each word

Table 5.7. Participation in school lunch program

Lunch program	Sample %
Regular	65.20%
Free or reduced	31.50%
Not reported	3.40%

Table 5.8. Coefficient alpha and split half coefficients–Spanish subtests

Subtest	Coefficient alpha by age group: 4	5	6	All	Split half coefficient over all ages
Phonology	0.91	0.88	0.86	0.89	0.88
Morphosyntax	0.96	0.96	0.95	0.96	0.96
Semantics	0.86	0.86	0.83	0.88	0.87

(segmental scores). The lower, but significant, correlation for both English and Spanish phonology compared to morphosyntax and semantics is likely due to children shifting from Spanish dominance to English dominance during this 1-year period.

Interrater Reliability

Interrater reliability represents the extent to which items answered by the same children can be consistently scored by different examiners. This consistency is important to ensure that the targets measured are represented appropriately. Scoring errors can lead to making inaccurate clinical decisions about a child's phonological or language ability. Application of detailed scoring guidelines, consistent administration procedures, and practice can reduce this type of potential error.

During BESA development, several studies of reliability were conducted to examine the amount of error due to different scorers. To assess the reliability of the Phonology subtest, 10 protocols were independently rescored by experienced bilingual testers; point-to-point agreement was 95% for both English and Spanish (see Table 5.11). For Morphosyntax and Semantics subtests, 21 protocols were independently rescored by experienced bilingual testers; point-to-point agreement ranged from 96% to 100%, providing evidence of high interrater reliability. When scoring the Pragmatics activity, 30 protocols were independently rescored; point-to-point agreement was 96%, indicating high interrater agreement.

Both intra- (consistency in scoring within a single rater) and inter- (consistency in scoring among raters) rater reliability for descriptive analysis has also been completed for Phonology. Point-to-point agreement on scoring the productions of typically developing children and those with phonological disorders has been greater than 90%, indicating a high degree of concordance (Shriberg & Lof, 1991).

Standard Error of Measurement and Confidence Intervals

Scores obtained from any test are a composite of a person's "true ability" and some amount of error. Therefore, it is important to have a way to estimate the amount of error inherent in any set of observed scores. The standard error of measurement *(SEM)*

Table 5.9. Coefficient alpha and split half coefficients–English subtests

Subtest	Coefficient alpha by age group: 4	5	6	All	Split half coefficient over all ages
Phonology	0.91	0.90	0.86	0.91	0.86
Morphosyntax	0.94	0.96	0.95	0.95	0.97
Semantics	0.82	0.80	0.75	0.86	0.89

Table 5.10. Temporal stability of raw scores over 1 year

English (*r*)	Spanish (*r*)
0.27	0.56
0.83	0.88
0.65	0.71

Note: All $p < .001$.

provides an estimate of error and is derived from the reliability coefficient of a score. The *SEM* is calculated using the formula

$$SEM = SD \sqrt{1 - r}$$

where *SD* is the standard deviation of the distribution (e.g., 15 for standard scores) and *r* is the reliability coefficient, in this case Chronbach's alpha.

The more reliable the test, the smaller is the *SEM*. Using the *SEM*, a confidence interval within which the true score is likely to be found can be calculated. The calculated confidence interval is based on a specified degree of confidence. Table 5.12 lists the *SEMs* for standard scores for all age groups at the 95% confidence level.

Confidence intervals are based on the *SEM* and provide a band of scores within which an examinee's true score will fall. Classical test theory (Lord & Novick, 2008) posits that there is always some error inherent in any measurement, and the observed score is the combination of the person's "true score" (a theoretical construct) and measurement error. Confidence intervals are another way to show the precision of the observed test scores; the smaller the confidence interval, the more accurately the observed score will reflect the person's true ability. Confidence intervals for BESA standard scores were calculated using the formula

$$p\% \text{ Confidence Interval} = \text{Obtained Score} \pm z_p\,(SEM)$$

where *p* is the intended confidence interval level (here, 90% and 95%) and z_p is the corresponding *z* value (found on a standard curve table). Table 5.12 shows the 90% and 95% level confidence intervals for standard scores by age group.

The reliability of the BESA is very good. This is indicated by stability in test scores and correlation alpha and by stable confidence intervals across subtests and ages. Reliability estimates suggest that information obtained from the BESA is consistent. Reliability is an important component of test evaluation, but a test must also demonstrate good validity.

VALIDITY

Validity is an important aspect of evaluating tests. Questions of validity focus on whether the test measures what it is proposed to measure. Types of validity include both logical and empirical evidence of validity. According to Hutchinson (1996), both

Table 5.11. Interrater reliability

Subtest	English	Spanish
Phonology	95%	95%
Morphosyntax	96%	96%
Semantics	100%	98%

Table 5.12. Standard errors of measurement (*SEMs*) and confidence intervals (CIs) for standard scores by age

		Age group			
Subtest		4	5	6	Overall
Spanish Phonology	*SEM*	4.47	4.67	5.63	4.60
	90% CI	7.38	7.71	9.29	7.59
	95% CI	8.77	9.16	11.04	9.01
	N	*92*	*146*	*118*	*356*
English Phonology	*SEM*	4.62	5.15	5.69	5.02
	90% CI	7.63	8.50	9.39	8.28
	95% CI	9.06	10.10	11.16	9.84
	N	*66*	*111*	*115*	*292*
Spanish Morphosyntax	*SEM*	3.00	3.00	3.35	3.00
	90% CI	4.95	4.95	5.53	4.95
	95% CI	5.88	5.88	6.57	5.88
	N	*65*	*71*	*88*	*224*
English Morphosyntax	*SEM*	2.92	3.04	3.29	2.92
	90% CI	4.82	5.01	5.42	4.82
	95% CI	5.73	5.95	6.44	5.73
	N	*93*	*91*	*105*	*289*
Spanish Semantics	*SEM*	6.42	6.72	7.45	5.67
	90% CI	10.59	11.10	12.30	9.36
	95% CI	12.58	13.18	14.61	11.12
	N	*106*	*156*	*142*	*404*
English Semantics	*SEM*	5.71	5.59	6.11	5.13
	90% CI	9.42	9.23	10.08	8.47
	95% CI	11.20	10.96	11.98	10.06
	N	*121*	*167*	*147*	*435*

types of validity are important for judging whether a test is appropriate for the intended use. Logical validity includes questions about test clarity and purpose, clearly defined concepts, and the rationale for selection of test content. Empirical validity includes evidence of the test's relationship with other (similar and dissimilar) tests and measures, relationship among the components of the test, and classification accuracy.

Logical Validity

Logical validity is a form of face or content validity and refers to test purpose or test construct. The test and subtest organization should make sense given the intended purpose. Test items should be those that represent the construct being tested.

Test Purpose

As stated in Chapter 1, the BESA was developed in response to the need for an assessment of speech and language that is culturally and linguistically appropriate for Spanish–English bilingual children. Its purpose is to identify LI and/or speech impairment in Spanish–English speakers ages 4 through 6. In addition, it was specifically developed in both Spanish and English to help clinicians differentiate typical speech-language differences from true speech-language impairment.

Bilingual Concept Definitions

The BESA uses many concepts and ideas that are commonly known to speech-language pathologists and school personnel, which are detailed in Chapter 3. In addition, there are concepts used here that are specific to the process of conducting a bilingual assessment. These concepts and definitions are presented in Chapter 3, but we highlight some here again that may be less familiar.

Language input and output refers to the percentage of time children currently hear (input) and use (output) Spanish and English. Input and output are used in the BIOS to determine which language(s) should be used for testing.

Age of first exposure to English refers to the age at which the child was first regularly exposed to English as a second language; this information helps clinicians to interpret child performance in each language.

Mixed dominance refers to the notion that bilingual children may show relative strength in a given domain (e.g., semantics) in one language (e.g., English) while demonstrating strength in a different domain (e.g., morphosyntax) in the other language (e.g., Spanish). Mixed dominance has been documented for a significant proportion of bilingual children (Bedore et al., 2010; Bedore et al., 2012; Kohnert & Bates, 2002; Kohnert, Bates, & Hernández, 1999) and is not considered an indicator of impairment. Children both with and without LI may present with "mixed dominance" (Paradis et al., 2003).

Rationale for the Selection of Subtest Content

The content for each subtest was based on a thorough review of the developmental and clinical literature for each of the test domains. For each of the subtests, we developed and tested items that potentially differentiated LI and/or speech impairment in Spanish and English. During the initial development phase, a large number of items for each domain was generated and tested with small groups of bilingual children, with and without LI. Items were based on the literature and our own clinical experiences with bilingual children, as indicated the following sections (see Tables 5.13–5.16). Through tryout testing, items that differentiated between children with and without LI were retained. This smaller set of items was then tested with larger numbers of children for further item reduction. Item analysis identified the best set of items for inclusion in the final, normed test.

Pragmatics

The Pragmatics activity is set up by asking the child to wrap a gift for a friend named "Diego." The items were developed based on Fey's (1986) system for conversational acts. The activity elicits mainly assertive acts. Table 5.13 includes a list of conversational acts, definitions, and examples from the Pragmatics activity.

Phonology

The Phonology subtest includes whole-word scoring. In addition, selected target items include syllable initial and syllable final consonants based on the structure of Spanish and English. Descriptive analyses include percentage correct determinations for whole-word production, initial syllables, final syllables, consonants, vowels, and total segments. Table 5.14 provides the background citations that justify inclusion of these levels of analysis.

Morphosyntax

Items for the Morphosyntax subtest were selected based on previous research indicating the difficulties that children have in the grammatical area. Items that had been demonstrated to be difficult for Spanish monolinguals with LI and/or for bilingual

Table 5.13. Pragmatics activity tasks

Conversational act	Definition	Example
Request for information	Questions, solicitation of new information	*What is it? What's in the box?*
Request for action	Solicitation of an action to be performed by the conversational partner	*Give me the tape.*
Request for clarification	Questions that request clarification of the conversational partner's previous statement	*What's a mushki?*
Comments	Making comment in the form of naming or description of objects in view	*The tape dispenser is empty. We're out of tape.*
Disagreements	Use of negation	*That's not the blue one, it's green.*
Statement	Explanations, description of rules and steps	*First, wrap the paper around the box, then tape it.*

Spanish–English speakers with LI were selected for testing. Likewise, items were developed that targeted the difficulties documented in monolingual English and bilingual Spanish–English speakers with LI. Table 5.15 displays the types of items included in the Spanish and English versions of the Morphosyntax subtest of the BESA. Justification for inclusion of these items is detailed in the Source Literature column.

Semantics

The Semantics items were selected to elicit concepts and word associations. The Semantics subtest includes seven item types (these are listed in Table 5.16) and includes both expressive and receptive items. Semantic concept items were selected for the BESA for two main reasons. First, they allow children to respond in different ways without penalizing for diverse individual experiences. Second, it is documented that children with LI

Table 5.14. Phonology subtest levels of analysis

Level of analysis	English examples*	Source literature	Spanish examples	Source literature
Whole word	/fɹɑg/ [fɹɑg]	Ingram (2002)	/tɾen/ "train" → [tɾen]	(Acevedo, 1993; Anderson & Smith, 1987; Jimenez, 1987)
Syllable initial	/fɹɑg/	(Gildersleeve-Neumann, Kester, Davis, & Peña, 2008; Smit, Hand, Freilinger, Bernthal, & Bird, 1990; Stoel-Gammon & Dunn, 1985)	/tɾen/	(Acevedo, 1993; Anderson & Smith, 1987; Jimenez, 1987)
Syllable final	/fɹɑg/	(Gildersleeve-Neumann et al., 2008; Stoel-Gammon & Dunn, 1985)	/tɾen/	(Acevedo, 1993; Anderson & Smith, 1987; Jimenez, 1987)
Total consonants	/fɹɑg/	(Austin & Shriberg, 1996; Gildersleeve-Neumann et al., 2008; Shriberg, 1993; Shriberg, Austin, Lewis, McSweeny, & Wilson, 1997; Shriberg & Kwiatkowski, 1994)	/tɾen/	(Acevedo, 1993; Anderson & Smith, 1987; Jimenez, 1987)
Vowels	/fɹɑg/	(Austin & Shriberg, 1996; Gildersleeve-Neumann et al., 2008; Shriberg, 1993; Shriberg et al., 1997; Shriberg & Kwiatkowski, 1994)	/tɾen/	(Acevedo, 1993; Anderson & Smith, 1987; Jimenez, 1987)
Total segments	/fɹɑg/	(Austin & Shriberg, 1996; Gildersleeve-Neumann et al., 2008; Shriberg, 1993; Shriberg et al., 1997; Shriberg & Kwiatkowski, 1994)	/tɾen/	(Acevedo, 1993; Anderson & Smith, 1987; Jimenez, 1987)

Table 5.15. Morphosyntax subtest item types

Target	English	Spanish	Examples	Source literature
Articles		✓	*el niño*	Ambert, 1986; Anderson & Souto, 2005; Bosch & Serra, 1997; Eng & O'Connor, 2000; Leonard, Eyer, Bedore, & Grela, 1997; Restrepo & Gutiérrez-Clellen, 2001
Clitics		✓	*lo rompió* (*it* [masculine] *broke-third person singular present tense*)	Ambert, 1986; Bedore & Leonard, 2001; Bosch & Serra, 1997; Jacobson & Livert, 2010; Jacobson & Schwartz, 2002; Restrepo & Gutiérrez-Clellen, 2001
Plural -*s*	✓		*boxes*	Leonard et al., 1997
Possessive -*s*	✓		*teacher's*	Leonard et al., 1997
Third-person singular present	✓		*runs*	Leonard et al., 1997; Rice & Wexler, 1996; Rice, Wexler, & Cleave, 1995
Regular and irregular past tense	✓		*dropped; broke*	Ambert, 1986; Centeno & Anderson, 2011; Jacobson & Livert, 2010; Jacobson & Schwartz, 2005; Leonard et al., 1997; Restrepo & Kruth, 2000
Copula	✓		*He is tall.*	Rice et al., 1995
Present and past auxiliary	✓	✓	*They are going to . . .* *They were going to . . .; Lo estan haceindo (they are doing it), Estaban comiendo (they were eating)*	Rice et al., 1995
Subjunctive		✓	*camine (walk, subjunctive)*	Bedore & Leonard, 2001; Gutiérrez-Clellen, Restrepo, Bedore, Peña, & Anderson, 2000
Prepositional phrases (SR)	✓	✓	*between the houses;* *entre las casas*	Ambert, 1986; Slobin & Bocaz, 1988
Relative clauses (SR)	✓	✓	*. . . that was on the stove; . . . que estaba en la estufa*	Barriga Villanueva, 1985; Gutiérrez-Clellen, 1998; Gutiérrez-Clellen & Hofstetter, 1994
Negative	✓	✓	*don't burn the toast; no hay ninguna ([there] are none)*	Padilla & Lindholm, 1976
Questions with inversion (SR)	✓		*Is the bus at the school?*	Merino, 1983; Padilla & Lindholm, 1976
Adjective agreement (SR)		✓	*las manzanas son rojas (the apples are red)*	Bedore & Leonard, 2001; Torrens & Wexler, 2001

Key: SR, Sentence repetition.

Table 5.16. Item types included in the Semantics subtest

Target	Examples	Background literature
Analogies	*Hamburger is to plate as soup is to _____.*	Rattermann & Gentner, 1998
Descriptions	*Tell me three things about a school bus.*	Clark, 2001
Category generation	*Tell me the names of as many zoo animals as you can think of.*	Nelson & Nelson, 1990
Similarities and differences	*What makes these two cards go together?*	Bloom, 2000; Choi, McDonough, Bowerman, & Mandler, 1999
Functions	*What do you use a pencil for?*	Crystal, 1998; Peña & Quinn, 1997
Linguistic concepts	*What color is this balloon?*	Golomb, 2013; Vermeer & Shohov, 2004; Wilcox, 1999

have difficulty in the expression of semantic associations. Even if they have vocabulary knowledge in the normal age range (i.e., breadth of semantic knowledge), research indicates that these children have particular difficulties with depth of semantic knowledge.

Empirical Validity

Beyond logical or content validity, it is also important to establish empirical evidence of validity. Empirical evidence of validity includes evaluation of item difficulty and item discrimination.

Item Difficulty Analysis

Item difficulty analysis provides information about test ease and difficulty and is a quantitative measure of content validity. Item difficulty analysis is used to examine the test's content relative to children of different ages, and with and without impairment. Item difficulty values range from 0 to 1 and represent the proportion of children who responded correctly to an item. Items with values close to 1 are considered easy, and items with values close to 0 are considered very difficult (Allen & Yen, 1979; Friedenberg, 1995). Item difficulty analysis helps to identify the items that are of appropriate difficulty for the target age range. Items that are too easy or too hard are eliminated from the test.

Tables 5.17 and 5.18 display the average item difficulty for each subtest by age and ability. In general, there are age differences for Morphosyntax and Semantics, as predicted. The literature indicates that children continue to make changes in both morphosyntax and semantics in the target age range. There were virtually no age-related differences for Spanish Phonology and very small differences for English Phonology. This is consistent with the literature reporting that children have good phonological skills by about age 4, and that children's speech is highly intelligible at that age as well. Finally, there are no age-related differences for Pragmatics; this is consistent with the characteristics of this language domain.

Tables 5.17 and 5.18 also display item difficulty statistics for children with and without language or phonological impairment. Item difficulty statistics for each subgroup at each age show that the typically developing group consistently scores higher in comparison to the group with phonological impairment (on the Phonology subtest) and higher than the group with LI for Morphosyntax and Semantics. There are also small differences for the Pragmatics subtest, but generally this was an area of strength even for children with LI. Because the Pragmatics activity did not differentiate either by age or by LI status, it was not included as a scored component in the final form of the BESA.

Item Discrimination

Item discrimination is another quantitative measure used to evaluate test content. Item discrimination is the difference between the item difficulty values for children with and without communication impairment. This quantitative analysis was used to identify

Table 5.17. Spanish item difficulty statistics: age and ability

	Phonology		Morphosyntax		Semantics	
Age group	Normal language	Phonologically impaired	Normal language	Language impaired	Normal language	Language impaired
4	0.91	0.51	0.55	0.21	0.55	0.26
5	0.86	0.48	0.69	0.30	0.67	0.37
6	0.88	0.45	0.78	0.34	0.79	0.48

Table 5.18. English item difficulty statistics: age and ability

	Phonology		Morphosyntax		Semantics	
Age group	Normal language	Phonologically impaired	Normal language	Language impaired	Normal language	Language impaired
4	0.80	0.38	0.69	0.33	0.57	0.26
5	0.81	0.49	0.68	0.27	0.65	0.35
6	0.86	0.53	0.79	0.39	0.80	0.49

items that would best differentiate children with and without language and/or speech impairments, depending on the subtest. Discrimination values of .30 or greater are considered good (Friedenberg, 1995). Thus, items with poor discrimination values were excluded from the final version of the test.

Table 5.19 displays the average discrimination values for each subtest by age and language. Children with and without LI are compared in terms of Pragmatics, Phonology, Morphosyntax, and Semantics tasks. Discrimination values on the BESA subtests consistently show good discrimination on Phonology, Morphosyntax, and Semantics in both languages. Although there are no ability differences on the Pragmatics items, correlation analysis found that total Pragmatics scores were significantly associated with severity of LI.

Construct Validity

Construct validity evaluates the extent to which a measure represents the trait measured (Anastasi & Urbina, 1997). Empirical evidence of construct validity on the BESA includes associations with age. It is expected that in language acquisition, older children perform more accurately than younger children. Furthermore, a test that is designed to identify children with impairment should show differences between children with and without impairment. Finally, factor analysis evaluates the extent to which items on the different subtests group within each subtest.

Correlations With Age

On the BESA, age differentiation is one construct proposed to account for differences in test performance. More specifically, within each language it is expected that age would account for some of the differences in performance, particularly in morphosyntax and semantics. It is expected that correlation with phonology would be more modest, given that children with typical development generally master most of their sound inventory by about age 4 (Bedore, 1999). With respect to pragmatics, correlations by age would be very modest because interactional turn-taking forms the basis for communication from a very young age. In this section, we investigate the extent to which the subtests are sensitive to age in months.

Table 5.19. Median item discrimination indices by age, subtest, and language

	Phonology		Morphosyntax		Semantics	
Age group	Spanish	English	Spanish	English	Spanish	English
4	0.41	0.42	0.34	0.42	0.29	0.31
5	0.39	0.32	0.38	0.36	0.29	0.30
6	0.44	0.33	0.44	0.40	0.31	0.31

Table 5.20a. Unsmoothed mean raw scores by age

	Spanish			English		
Age group	Phonology (28)	Morphosyntax (58)	Semantics (25)	Phonology (31)	Morphosyntax (57)	Semantics (25)
4	20.24	23.83	9.97	22.83	26.33	9.34
5	21.81	28.91	16.82	23.41	30.50	16.05
6	24.44	37.03	18.67	23.95	37.76	17.27

Table 5.20a shows the expected trend for scores to increase with age. Table 5.20b shows the correlations of raw score with age. Results demonstrate significant, moderate to large age effects on all the measures in both languages, as expected. (For all correlations, $p < .001$.)

Children With and Without Language Impairment

It would be expected that typically developing children and those who had been previously diagnosed with LI would perform differently on the subtests. Tables 5.21 and 5.22 show the score differences seen in the raw (unsmoothed) scores, with the group with LI scoring lower than the typically developing group for all subtests and all ages.

Factor Analysis

Another aspect of construct validity is the extent to which the different domains of the test are distinct or uniquely identified. One way to establish these different traits (or factors) is to subject data to factor analysis to determine their factor structure. Principal components factor analyses (PCAs) were completed separately for the English and Spanish scores (the three subtests and the Pragmatics activity) in order to identify the factor structure underlying the BESA. Subsequent analyses utilizing *all item answers* for English and Spanish components confirmed that the items within each of the four sets of items (for both languages) loaded distinctly on separate factors (see Appendix I: Factor Loadings—BESA Items). (*Note:* Although the published version of the BESA does not include Pragmatics scores, the normative study did, and those data were used in these analyses. Pragmatics scores did not differentiate between ages or impairment status, so those items were designated to be an unscored activity instead of a standardized subtest.)

Analysis of English Subtests and Items

The initial PCAs utilized English *subtest total scores*, and later PCAs with varimax rotation confirmed that the subtests each loaded onto separate factors (see Table 5.23). Analysis of the 124 English items (25 Semantics, 31 Phonology, 11 Pragmatics, and 57 Morphosyntax) yielded five factors due to the cloze and sentence repetition items in the English Morphosyntax subtest loading onto two separate factors. For scoring and interpretation of both languages, separate scores are derived for the Morphosyntax cloze and sentence repetition items, which are then combined for one subtest score.

Table 5.20b. Subtest raw score correlations with age

Subtest	Spanish	English
Phonology	0.38	0.37
Morphosyntax	0.57	0.44
Semantics	0.69	0.72

Note: ps < .001.

Table 5.21. Subtest raw score data for typically developing sample

		Typically developing sample					
		Spanish Phono.	English Phono.	Spanish Morpho.	English Morpho.	Spanish Seman.	English Seman.
Age 4.0	Mean	20.67	25.90	25.92	33.50	11.80	10.80
	SD	5.35	3.11	14.14	11.95	3.85	6.13
Age 4.25	Mean	23.00	23.43	27.29	40.33	11.82	15.00
	SD	4.55	5.03	9.14	13.44	5.18	4.82
Age 4.5	Mean	21.48	23.93	28.06	35.82	11.73	12.00
	SD	6.32	5.19	9.83	15.30	4.38	5.68
Age 4.75	Mean	22.11	24.79	26.17	39.69	12.90	14.36
	SD	5.18	4.65	12.45	12.28	4.80	4.92
Age 5.0	Mean	22.03	24.03	31.20	41.63	13.77	13.93
	SD	5.62	4.67	10.34	9.08	4.44	5.17
Age 5.25	Mean	23.64	24.14	30.44	36.00	15.00	15.46
	SD	4.90	5.41	11.51	12.38	5.32	4.33
Age 5.5	Mean	22.88	25.04	33.27	35.33	17.61	16.94
	SD	4.55	3.77	10.67	13.41	2.93	4.63
Age 5.75	Mean	24.15	24.39	32.52	37.40	16.74	15.90
	SD	3.35	4.71	12.54	11.39	4.14	5.95
Age 6.0	Mean	23.18	26.08	34.11	43.38	17.69	17.58
	SD	4.52	3.48	12.98	11.31	4.89	4.49
Age 6.25	Mean	25.77	27.24	33.67	44.41	19.00	19.67
	SD	2.56	2.95	13.95	7.99	3.77	3.40
Age 6.50	Mean	25.97	25.67	37.91	42.52	19.39	17.69
	SD	3.80	4.05	10.57	11.53	3.69	5.06
Age 6.75	Mean	24.50	25.75	38.96	45.13	19.38	19.95
	SD	3.05	3.26	9.37	10.90	3.12	3.87

Notes: Data are unsmoothed; SD, standard deviation.

The initial analysis of eigenvalues (Tables 5.24 and 5.25) utilizing BESA English subtest scores showed that the Semantics (receptive) and Semantics (expressive) scores, loading on the first factor, explained 54.2% and 16.3% of the variance, respectively; the Morphosyntax (cloze) and Morphosyntax (sentence repetition) scores, loading on the second factor, explained 12.3% and 7.5% of the variance; the Pragmatics subtest score explained 5.5% of the variance, and the last, Phonology, explained 4.2% of the variance.

Further analysis utilizing English item scores yielded a Kaiser-Meyer-Olkin measure of sampling adequacy of 0.856, well above the recommended value of 0.6. Bartlett's test of sphericity was significant, with X^2 (7,503) = 13,437.36, $p < .001$. The rotated component matrix results from analysis of item scores show the factor loadings of the items have the same pattern as the subtest scores (see Appendix I: Factor Loadings—BESA Items).

Analysis of Spanish Subtests and Items

The initial PCA analysis utilizing BESA Spanish *subtest scores*, and then subsequent PCA with varimax rotation (Tables 5.26 and 5.27), showed patterns similar to those of the English subtests. Further analysis of the 115 Spanish *item scores* (25 Semantics, 28 Phonology, 11 Pragmatics, and 51 Morphosyntax) confirmed that the items loaded distinctly on four separate factors corresponding to Phonology, Morphosyntax,

Table 5.22. Subtest raw score data for clinical sample

		PI		LI			
		Spanish Phono.	English Phono.	Spanish Morpho.	English Morpho.	Spanish Seman.	English Seman.
Age 4.0	Mean	16.50	16.27	13.00	12.08	5.75	5.69
	SD	6.46	6.93	9.57	6.01	2.66	3.20
Age 4.25	Mean	13.83	16.50	9.61	16.00	6.39	4.57
	SD	6.36	7.93	4.37	12.28	3.09	2.30
Age 4.5	Mean	18.62	22.00	11.00	16.25	6.26	6.22
	SD	6.72	5.08	6.15	6.22	2.60	4.00
Age 4.75	Mean	20.67	16.60	9.67	22.80	7.17	8.38
	SD	4.93	3.13	5.51	13.18	4.07	4.69
Age 5.0	Mean	14.73	18.06	15.18	15.86	8.54	7.55
	SD	6.50	5.18	10.44	12.91	6.13	4.26
Age 5.25	Mean	17.57	20.63	12.00	21.00	6.88	8.00
	SD	6.75	8.43	7.98	10.20	4.64	3.91
Age 5.5	Mean	18.67	17.71	11.40	16.00	9.00	12.50
	SD	6.98	4.89	7.37	8.85	3.61	5.98
Age 5.75	Mean	15.75	20.56	19.75	16.38	7.86	10.70
	SD	11.00	5.86	16.88	5.98	5.40	6.06
Age 6.0	Mean	20.00	21.33	10.33	17.80	10.00	9.78
	SD	5.29	4.93	5.20	11.32	4.16	5.31
Age 6.25	Mean	17.75	23.67	19.33	30.67	12.00	7.75
	SD	9.54	4.73	10.69	23.01	1.41	2.99
Age 6.50	Mean	12.25	18.22	22.50	22.88	11.25	15.44
	SD	5.74	6.04	2.12	8.15	4.79	3.32
Age 6.75	Mean	17.67	25.00	16.50	20.00	12.20	14.40
	SD	6.66	7.81	2.12	1.41	3.77	3.78

Notes: Data are unsmoothed; PI, phonological impairment; LI, language impairment; SD, standard deviation.

and Semantics subtests, and Pragmatics activity (see Appendix I: Factor Loadings—BESA Items).

An analysis of eigenvalues utilizing BESA Spanish subtest scores showed that Semantics (receptive) and Semantics (expressive) subtests, loading on the first factor, explained 52.4% and 16.2% of the variance; Morphosyntax (cloze) and Morphosyntax (sentence repetition) subtests, loading on the second factor, explained 10.6% and 10.3% of the variance; Pragmatics subtest score explained 6.1% of the variance, and Phonology explained 4.4% of the variance (see Tables 5.28 and 5.29).

Table 5.23. BESA English scores: PCA factor analysis with varimax rotation

Component	1	2	3	4
Semantics (receptive)	0.891	0.270	0.134	0.014
Semantics (expressive)	0.842	0.342	0.166	0.060
Morphosyntax (cloze)	0.325	0.761	0.344	0.077
Morphosyntax (sentence repetition)	0.343	0.855	0.158	0.049
Pragmatics	0.040	0.065	0.030	0.996
Phonology	0.186	0.279	0.936	0.032

Notes: Extraction method: principal component analysis; rotation method: varimax with Kaiser normalization.

Table 5.24. PCA of English components—eigenvalues

	Initial eigenvalues			Extraction sums of squared loadings		
English component	Total	Variance (%)	Cumulative (%)	Total	Variance (%)	Cumulative (%)
Semantics (receptive)	3.255	54.246	54.246	3.255	54.246	54.246
Semantics (expressive)	0.978	16.295	70.541	0.978	16.295	70.541
Morphosyntax (cloze)	0.737	12.275	82.816	0.737	12.275	82.816
Morphosyntax (sentence repetition)	0.450	7.497	90.313	0.450	7.497	90.313
Pragmatics	0.331	5.520	95.833			
Phonology	0.250	4.167	100.000			

PCA, principal component factor analysis.

Table 5.25. Principal component factor analysis of English subtests—total variance explained, rotated

	Rotation sums of squared loadings		
English component	Total	Variance (%)	Cumulative (%)
Semantics (receptive)	1.763	29.39	29.39
Semantics (expressive)	1.584	26.392	55.782
Morphosyntax (cloze)	1.066	17.763	73.545
Morphosyntax (sentence repetition)	1.006	16.768	90.313
Pragmatics			
Phonology			

Table 5.26. BESA Spanish Scores—principal components factor analysis; unrotated component matrix

Spanish component	1	2	3	4
Semantics (receptive)	0.818	–0.201	0.271	–0.292
Semantics (expressive)	0.839	–0.089	0.128	–0.353
Morphosyntax (cloze)	0.764	–0.032	–0.413	0.341
Morphosyntax (sentence repetition)	0.795	–0.064	–0.412	–0.065
Pragmatics	0.258	0.954	–0.019	–0.14
Phonology	0.699	0.098	0.455	0.518

Note: Extraction method: principal component analysis.

Table 5.27. BESA Spanish Scores—principal component factor analysis with varimax rotation

Spanish component	1	2	3	4
Semantics (receptive)	0.867	0.217	0.262	–0.021
Semantics (expressive)	0.849	0.312	0.153	0.107
Morphosyntax (cloze)	0.177	0.864	0.303	0.038
Morphosyntax (sentence repetition)	0.459	0.769	0.028	0.087
Pragmatics	0.047	0.066	0.077	0.992
Phonology	0.276	0.220	0.917	0.095

Notes: Extraction method: principal component analysis; rotation method: varimax with Kaiser normalization.

Table 5.28. Principal components factor analysis of Spanish subtests—total variance explained

	Initial eigenvalues			Extraction sums of squared loadings		
Spanish component	Total	Variance (%)	Cumulative (%)	Total	Variance (%)	Cumulative (%)
Semantics (receptive)	3.144	52.401	52.401	3.144	52.401	52.401
Semantics (expressive)	0.973	16.223	68.624	0.973	16.223	68.624
Morphosyntax (cloze)	0.637	10.618	79.242	0.637	10.618	79.242
Morphosyntax (sentence repetition)	0.618	10.299	89.541	0.618	10.299	89.541
Pragmatics	0.363	6.056	95.597			
Phonology	0.264	4.403	100.000			

Subsequent analysis of Spanish item scores yielded a Kaiser-Meyer-Olkin measure of sampling adequacy of 0.872, which is above the recommended value of 0.6. Bartlett's test of sphericity was significant, with X^2 (6,555) = 12,494.14, $p < .001$. The item scores loading patterns were consistent with the four BESA subtests (see Appendix I: Factor Loadings—BESA Items).

Correlations Among Subtests

Correlations among the tests and subtests within each language, and correlations between languages for the test and subtests, were calculated. These correlation analyses are used to understand the relationships between the components of the subtest within and between languages; Figure 5.1 displays the correlations for English. The subtests are significantly correlated to each other, with the exception of Pragmatics. This finding is consistent with expectations. Morphosyntax and Semantics are most strongly correlated. Phonology is more strongly correlated to Morphosyntax than other domains, but moderately associated with Semantics. This pattern is consistent with that reported in the literature.

Figure 5.2 displays the correlations for Spanish. All subtests are significantly correlated to each other. The strongest correlations are between Morphosyntax and Semantics. The weakest correlations are between Pragmatics and the other domains. Phonology is moderately correlated to both Morphosyntax and Semantics.

Cross-language correlations by domain demonstrate significant and positive correlations for Phonology, Morphosyntax, and Semantics between the two languages. These correlations are moderate to large (see Figure 5.3).

Table 5.29. Principal components factor analysis of Spanish subtests—total variance explained, rotated

	Rotation sums of squared loadings		
Spanish component	Total	Variance (%)	Cumulative (%)
Semantics (receptive)	1.793	29.886	29.886
Semantics (expressive)	1.534	25.572	55.458
Morphosyntax (cloze)	1.031	17.179	72.638
Morphosyntax (sentence repetition)	1.014	16.904	89.541
Pragmatics			
Phonology			

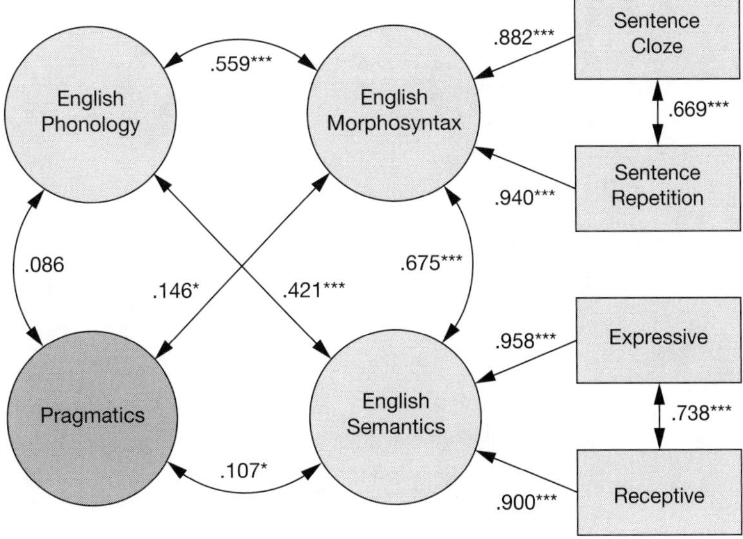

Figure 5.1. Correlations among BESA English components.

CORRELATIONS WITH OTHER MEASURES

Examination of the relationship between other tests and subtests that are both similar and dissimilar provides evidence about the test construct. It is expected that tests that have similar constructs would be more highly correlated than tests that have dissimilar constructs. We compared the four BESA subtests to other language sample measures in each language. Language sampling is considered to be a gold-standard measure for

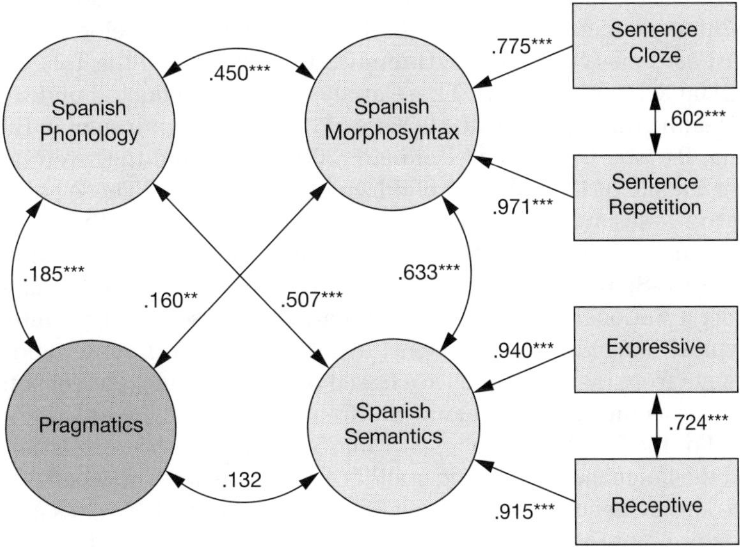

Figure 5.2. Correlations among BESA Spanish components.

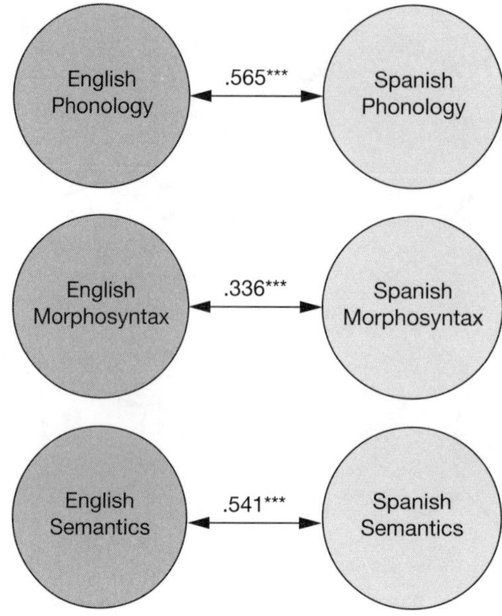

Note: **p* < .05; ***p* < .01; ****p* < .001

Figure 5.3. Cross-language correlations for BESA subtests.

assessment of language (Dunn, Flax, Sliwinski, & Aram, 1996; Heilmann et al., 2008; Heilmann, Nockerts, & Miller, 2010; Hewitt, Hammer, Yont, & Tomblin, 2005). For children from minority language backgrounds for whom there are no standardized tests available, language sampling is often recommended (Gutiérrez-Clellen et al., 2000; Gutiérrez-Clellen & Simon-Cereijido, 2009; Patterson, 2000; Seymour, Bland-Stewart, & Green, 1998; Washington, Kamhi, & Pollock, 1996). In addition, for English, we used two additional standardized tests: the Test of Language Development–Primary second and third editions (Newcomer & Hammill, 1991, 1997) and the Test of Narrative Language (Gillam & Pearson, 2004). These analyses were conducted under a National Institutes of Health grant (Diagnostic Markers of Language Impairment in Bilinguals) awarded to Peña, Bedore, Gillam, and Bohman (2006–2011), and they were based on an independent sample of 180 bilingual children in kindergarten. These children were residing in central Texas and northern Utah. In addition, we used the Expressive One-Word Picture Vocabulary Test–2000 (Brownell, 2000) and the Expressive One-Word Picture Vocabulary Test–Spanish Bilingual Edition (Brownell, 2001). These analyses were conducted under a National Institutes of Health grant (Cross-Language Outcomes in Typical and Atypical Language Development) awarded to Peña, Bedore, and Griffin (2010–2017). Results from these analyses are based on another independent sample of 64 kindergarten and second-grade bilingual children from central Texas.

For the BESA English tests, Table 5.30 displays the correlations between the BESA and the language sample and standardized measures. In general, the pattern of results provides evidence of content and construct validity. Semantics and Morphosyntax subtests are more strongly correlated with language sample measures and standardized tests than are the Pragmatics activity and the Phonology subtest. Within language samples, number of different words, total words, and number of main verbs more strongly correlated with Semantics (ranging from .416 to .564), whereas percentage grammatical

Table 5.30. English BESA component correlations with language sample measures and standardized tests

BESA English	Phonology	Morphosyntax	Semantics	Pragmatics
Language sample measures				
Number of different words	0.229**	0.524***	0.564***	0.384***
Number of total words	0.169*	0.429***	0.440***	0.362***
Number of main verbs	0.151*	0.381***	0.416***	0.345***
Percentage grammatical	0.383***	0.649***	0.414***	0.223**
Standardized tests				
TNL composite	0.201**	0.643***	0.649***	0.374***
TOLD relational vocabulary	0.154*	0.433***	0.455***	0.186*
TOLD oral vocabulary	0.207**	0.477***	0.520***	0.212**
TOLD grammar understanding	0.076	0.345***	0.421***	0.238**
TOLD sentence imitation	0.328***	0.674***	0.431***	0.192**
TOLD grammar completion	0.265***	0.643***	0.541***	0.224**
TOLD spoken language quotient	0.272***	0.704***	0.690***	0.321***
TOLD listening quotient	0.131	0.402***	0.527***	0.317***
TOLD organizing quotient	0.275***	0.646***	0.537***	0.228**
TOLD speaking quotient	0.273***	0.655***	0.601***	0.243**
TOLD semantics quotient	0.207**	0.555***	0.624***	0.286***
EOWPVT–2000 raw scores	0.511***	0.715***	0.818***	–

Notes: *$p < .05$; **$p < .01$; ***$p < .001$; TNL, Test of Narrative Language (Gillam & Pearson, 2004); TOLD, Test of Language Development–Primary second and third editions (Newcomer & Hammill, 1991, 1997); EOWPVT–2000, Expressive One-Word Picture Vocabulary Test–2000 (Brownell, 2000).

correlated more strongly with Morphosyntax ($r = .649$). Similarly, Semantics and Morphosyntax correlated more highly with the standardized measures of language than did the Pragmatics activity and Phonology subtest. Raw scores from the Expressive One-Word Picture Vocabulary Test–2000 and raw scores from the BESA subtests correlated significantly.

For the BESA Spanish subtests, Table 5.31 displays the correlations between BESA subtests and all the measures. The language sample scores come from an independent sample of 180 kindergarten-age children (drawn from the Diagnostic Markers of

Table 5.31. Spanish BESA component correlations with language sample measures and a standardized test

BESA Spanish	Phonology	Morphosyntax	Semantics	Pragmatics
Language sample measures				
Number of different words	0.175*	0.468***	0.412***	0.178*
Number of total words	0.136	0.355***	0.315***	0.166*
Number of main verbs	0.094	0.320***	0.301***	0.164*
Percentage grammatical	0.279***	0.534***	0.314***	0.159*
Standardized test				
EOWPVT–Bilingual raw scores	0.265*	0.284*	0.406***	–

Notes: *$p < .05$; **$p < .01$; ***$p < .001$; EOWPVT–Bilingual, Expressive One-Word Picture Vocabulary Test–Spanish Bilingual Edition (Brownell, 2001).

Language Impairment in Bilinguals study); raw scores on the Expressive One-Word Picture Vocabulary Test–Spanish Bilingual Edition (Brownell, 2001) shown on Table 5.31 are from a separate sample of 64 kindergarten and second-grade children from the Cross-language Outcomes in Typical and Atypical Bilingual Development study. In general, the patterns of results provide evidence of content and construct validity. The BESA Semantics and Morphosyntax subtests are more strongly correlated with language sample measures and standardized subtests than are the Pragmatics activity and Phonology subtest. Within language samples, number of different words, total words, number of main verbs, and percentage grammatical correlated more strongly with Morphosyntax than with Semantics, but both were significant at the $p < .01$ level. Phonology correlated most significantly with percentage grammatical, followed by number of different words.

DIAGNOSTIC ACCURACY

For a diagnostic test, classification or diagnostic accuracy is one of the most important considerations (Dollaghan, 2004; Dollaghan & Horner, 2011; Friberg, 2010; Gray, Plante, Vance, & Henrichsen, 1999; Peña, Spaulding, & Plante, 2006; Plante, 2004; Plante & Vance, 1994; Spaulding et al., 2006). Sensitivity and specificity should be 80% or above. Positive and negative likelihood ratios provide information about the probability that a result indicating impairment or no impairment is true. Positive likelihood ratios provide information about a positive result indicating impairment. Positive likelihood ratios of 4 or more and negative likelihood ratios of .4 or less are suggestive. Positive likelihood ratios of 10 or more and negative likelihood ratios of .2 or less are considered very likely. In this section, we examine classification accuracy for each test in each language with their positive and negative likelihood ratios, as well as with composites of tests. Finally, we examine the use of composites across Spanish and English to make recommendations for clinical use.

For this set of studies, children were identified with LI on the basis of language sample measures, parent and teacher report, and clinical observation. Children were identified with LI if they met at least three of the following criteria: 1) more than 20% ungrammatical utterances in their better language on a conversational and narrative sample combined, mean length of utterance, or number of different words more than 1 standard deviation below the mean compared to same-age peers in the better language; 2) parent report of concern about the child's language development as compared to similar-age peers; 3) teacher concerns about language development as compared to similar-age peers; 4) clinical observation indicating concerns about LI or clinical diagnosis by a bilingual speech-language pathologist.

For assessment of phonology, children were reported to be typically developing, based on parent and teacher report. Neither teacher nor parents expressed concern about being able to understand the child's speech. Moreover, none of the children identified as typically developing had received services for a speech and/or language disorder. Children identified with a phonological disorder were those who were reported to be difficult to understand by either teacher or parent.

Table 5.32 displays the classification accuracy data for the individual English subtests. In general, classification accuracy for the English subtests is acceptable for all ages of children who were balanced bilingual, bilingual dominant in English, and functionally English monolingual. The subtests demonstrated fair to good classification accuracy for identification of LI using either the Semantics or Morphosyntax subtests and for identification of phonological impairment using the Phonology subtest. Similarly, likelihood ratios are in the suggestive to very likely ranges for all the subtests individually. The Phonology subtest likelihood ratios indicate virtual certainty that results are accurate.

Table 5.32. BESA English—classification accuracy

BESA subtest	As a measure of:	Age group	Cut score	Sensitivity	Specificity	Positive likelihood ratio	Negative likelihood ratio
Phonology	Phonological impairment	4	73	100.0	93.0	14.29	0
		5	75	90.5	89.9	8.96	0.106
		6	79	90.0	96.5	25.86	0.098
Semantics	Language impairment	4	88	83.3	78.5	3.87	0.213
		5	87	80.0	80.5	4.10	0.248
		6	82	81.5	86.9	6.22	0.213
Morphosyntax		4	86	87.5	84.5	5.65	0.148
		5	85	88.6	81.6	4.82	0.140
		6	81	88.9	88.2	7.53	0.126

Table 5.33 displays the classification accuracy data for the individual Spanish subtests. In general, classification accuracy for the Spanish subtests is acceptable for all ages of children who were balanced bilingual, bilingual dominant in Spanish, or functionally Spanish monolingual. The subtests demonstrated fair to good classification accuracy for identification of LI using either the Semantics or Morphosyntax subtests and for identification of phonological impairment using the Phonology subtest. There was slightly lower sensitivity for the Semantics subtest for 5-year-olds, and for the Phonology subtest for 6-year-olds. The likelihood ratios are also in the acceptable range.

Table 5.34 displays the classification accuracy data based on the best score obtained of the English and Spanish scores of the bilingual children. Although amount of language exposure is associated with language performance, children may show variability in performance across their two languages (Bedore et al., 2010; Bedore et al., 2012; Oller, Pearson, & Cobo-Lewis, 2007; Pearson & Fernández, 1994); thus, it is important to determine performance in the child's best language. For this analysis, scores in each language were compared and the higher score was entered. For example, if a child's score was 92 in Spanish and 87 in English, 92 was the best score and was recorded. In general, the classification accuracy using the best score was consistent with the classification accuracy obtained in each language. In some cases, however, classification accuracy improved using the best language score. Positive and negative likelihood ratios indicate the accuracy of each subtest result at each age. These are in the acceptable range.

Table 5.33. BESA Spanish—classification accuracy

BESA subtest	As a measure of:	Age group	Cut score	Sensitivity	Specificity	Positive likelihood ratio	Negative likelihood ratio
Phonology	Phonological impairment	4	71	100.0	96.7	30.30	0
		5	78	84.0	93.1	12.17	0.172
		6	69	66.7	95.3	14.19	0.349
Semantics	Language impairment	4	80	89.7	78.3	4.13	0.131
		5	82	72.0	88.5	6.26	0.316
		6	81	87.5	87.4	6.94	0.143
Morphosyntax		4	83	93.8	81.4	5.04	0.076
		5	83	87.8	83.7	5.39	0.145
		6	79	91.7	88.7	8.12	0.094

Table 5.34. Classification accuracy of best language score (English or Spanish)

Subtest	As a measure of	Age group	Cut score	Sensitivity	Specificity	Positive likelihood ratio	Negative likelihood ratio
Phonology	Phonological impairment	4	74	100.0	94.8	19.23	0
		5	79	85.4	92.1	10.81	0.012
		6	73	80.0	96.0	20.00	0.208
Semantics	Language impairment	4	88	85.2	80.6	4.39	0.184
		5	88	75.0	82.2	4.21	0.304
		6	82	82.4	87.3	6.49	0.202
Morphosyntax		4	84	90.9	83.2	5.41	0.109
		5	85	89.7	84.7	5.86	0.122
		6	81	96.4	89.9	9.54	0.040

The BESA subtests were designed to be used in combination to make a diagnostic decision. Thus, in this section, data are presented examining classification accuracy for LI using a composite that combines Semantics and Morphosyntax (see Table 5.35). Because bilingual children often present with "mixed dominance" (Bedore et al., 2010; Bedore et al., 2012), that composite combines the best score in each domain. For example, if a child scores 82 in Spanish Morphosyntax, 93 in English Morphosyntax, 102 in Spanish Semantics, and 78 in English Semantics, the higher score in Morphosyntax (93) is combined with the higher score in Semantics (102) even if the stronger scores are in different languages. This approach allows analysis of English monolingual, English dominant, bilingual, Spanish dominant, and Spanish monolingual in one analysis. Using this method, we found that the combination of Semantics and Morphosyntax demonstrates very good to excellent classification accuracy (see Table 5.35).

BIAS ANALYSES

We made every attempt to reduce bias in developing the subtest items, so that scoring would not penalize differences by sex, region, dialect use, and/or developmental differences in the acquisition of the two languages.

For the Phonology subtest, all stimulus words depict objects and attributes that are familiar to children and are easily represented. We chose items that would be appropriate across United States geographic regions where certain dialect forms may be more prevalent than others. Normal differences in pronunciation are directly addressed in the scoring and analysis of the target items.

There are two potential sources for bias in the Pragmatics activity: the task and the construct. Among the several tasks selected, wrapping a present was judged by the authors and others to be a task that is common across all of the target groups—even very young children. The construct assessed provides an index of the assertiveness of

Table 5.35. Classification accuracy of language index composite as a measure of language impairment

Age group	Sensitivity	Specificity	Positive likelihood ratio	Negative likelihood ratio
4	92.3	85.8	6.50	0.09
5	88.9	84.9	5.88	0.13
6	96.0	92.4	11.32	0.15

the children. Communication styles and degrees of assertiveness vary across groups, with greater assertiveness required in certain social situations, as in taking a test or performing as expected in school. Although low performance in this activity is not indicative of LI and the task does not contribute to any BESA score, the interactions noted during the task could point to mediating factors in a child's performance on other components of the BESA and, as such, the activity provides a valuable opportunity to observe behaviors associated with language use.

Semantics subtest items were also selected to minimize bias. Three key considerations guided the selection of items. First, items were selected that related to themes likely to be familiar to children from the different cultural and dialectal groups that make up the Hispanic population in the United States. Next, items were designed to which children could respond based on semantic knowledge rather than targeting specific vocabulary that might not be familiar to children in the process of acquiring Spanish or English. Finally, dialect-specific alternatives were presented to responses to ensure that children's responses were accurately credited.

The same approach was used for the selection of the items in the Morphosyntax subtest. The themes of the targeted phrases and sentences were selected to represent the experiences of children regardless of region of origin or cultural experience. Alternative scoring procedures for speakers of Caribbean Spanish dialects are provided so as not to penalize regional or dialectal variations. (See Appendix A: Acceptable and Unacceptable Responses for all subtests in English and Spanish.)

In addition to analysis of potential bias via clinical expertise and judgment, analysis of item bias was evaluated statistically. Specifically, item difficulty differences were evaluated for each item by sex and by region. We used the average item discrimination values derived in the comparison of children with and without language or phonological impairment. The logic of this approach is that if items showed differences between sex or regions that were equal to or greater than differences by ability, it could be potentially problematic because the differences at the item level were consistent with impairment. Follow-up analyses determined the degree to which there were systematic misclassifications. (*Note:* Usually, bias analyses are conducted to ensure that systematic item differences are not seen when performance of a minority group is compared to the remainder of the normative sample. The BESA, to be utilized primarily by bilingual children, a minority group by definition, focused on detecting sex and regional bias.)

Performance Differences by Sex

Item-level comparisons indicated no differences on any items by sex for Phonology, Morphosyntax, or Semantics in Spanish or English.

Performance Differences by Region

Items that demonstrated significant differences by region were flagged for further analysis. Tables 5.36 and 5.37 display the number of items on each subtest that demonstrated significant differences for each of the three subtests for each language that were retained for the final version of the BESA. We identified minimal item bias by region for all subtests, with the exception of English Morphosyntax. For this subtest, children from the Eastern region of the United States scored lower on 10 items compared to children in the Western and/or Central regions of the United States. Children in the Eastern region of the United States were more likely to use features of African American English (AAE). Specific items that were more differentially difficult for this group of children included possessive *'s* and third-person singular (Craig & Washington, 2005; Seymour & Roeper, 1999) and passives (Pruitt, Oetting, & Hegarty, 2011), consistent

Table 5.36. Item bias: number of biased items per English subtest

Comparisons	Phonology	Morphosyntax	Semantics
East > West	0	0	1
West > East	2	9	0
Central > West	0	0	0
West > Central	0	0	0
East > Central	0	0	1
Central > East	2	3	1
Total different items	2	10*	2*

*Same item(s) with difference for two comparisons.

with identified features of AAE. There were, in addition, three Spanish Morphosyntax items that were differentially more difficult for children in the Eastern region of the United States, including present progressive and direct-object clitics (plural form). The differential performance on plural forms of the direct-object clitics may be consistent with features of radical dialects. However, because these represented a very small portion of the item set, we judged that these differences were unlikely to affect test outcomes. Within the Morphosyntax subtests in both languages, sentence repetition items showed the least bias.

Ultimately, no tests are completely free of item bias. Children's individual experiences, backgrounds, and language exposure contribute to their performance on a given language test. What is critically important are the clinical decisions made on the basis of a child's performance. For a diagnostic measure, classification accuracy is of greatest interest. The overall classification accuracy on the basis of composite scores (including both Morphosyntax and Semantics subtests) was high. However, given that 17% of the English Morphosyntax subtest items flagged as potentially biased, it was possible that children from the Eastern United States might be prone to greater misclassification compared to the other two groups. There was an overall false positive rate of 11.5% and a false negative rate of 9%. The classification rate for the Eastern region was compared to the West and Central regions combined. This comparison showed a higher false positive rate of 21.2% for the Eastern region compared to a false positive rate of 8.6% for the other two regions. The false negative rate was 10% for the Eastern region, compared to a false negative rate of 8.4% for the West and Central regions combined. Although these rates of misclassification are within acceptable levels, there was a much higher false positive rate for the children in the Eastern group. Discriminant analyses were rerun,

Table 5.37. Item bias: number of biased items per Spanish subtest

Comparisons	Phonology	Morphosyntax	Semantics
East > West	0	0	0
West > East	1	3	0
Central > West	0	0	0
West > Central	0	0	0
East > Central	0	0	0
Central > East	0	2	0
Total different items	1	3*	0

*Same item(s) with difference for two comparisons.

this time with only the cases from the Eastern region. Using a slightly lower cut score for Morphosyntax, sensitivity for this group was 86% and specificity was 82.8%. These improved classification rates are in the fair to good range.

SUMMARY

The theoretical rationale and empirical evidence presented in this chapter strongly support that the BESA is a valid test that can be used to identify LI and/or speech impairment in Spanish–English speakers ages 4 through 6 years. The content areas sampled in the subtests have been identified in the research literature as demonstrating developmental differences (across age) and discriminating typically developing children from those identified as having LI. The strong association among the BESA subtests and with other existing language tests attests that the constructs being assessed are similar. Moreover, the high sensitivity and specificity demonstrated strongly support our conclusion that the BESA can confidently be used to identify Spanish–English speakers with LI.

References

Acevedo, M.A. (1993). Development of Spanish consonants in preschool children. *Journal of Childhood Communication Disorders,*15, 9–15.

Aguilar-Mediavilla, E., Sanz-Torrent, M., & Serra-Raventós, M. (2007). Influence of phonology on morpho-syntax in Romance languages in children with specific language impairment (SLI). *International Journal of Language and Communication Disorders, 42*, 525–347.

Allen, M., & Yen, W. (1979). *Introduction to measurement theory*. Belmont, CA: Wadsworth.

Ambert, A. N. (1986). Identifying language disorders in Spanish-speakers. *Journal of Reading, Writing, and Learning Disabilities International, 2*(1), 21–41. doi:10.1080/0748763860020104

Anastasi, A., & Urbina, S. (1997). *Psychological testing*. Upper Saddle River, NJ: Prentice Hall.

Anderson, R. T. (1995). Spanish morphological and syntactic development. In H. Kayser (Ed.), *Bilingual speech-language pathology: A Hispanic focus* (pp. 41–74). San Diego, CA: Singular.

Anderson, R. T. (2001). Lexical morphology and verb use in child first language loss: A preliminary case study investigation. *International Journal of Bilingualism, 5*(4), 377–401.

Anderson, R. T., & Souto, S. M. (2005). The use of articles by monolingual Puerto Rican Spanish-speaking children with specific language impairment. *Applied Psycholinguistics, 26*(4), 621–647. doi:10.1017/s0142716405050332

Arnold, B. R., & Matus, Y. E. (2000). Test translation and cultural equivalence methodologies for use with diverse populations. In I. Cuellar & F. A. Paniagua (Eds.), *Handbook of multicultural mental health* (pp. 121–136). San Diego, CA: Academic Press.

Austin, D., & Shriberg, L. D. (1996). *Lifespan reference data for ten measures of articulation competence using the speech disorders classification system (SDCS)* (Phonology Project Technical Report No. 3). Madison, WI: Waisman Center on Mental Retardation and Human Development, University of Wisconsin.

Auza, A., Harmon, M. T., & Murata, C. (2018). Retelling stories: Grammatical and lexical measures for identifying monolingual Spanish speaking children with specific language impairment (SLI). *Journal of Communication Disorders,, 71*, 52–60.

Barriga Villanueva, R. (1985). La producción de oraciones relativas en niños mexicanos de seis años. *Nueva revista de filología hispánica, 34*(1), 108–155.

Bedore, L. (1999). The acquisition of Spanish. In O. Taylor & L. Leonard (Eds.), *Language acquisition across North America: Cross-cultural and cross-linguistic perspectives* (pp. 157–207). San Diego, CA: Singular.

Bedore, L. M., & Leonard, L. B. (1998). Specific language impairment and grammatical morphology: A discriminant function analysis. *Journal of Speech, Language, and Hearing Research, 41*(5), 1185–1192.

Bedore, L. M., & Leonard, L. B. (2001). Grammatical morphology deficits in Spanish-speaking children with specific language impairment. *Journal of Speech, Language, and Hearing Research, 44*, 905–924.

Bedore, L. M., Peña, E. D., García, M., & Cortez, C. (2005). Conceptual versus monolingual scoring: When does it make a difference? *Language, Speech, and Hearing in Schools, 36*, 188–200.

Bedore, L. M., Peña, E. D., Gillam, R. B., & Ho, T.-H. (2010). Language sample measures and language ability in Spanish–English bilingual kindergarteners. *Journal of Communication Disorders, 43*(6), 498–510. doi:10.1016/j.jcomdis.2010.05.002

Bedore, L. M., Pena, E. D., Griffin, Z. M., & Hixon, J. G. (2016). Effects of age of English exposure, current input/output, and grade on bilingual language performance. *Journal of Child Language, 43*(3), 687–706.

Bedore, L. M., Peña, E. D., Summers, C., Boerger, K., Resendiz, M., Greene, K., . . . Gillam, R. B. (2012). The measure matters: Language dominance profiles across measures in Spanish/English bilingual children. *Bilingualism: Language and Cognition, 15*, 616–629.

Betz, S. K., Eickhoff, J. R., Sullivan, S. F., Nippold, M., & Schneider, P. (2013). Factors influencing the selection of standardized tests for the diagnosis of specific language impairment. *Language, Speech, and Hearing Services in Schools, 44*(2), 133–146. doi:10.1044/0161-1461(2012/12-0093

Bialystok, E. (2001). *Bilingualism in development: Language, literacy, and cognition*. New York, NY: Cambridge University Press.

Bland-Stewart, L., & Fitzgerald, S. M. (2001). Use of Brown's 14 grammatical morphemes by bilingual Hispanic preschoolers: A pilot study. *Communication Disorders Quarterly, 22*, 171–186.

Blom, E., & Boerma, T. (2017). Effects of language impairment and bilingualism across domains. *Linguistic Approaches to Bilingualism, 7*(3), 277–300.

Bloom, P. (2000). *How children learn the meanings of words*. Cambridge, MA: MIT Press.

Bohman, T. M., Bedore, L. M., Peña, E. D., Mendez-Perez, A., & Gillam, R. B. (2010). What you hear and what you say: Language performance in Spanish–English bilinguals. *International Journal of Bilingual Education and Bilingualism, 13*(3), 325–344. doi:10.1080/13670050903342019

Bonifacio, S., Girolametto, L., Bulligan, M., Callegari, M., Vignola, S., & Zocconi, E. (2007). Assertive and responsive conversational skills of Italian-speaking late talkers. *International Journal of Language and Communication Disorders, 42*(5), 607–623.

Bosch, L., & Serra, M. (1997). Grammatical morphology deficits of Spanish-speaking children with specific language impairment. In A. Baker, M. Beers, G. Bol, J. de Jong, & G. Leemans (Eds.), *Child language disorders in a cross-linguistic perspective: Proceedings of the Fourth Symposium of the European Group on Child Language Disorders* (pp. 33–45). Amsterdam, Netherlands: Universiteit van Amsterdam.

Botting, N., Conti-Ramsden, G., & Crutchley, A. (1997). Concordance between teacher/therapist opinion and formal language assessment scores in children with language impairment. *European Journal of Disorders of Communication, 32*(3), 317–327. doi:10.3109/13682829709017898

Bracken, B. A. (1988). Ten psychometric reasons why similar tests produce dissimilar results. *Journal of School Psychology, 26*, 155–166.

Bracken, B. A., & Barona, A. (1991). State of the art procedures for translating, validating and using psychoeducational tests in cross-cultural assessment. *School Psychology International, 12*, 119–132.

Brownell, R. (2000). *Expressive one-word picture vocabulary test–2000 edition*. Novato, CA: Academic Therapy Publications.

Brownell, R. (2001). *Expressive one-word picture vocabulary test–Spanish-bilingual edition*. Novato, CA: Academic Therapy Publications.

Caesar, L. G., & Kohler, P. D. (2007). The state of school-based bilingual assessment: Actual practice versus recommended guidelines. *Language, Speech, and Hearing Services in Schools, 38*(3), 190–200.

Canfield, D. L. (1981). *Spanish pronunciation in the Americas*. Chicago, IL: University of Chicago Press.

Carlo, M. S., August, D., McLaughlin, B., Snow, C. E., Dressler, C., Lippman, D. N., . . . White, C. E. (2004). Closing the gap: Addressing the vocabulary needs of English language learners in bilingual and mainstream classrooms. *Reading Research Quarterly, 39*(2), 188–215.

Castilla, A. P., Restrepo, M. A., & Perez-Leroux, A. T. (2009). Individual differences and language interdependence: A study of sequential bilingual development in Spanish–English preschool children. *International Journal of Bilingual Education and Bilingualism, 12*(5), 565–580.

Centeno, J. G., & Anderson, R. T. (2011). A preliminary comparison of verb tense production in Spanish speakers with expressive restrictions. *Clinical Linguistics and Phonetics, 25*(10), 864–880. doi:10.3109/02699206.2011.582225

Choi, S., McDonough, L., Bowerman, M., & Mandler, J. (1999). Early sensitivity to language-specific spatial categories in English and Korean. *Cognitive Development, 14*, 241–268.

Clark, E. V. (2001). Emergent categories in first language acquisition. In M. Bowerman & S. Levinson (Eds.), *Language acquisition and conceptual development* (pp. 379–405). Cambridge, United Kingdom: Cambridge University Press.

Cooperson, S. J., Bedore, L. M., & Peña, E. D. (2013). The relationship of phonological skills to language skills in Spanish–English-speaking bilingual children. *Clinical Linguistics and Phonetics, 27*(5), 371–389. doi:10.3109/02699206.2013.782568

Craig, H. K., & Washington, J. A. (2005). *Malik goes to school: Examining the language skills of African American students from preschool–5th grade*. New York, NY: Psychology Press.

Crystal, D. (1998). Sense: The final frontier. *Child Language Teaching and Therapy, 14*(1), 1–27.

Damico, J. S., Oller, J. W., & Storey, M. E. (1983). The diagnosis of language disorders in bilingual children: Surface-oriented and pragmatic criteria. *Journal of Speech and Hearing Disorders, 48*(4), 385–394.

Deuchar, M., & Quay, S. (2000). *Bilingual acquisition: Theoretical implications of a case study*. New York, NY: Oxford University Press.

Dollaghan, C. A. (2004). Evidence-based practice in communication disorders: What do we know, and when do we know it? *Journal of Communication Disorders, 37*(5), 391–400.

Dollaghan, C. A., & Horner, E. A. (2011). Bilingual language assessment: A meta-analysis of diagnostic accuracy. *Journal of Speech, Language, and Hearing Research, 54*(4), 1077–1088. doi:10.1044/1092-4388(2010/10-0093)

Dunn, M., Flax, J., Sliwinski, M., & Aram, D. (1996). The use of spontaneous language measures as criteria for identifying children with specific language impairment: An attempt to reconcile clinical and research incongruence. *Journal of Speech and Hearing Research, 39*(3), 643–654.

Eng, N., & O'Connor, B. (2000). Acquisition of definite article + noun agreement of Spanish–English bilingual children with specific language impairment. *Communication Disorders Quarterly, 21*(2), 114–124. doi:10.1177/152574010002100205

Ennis, S. R., Ríos-Vargas, M., & Albert, N. G. (2011). *The Hispanic population: 2010*. Washington, DC: U.S. Census Bureau.

Fabiano-Smith, L., & Barlow, J. A. (2010). Interaction in bilingual phonological acquisition: Evidence from phonetic inventories. *International Journal of Bilingual Education and Bilingualism, 13*(1), 81–97.

Fey, M. (1986). *Language intervention with young children*. Austin, TX: PRO-ED.

Fiestas, C. E., & Peña, E. D. (2004). Narrative discourse in bilingual children: Language and task effects. *Language, Speech, and Hearing Services in Schools, 35*(2), 155–168.

Frank, I., & Poulin-Dubois, D. (2002). Young monolingual and bilingual children's responses to violation of the mutual exclusivity principle. *International Journal of Bilingualism, 6*(2), 125–146.

Friberg, J. C. (2010). Considerations for test selection: How do validity and reliability impact diagnostic decisions? *Child Language Teaching and Therapy, 26*(1), 77–92. doi:10.1177/0265659009349972

Friedenberg, L. (1995). *Psychological testing: Design, analysis, and use.* Needham Heights, MA: Allyn & Bacon.

Gawlitzek-Maiwald, I., & Tracy, R. (1996). Bilingual bootstrapping. *Linguistics, 34*, 901–926.

Gildersleeve-Neumann, C. E., Kester, E. S., Davis, B. L., & Peña, E. D. (2008). English speech sound development in preschool-aged children from bilingual English–Spanish environments. *Language, Speech, and Hearing Services in Schools, 39*(3), 314–328.

Gildersleeve-Neumann, C. E., & Wright, K. L. (2010). English speech acquisition in 3- to 5-year-old children learning Russian and English. *Language, Speech, and Hearing Services in Schools, 41*(4), 429–444. doi:10.1044/0161-1461(2009/09-0059)

Gillam, R. B., & Pearson, N. (2004). *Test of Narrative Language.* Austin, TX: PRO-ED.

Goldstein, B. (2000, June). *Phonological disorders in bilingual (Spanish–English) children.* Paper presented at the Child Phonology Conference, Cedar Falls, IA.

Goldstein, B. (2001). Transcription of Spanish and Spanish-influenced English. *Communication Disorders Quarterly, 23*(1), 54–60.

Goldstein, B., Bunta, F., Lange, J., Burrows, L., Pont, S., & Bennett, J. (2008, November). *Interdependence in the phonological systems of bilingual children with speech sound disorders.* Paper presented at the meeting of American Speech-Language-Hearing Association, Chicago, IL.

Goldstein, B., & Gildersleeve-Neumann, C. E. (2012). Phonological development and disorders. In B. Goldstein (Ed.), *Bilingual language development and disorders in Spanish–English Speakers* (2nd ed.). Baltimore, MD: Paul H. Brookes Publishing Co.

Golomb, C. (2013). *The child's creation of a pictorial world.* New York, NY: Psychology Press.

Gray, S., Plante, E., Vance, R., & Henrichsen, M. (1999). The diagnostic accuracy of four vocabulary tests administered to preschool-age children. *Language, Speech, and Hearing Services in Schools, 30*(2), 196–206.

Grech, H., & Dodd, B. (2008). Phonological acquisition in Malta: A bilingual learning context. *International Journal of Bilingualism, 12*(3), 155–171.

Greene, K. J., Peña, E. D., & Bedore, L. M. (2013). Lexical choice and language selection in bilingual preschoolers. *Child Language Teaching and Therapy, 29*(1), 27–39. doi:10.1177/0265659012459743

Greet Cotton, E., & Sharp, J. M. (1988). *Spanish in the Americas.* Washington, DC: Georgetown University Press.

Guitart, J. M. (1976). *Markedness and a Cuban dialect of Spanish.* Washington, DC: Georgetown University Press.

Gutiérrez-Clellen, V. F. (1998). Syntactic skills of Spanish-speaking children with low school achievement. *Language, Speech, and Hearing Services in Schools, 29*(4), 207–215.

Gutiérrez-Clellen, V. F. (2002). Narratives in two languages: Assessing performance of bilingual children. *Linguistics and Education, 13*(2), 175–197.

Gutiérrez-Clellen, V. F., & Hofstetter, R. (1994). Syntactic complexity in Spanish narratives: A developmental study. *Journal of Speech and Hearing Research, 37*, 645–654.

Gutiérrez-Clellen, V. F., & Iglesias, A. (1992). Causal coherence in the oral narratives of Spanish-speaking children. *Journal of Speech and Hearing Research, 35*, 363–372.

Gutiérrez-Clellen, V. F., Restrepo, M. A., Bedore, L. M., Peña, E. D., & Anderson, R. T. (2000). Language sample analysis in Spanish-speaking children: Methodological considerations. *Language, Speech, and Hearing Services in Schools, 31*(1), 88–98.

Gutiérrez-Clellen, V. F., Restrepo, M. A., & Simon-Cereijido, G. (2006). Evaluating the discriminant accuracy of a grammatical measure with Spanish-speaking children. *Journal of Speech, Language, and Hearing Research, 49*(6), 1209–1223.

Gutiérrez-Clellen, V. F., & Simon-Cereijido, G. (2007). The discriminant accuracy of a grammatical measure with Latino English-speaking children. *Journal of Speech, Language, and Hearing Research, 50*(4), 968–981.

Gutiérrez-Clellen, V. F., & Simon-Cereijido, G. (2009). Using language sampling in clinical assessments with bilingual children: Challenges and future directions. *Seminars in Speech and Language, 30*(4), 234–245. doi:10.1055/s-0029-1241722

Gutiérrez-Clellen, V. F., Simon-Cereijido, G., & Leone, A. (2009). Codeswitching in bilingual children with specific language impairment. *International Journal of Bilingualism, 13*, 91–109.

Gutiérrez-Clellen, V. F., Simon-Cereijido, G., & Wagner, C. (2008). Bilingual children with language impairment: A comparison with monolinguals and second language learners. *Applied Psycholinguistics, 29*(1), 3–19.

Hammond, R. M. (2001). *The sounds of Spanish: Analysis and application.* Somerville, MA: Cascadilla Press.

Heilmann, J., Miller, J. F., Iglesias, A., Fabiano-Smith, L., Nockerts, A., & Andriacchi, K. D. (2008). Narrative transcription accuracy and reliability in two languages. *Topics in Language Disorders, 28*(2), 178–188.

Heilmann, J., Nockerts, A., & Miller, J. F. (2010). Language sampling: Does the length of the transcript matter? *Language, Speech, and Hearing Services in Schools, 41*(4), 393–404.

Hewitt, L. E., Hammer, C. S., Yont, K. M., & Tomblin, J. B. (2005). Language sampling for kindergarten children with and without SLI: Mean length of utterance, IPSyn, and NDW. *Journal of Communication Disorders, 38*(3), 197–213.

Huerta, A. (1977). The development of codeswitching in a young bilingual. *Working Papers in Sociolinguistics, 21*, 1–27.

Hutchinson, T. A. (1996). What to look for in the technical manual: Twenty questions for users. *Language, Speech, and Hearing Services in Schools, 27*(2), 109–121.

Individuals with Disabilities Education Improvement Act (IDEA) of 2004, PL 108-446, 20 U.S.C. §§ 1400 *et seq.*

Ingram, D. (2002). The measurement of whole-word productions. *Journal of Child Language, 29,* 713–733.

Jackson-Maldonado, D., Hoist, J., Mejia, A. S., Peña, E. D., & Bedore, L. M. (2015, June). *The use of* BESA *as a bilingual test with monolingual Spanish-speaking children.* Poster session presented at the Symposium for Research in Child Language Disorders, Madison, WI.

Jacobson, P. F., & Livert, D. (2010). English past tense use as a clinical marker in older bilingual children with language impairment. *Clinical Linguistics and Phonetics, 24*(2), 101–121. doi:10.3109/02699200903437906

Jacobson, P. F., & Schwartz, R. G. (2002). Morphology in incipient bilingual Spanish-speaking preschool children with specific language impairment. *Applied Psycholinguistics, 23*(1), 23–41.

Jacobson, P. F., & Schwartz, R. G. (2005). English past tense use in bilingual children with language impairment. *American Journal of Speech-Language Pathology, 14*(4), 313–323. doi:10.1044/1058-0360(2005/030)

Jiménez, B. C. (1987). Acquisition of Spanish consonants in children aged 3-5 years, 7 months. *Language, Speech, and Hearing Services in Schools, 18,* 357–363.

Kapantzoglou, M., Fergadiotis, G., & Restrepo, M. A. (2017). Language sample analysis and elicitation technique effects in bilingual children with and without language impairment. *Journal of Speech, Language, and Hearing Research, 60,* 1–13.

Kohnert, K. J., & Bates, E. (2002). Balancing bilinguals II: Lexical comprehension and cognitive processing in children learning Spanish and English. *Journal of Speech, Language, and Hearing Research, 45,* 347–359.

Kohnert, K. J., Bates, E., & Hernández, A. (1999). Balancing bilinguals: Lexical-semantic production and cognitive processing in children learning Spanish and English. *Journal of Speech, Language, and Hearing Research, 42*(6), 1400–1413.

Kohnert, K. J., Hernández, A. E., & Bates, E. (1998). Bilingual performance on the Boston naming test: Preliminary norms in Spanish and English. *Brain and Language, 65*(3), 422–440. doi:10.1006/brln.1998.2001

Leonard, L. B. (2014). Specific language impairment across languages. *Child Development Perspectives, 8*(1), 1–5.

Leonard, L., Eyer, J. A., Bedorc, L. M., & Grela, B. G. (1997). Three accounts of the grammatical morpheme difficulties of English-speaking children with specific language impairment. *Journal of Speech, Language, and Hearing Research, 40,* 741–753.

Lombardi, R. P., & de Peters, A. B. (1981). *Modern spoken Spanish: An interdisciplinary perspective.* Washington, DC: University Press of America.

Lord, F. M., & Novick, M. R. (2008*). Statistical theories of mental test scores.* Chicago, IL: Information Age Publishing.

Martin, D., Krishnamurthy, R., Bhardwaj, M., & Charles, R. (2003). Language change in young Panjabi/English children: Implications for bilingual language assessment. *Child Language Teaching and Therapy, 19*(3), 245–265. doi:10.1191/0265659003ct254oa

McCauley, R. J., & Swisher, L. (1984a). Psychometric review of language and articulation tests for preschool children. *Journal of Speech and Hearing Disorders, 49,* 34–42.

McCauley, R. J., & Swisher, L. (1984b). Use and misuse of norm-referenced test in clinical assessment: A hypothetical case. *Journal of Speech and Hearing Disorders, 49,* 338–348.

McGregor, K. K. (2009). Semantics in child language disorders. In: R. Schwartz (Ed.), *Handbook of child language disorders* (pp. 365–387). New York, NY: Psychology Press.

McLeod, S., & Verdon, S. (2014). A review of 30 speech assessments in 19 languages other than English. *American Journal of Speech-Language Pathology, 23*(4), 708–723.

Merino, B. J. (1983). Language development in normal and language handicapped Spanish-speaking children. *Hispanic Journal of Behavioral Sciences, 5*(4), 379–400.

Merriman, W. E., & Kutlesic, V. (1993). Bilingual and monolingual children's use of two lexical acquisition heuristics. *Applied Psycholinguistics, 14*(2), 229–249. doi:10.1017/s0142716400009565

Montrul, S. (2002). Incomplete acquisition and attrition of Spanish tense/aspect distinctions in adult bilinguals. *Bilingualism: Language and Cognition, 5*(1), 39–68. doi:10.1017/s1366728902000135

Navarro Tomás, T. (1966). *Estudios de fonología española* (Vol. 1). New York, NY: Las Americas Publishing.

Nelson, K., & Nelson, A. P. (1990). Category production in response to script and category cues by kindergarten and second-grade children. *Journal of Applied Developmental Psychology, 11,* 431–446.

Newcomer, P., & Hammill, D. (1991). *Test of Language Development–Primary* (2nd ed.). Austin, TX: PRO-ED.

Newcomer, P., & Hammill, D. (1997). *Test of Language Development–Primary* (3rd ed.). Austin, TX: PRO-ED.

Oller, D. K., Pearson, B. Z., & Cobo-Lewis, A. B. (2007). Profile effects in early bilingual language and literacy. *Applied Psycholinguistics, 28*(2), 191–230.

Ordóñez, C. L., Carlo, M. S., Snow, C. E., & McLaughlin, B. (2002). Depth and breadth of vocabulary in two languages: Which vocabulary skills transfer? *Journal of Educational Psychology, 94*(4), 719–728. doi:10.1037/0022-0663.94.4.719

O'Toole, C., & Hickey, T. M. (2013). Diagnosing language impairment in bilinguals: Professional experience and perception. *Child Language Teaching and Therapy, 29*(1), 91–109. doi:10.1177/0265659012459859

Padilla, A. M., & Lindholm, K. J. (1976). Development of interrogative, negative and possessive forms in the speech of young Spanish/English bilinguals. *Bilingual Review/La Revista Bilingüe, 3,* 122–152.

Paradis, J., Crago, M., Genesee, F., & Rice, M. (2003). French–English bilingual children with SLI: How do they compare with their monolingual peers? *Journal of Speech, Language, and Hearing Research, 46,* 113–127.

Paradis, J., Jia, R., & Arppe, A. (2017). The acquisition of tense morphology over time by English second language children with specific language impairment: Testing the cumulative effects hypothesis. *Applied Psycholinguistics, 38,* 881–908.

Patterson, J. L. (2000). Observed and reported expressive vocabulary and word combinations in bilingual toddlers. *Journal of Speech, Language, and Hearing Research, 43*(1), 121–128.

Pearson, B. Z., & Fernández, S. C. (1994). Patterns of interaction in the lexical growth in two languages of bilingual infants and toddlers. *Language Learning, 44*(4), 617–653.

Peña, E. D. (2007). Lost in translation: Methodological considerations in cross-cultural research. *Child Development, 78*(4), 1255–1264.

Peña, E. D., & Bedore, L. M. (2009). Bilingualism in child language disorders. In R. G. Schwartz (Ed.), *Handbook of child language disorders* (pp. 281–307). New York, NY: Psychology Press.

Peña, E. D., Bedore, L. M., Gillam, R. B., & Bohman, T. (2006–2011). R01 DC007439 Diagnostic Markers of Language Impairment in Bilinguals, National Institutes of Health, NIDCD.

Peña, E. D., Bedore, L. M., & Griffin, Z. (2010–2017). R01 DC010366 Cross-Language Outcomes of Typical and Atypical Language Development, National Institutes of Health, NIDCD.

Peña, E. D., Bedore, L. M., & Kester, E. S. (2016). Assessment of language impairment in bilingual children using semantic tasks: Two languages classify better than one. *International Journal of Language and Communication Disorders, 51*, 192–202.

Peña, E. D., Gillam, R. B., Bedore, L. M., & Bohman, T. (2011). Risk for poor performance on a language screening measure for bilingual preschoolers and kindergarteners. *American Journal of Speech Language Pathology, 20*, 302–314.

Peña, E. D., & Quinn, R. (1997). Task familiarity: Effects on the test performance of Puerto Rican and African American children. *Language, Speech, and Hearing Services in Schools, 28*(4), 323–332.

Peña, E. D.., Spaulding, T. J., & Plante, E. (2006). The composition of normative groups and diagnostic decision making: Shooting ourselves in the foot. *American Journal of Speech-Language Pathology, 15*, 247–254.

Plante, E. (2004). Evidence based practice in communication sciences and disorders. *Journal of Communication Disorders, 37*, 389–390.

Plante, E., & Vance, R. (1994). Selection of preschool language tests: A data-based approach. *Language, Speech, and Hearing Services in Schools, 25*, 15–24.

Poulin-Dubois, D., Frank, I., Graham, S. A., & Elkin, A. (1999). The role of shape similarity in toddlers' lexical extensions. *British Journal of Developmental Psychology, 17*(Part 1), 21–36. doi:10.1348/026151099165131

Pruitt, S. L., Oetting, J. B., & Hegarty, M. (2011). Passive participle marking by African American English-speaking children reared in poverty. *Journal of Speech, Language, and Hearing Research, 54*(2), 598–607.

Rattermann, M. J., & Gentner, D. (1998). More evidence for a relationship shift in the development of analogy: Children's performance on a causal mapping task. *Cognitive Development, 13*, 453–478.

Restrepo, M. A., & Gutiérrez-Clellen, V. F. (2001). Article use in Spanish-speaking children with specific language impairment. *Journal of Child Language, 28*(2), 433–452. doi:10.1017/s0305000901004706

Restrepo, M. A., & Kruth, K. (2000). Grammatical characteristics of a Spanish–English bilingual child with specific language impairment. *Communication Disorders Quarterly, 21*(2), 66–76.

Restrepo, M. A., Morgan, G. P., & Thompson, M. S. (2013). The efficacy of a vocabulary intervention for dual-language learners with language impairment. *Journal of Speech, Language, and Hearing Research, 56*(2), 748–765.

Rice, M. L., & Wexler, K. (1996). Toward tense as a clinical marker of specific language impairment in English-speaking children. *Journal of Speech and Hearing Research, 39*(6), 1239–1257.

Rice, M. L., Wexler, K., & Cleave, P. L. (1995). Specific language impairment as a period of extended optional infinitive. *Journal of Speech, Language, and Hearing Research, 38*(4), 850–863.

Rodriguez, E., Bustamante, K., Wood, C., & Sunderman, G. (2017). A comparison of the grammatical production of child heritage speakers of Spanish across language and grade: Kindergarten and grade 1. *Languages, 2*(4), 27.

Rothweiler, M., Chilla, S., & Clahsen, H. (2012). Subject–verb agreement in specific language impairment: A study of monolingual and bilingual German-speaking children. *Bilingualism: Language and Cognition, 15*(1), 39–57. doi:10.1017/s136672891100037x

Royle, P., & Stine, I. (2013). The French noun phrase in preschool children with SLI: Morphosyntactic and error analyses. *Journal of Child Language, 40*, 945–970. doi:10.1017/S0305000912000414.

Salameh, E.-K., Håkansson, G., & Nettelbladt, U. (2004). Developmental perspectives on bilingual Swedish–Arabic children with and without language impairment: A longitudinal study. *International Journal of Language and Communication Disorders, 39*(1), 65–91. doi:10.1080/13682820310001595628

Schiff-Meyers, N. B. (1992). Considering arrested language development and language loss in the assessment of second language learners. *Language, Speech, and Hearing Services in Schools, 23*, 28–33.

Seymour, H. N., Bland-Stewart, L., & Green, L. J. (1998). Difference versus deficit in child African American English. *Language, Speech, and Hearing Services in Schools, 29*, 96–108.

Seymour, H. N., & Roeper, T. (1999). Grammatical acquisition of African American English. In O. Taylor & L. Leonard (Eds.), *Language acquisition across North America: Cross-cultural and cross-linguistic perspectives* (pp. 100–152). San Diego, CA: Singular Press.

Sheng, L., Bedore, L. M., Peña, E. D., & Fiestas, C. (2013). Semantic development in Spanish–English bilingual children: Effects of age and language experience. *Child Development, 84*, 1034–1045. doi:10.1111/cdev.12015

Sheng, L., Bedore, L. M., Peña, E. D., & Taliancich-Klinger, C. (2013). Semantic convergence in Spanish–English bilingual children with primary language impairment. *Journal of Speech, Language, and Hearing Research, 56*(2), 766–777. doi:10.1044/1092-4388(2012/11-0271

Sheng, L., McGregor, K. K., & Marian, V. (2006). Lexical-semantic organization in bilingual children: Evidence from a repeated word association task. *Journal of Speech, Language, and Hearing Research, 49*(3), 572–587.

Sheng, L., Peña, E. D., Bedore, L. M., & Fiestas, C. E. (2012). Semantic deficits in Spanish–English bilingual children with language impairment. *Journal of Speech, Language, and Hearing Research, 55*, 1–15.

Shriberg, L. D. (1993). Four new speech and prosody-voice measures for genetics research and other studies in developmental phonological disorders. *Journal of Speech, Language, and Hearing Research, 36*, 105–140.

Shriberg, L., & Austin, D. (1998). Comorbidity of speech-language disorder. In R. Paul (Ed.), *Exploring the speech–language connection* (pp. 73–115). Baltimore, MD: Paul H. Brookes Publishing Co.

Shriberg, L. D., Austin, D., Lewis, B. A., McSweeny, J. L., & Wilson, D. L. (1997). The percentage of consonants correct (PCC) metric: Extensions and reliability data. *Journal of Speech, Language, and Hearing Research, 40*(4), 708–722.

Shriberg, L. D., & Kwiatkowski, J. (1982). Phonological disorders: A procedure for assessing severity of involvement. *Journal of Speech and Hearing Disorders, 47*(3), 256–270.

Shriberg, L. D., & Kwiatkowski, J. (1994). Developmental phonological disorders: A clinical profile. *Journal of Speech, Language, and Hearing Research, 37*(5), 1100–1126.

Shriberg, L. D., & Lof, G. L. (1991). Reliability studies in broad and narrow phonetic transcription. *Clinical Linguistics and Phonetics, 5*(3), 225–279.

Silliman, E. R., Huntley Bahr, R., Brea, M. R., Hnath-Chisolm, T., & Mahecha, N. R. (2001). Spanish and English proficiency in the linguistic encoding of mental states in narrative retellings. *Linguistics and Education, 12*(4), 1–37.

Simon-Cereijido, G., & Gutiérrez-Clellen, V. F. (2007). Spontaneous language markers of Spanish language impairment. *Applied Psycholinguistics, 28*(2), 317–339. doi:10.1017/s0142716407070166

Slobin, D. I., & Bocaz, A. (1988). Learning to talk about movement through time and space: The development of narrative abilities in Spanish and English. *Lenguas Modernas, 15*, 5–24.

Smit, A. B., Hand, L., Freilinger, J. J., Bernthal, J. E., & Bird, A. (1990). The Iowa articulation norms project and its Nebraska replication. *Journal of Speech and Hearing Disorders, 55*, 779–798.

Spaulding, T. J., Plante, E., & Farinella, K. A. (2006). Eligibility criteria for language impairment: Is the low end of normal always appropriate? *Speech, Language, and Hearing Services in Schools, 37*, 61–72.

Spoelman, M., & Bol, G. W. (2012). The use of subject–verb agreement and verb argument structure in monolingual and bilingual children with specific language impairment. *Clinical Linguistics and Phonetics, 26*, 357–379. doi:10.3109/02699206.2011.637658

Stoel-Gammon, C., & Dunn, C. (1985). *Normal and disordered phonology in children*. Baltimore, MD: University Park Press.

Thordardottir, E. T., Ellis Weismer, S., & Evans, J. L. (2002). Continuity in lexical and morphological development in Icelandic and English-speaking 2-year-olds. *First Language, 22*(64), 3–28.

Thordardottir, E. T., Ellis Weismer, S., & Smith, M. E. (1997). Vocabulary learning in bilingual and monolingual clinical intervention. *Child Language Teaching and Therapy, 13*(3), 215–227.

Torrens, V., & Wexler, K. (2001). El retraso del lenguaje en la adquisición del castellano y el catalán [language delay in the acquisition of Castillian and Catalán]. *Aloma, 9*, 131–148.

Vermeer, A., & Shohov, S. P. (2004). Exploring the lexicon: Quantitative and qualitative aspects of children's L1/L2 word knowledge. In Shohov, S. P. (Ed.), *Advances in psychology research* (Vol. 32, pp. 42–67). Hauppauge, NY: Nova Science.

Washington, J. A., Kamhi, A. G., & Pollock, K. E. (1996). Issues in assessing the language abilities of African American children. In A. G. Kamhi, K. E. Pollock, and J. L. Harris (Eds.), *Communication development and disorders in African American Children: Research, assessment, and intervention* (pp. 35). Baltimore, MD: Paul H. Brookes Publishing Co.

Wilcox, T. (1999). Object individuation: Infants' use of shape, size, pattern, and color. *Cognition, 72*(2), 125–166.

Wilson, C., Davidson, L., & Martin, S. (2014). Effects of acoustic–phonetic detail on cross-language speech production. *Journal of Memory and Language, 77*, 1–24.

Winter, K. (1999). Speech and language therapy provision for bilingual children: Aspects of the current service. *International Journal of Language and Communication Disorders, 34*, 85–98.

Xuereb, R., Grech, H., & Dodd, B. (2011). The development of a literacy diagnostic tool for Maltese children. *Clinical Linguistics and Phonetics, 25*(5), 379–398. doi:10.3109/02699206.2010.540734

Appendices

APPENDIX A

Acceptable and Unacceptable Responses

Table A.1. Pragmatics activity: Spanish

Items	Acceptable responses	Unacceptable responses
S-PR1: Adivina lo que es.	Pelota, campana, monedas, pulsera, [gestures ringing]	[Shoulder shrug] No sé [No response] (NR)
S-PR2: Es un mushki. (mumbled)	¿Hmmm? ¿oh? ¿Qué es eso? ¿Qué es un mushki? ¿Hmmm? [Purses lips, questioning look] [Tilts head, questioning look]	[Shoulder shrug] No sé [No response] Para bebé
S-PR3: Un mushki, (open box) ¿Y ves?. El mushki se usa para poquilar las mungas.	¿Mushki? ¿como? ¿Poquilar (las) mungas? ¿como? ¿Qué es un mushki? ¿como? ¿Para qué (es)? ¿como? ¿Hmmm? ¿como?	Me gusta Qué bonito [Smiles]
S-PR4: ¿Tú sabes cómo envolver un regalo? Cuales son los pasos a sequir?	[Any sequence for present wrapping] Saca papel, luego tape, luego listón/cinta; Sortar papel, envolver regalo	[No response] No sé
S-PR5: Dame la cinta/el listón (not on table).	No sé dónde está No hay cinta/listón Allí están [Looks around and shrugs to indicate it's not there]	[Looks in box, opens box and closes it (but doesn't indicate it's missing)] [No response]

(continued)

Table A.1. *(continued)*

Items	Acceptable responses	Unacceptable responses
S-PR6: Aquí está la cinta/el listón. (Give child the wrong ribbon.)	[Makes comment about wrong color] Yo quería la cinta/el listón xx Este no es el qué quería [Gives ribbon back and indicates no] [Looks at wrong color and pauses, or looks at examiner] [Gives ribbon back to examiner and nods no, points to other ribbon]	[Continues to wrap present] [No response]
S-PR7: Dame un pedacito de tape (tape dispenser has no tape).	¿Dónde está el tape? ¿Tomaste el tape? [Gestures with hands that there's no tape] [Shakes head no and looks at examiner] [Looks around table, shows examiner empty tape dispenser]	[Continues to try to get tape from the dispenser] [No comment (or awareness) about tape dispenser being empty] [No response]
S-PR8: (Keep ribbons with puppet.) Put the ribbon on.	Dame la cinta/el listón [looks for ribbon actively] [gestures for ribbon]	[No response]
S-PR9: (Ribbon is too short.)	Es muy corta/o (chica/o) No es bastante grande Necesito una/o mas largo [Gestures too small]	[Continues to try tying small ribbon on the box, does not ask for assistance, no comment that ribbon is too short] [No response]
S-PR10: ¿Qué crees que debemos de hacer?	Juntar dos cintas/listones Saca una/o más largo/a Pegarla/o [Gestures taping or longer ribbon]	No sé [No response]
S-PR11: ¿Qué crees que Diego va a decir cuando yo se lo dé?	Gracias Le va a gustar Que sorpresa Que le gustará jugar con el [Gestures thank you]	No sé [No response]

Table A.2. Pragmatics activity: English

Items	Acceptable responses	Unacceptable responses
E-PR1: What do you think it is?	Any toy that might make a noise: A ball, a quarter, a bell, tools, a shake toy, a car, coins, a bracelet [Gestures ringing a bell]	[Shrug] [No response] I don't know
E-PR2: It's a mushki.	Oh! What is that? Huh?? A mushki?? Hmm? [Tilted head. . .look of confusion, purses lips to the side in confusion]	Oh, it's for babies [No response] I don't know
E-PR3: We use mushkis to bingle the waddle.	Mushki? Bingle? Waddle? To do what? I don't know what that is. [Look of confusion, open palm, shoulder shrug]	I like that It's pretty. [Smiles] [No response] I don't know.
E-PR4: What do I do next?	Any two-step sequence for present wrapping: Wrap the gift (get paper, then tape, then ribbon) Give it to somebody, cut paper	[No response] I don't know
E-PR5: Let me have the ribbon. (Not on table.)	I don't know where it is. Where is it? Where is the ribbon? I don't have the ribbon. [Looks around for ribbon] [Open palm for I don't know, pointing to the box]	[Looks in box without indicating that there's no ribbon] [Opens box and closes it without indicating that it's missing]
E-PR6: Here's the _______. (Wrong ribbon.)	[Makes comment about wrong color (e.g., "But I wanted the blue one," "I want the red ribbon," "This is not green").] That's not right. [Gives ribbon back to examiner and nods no.] [Points to other ribbon, looks at wrong color ribbon and pauses, looks at wrong color ribbon and looks at examiner.]	[Continues to wrap present] [No response]

(continued)

Table A.2. *(continued)*

Items	Acceptable responses	Unacceptable responses
E-PR7: Please give me some tape. (Tape dispenser has no tape.)	Where's the tape? There's nothing, no tape, this has no tape. How do you take the tape out? Looks like it's all gone. It's broken. [Gestures with hands, no tape] [Nods no and looks at examiner, looks around table/darts eyes] [Shows examiner empty tape dispenser]	[Continues to try to get tape from the dispenser, no comment about tape dispenser being empty] [No response]
E-PR8: Put the ribbon on.	Where's the ribbon? How can I tie this? I need the ribbon. [Holds box and looks for ribbon actively]	[No response]
E-PR9: (Give short ribbon.)	It's too little. It's not big enough. I need more ribbon. This is a short ribbon. [Hand gesture for too small]	[Continues to get small ribbon on the box, does not ask for assistance, no comment that ribbon is too short]
E-PR10: What should we do?	Maybe we should tape/tie two pieces together, get a longer ribbon. Tape it on. [Gestures taping two pieces of ribbon together] [Gestures getting a longer ribbon]	[No response] I don't know
E-PR11: What do you think Diego is going to say?	Thank you, Wow! He'll be happy, he will love/like it. He'll be surprised. He'll want to play with it. Yeah!	[No response] I don't know.

Table A.3. Spanish Phonology

Items	Acceptable responses
S-P1: señor	[seɲoɾ], [seɲol]
S-P2: radio	[raðio], [xaðio], [ʀaðio]
S-P3: leche	[let͡ʃe]
S-P4: tren	[tren]
S-P5: negro	[negro]
S-P6: clavo	[klaβo]
S-P7: bloque	[bloke]
S-P8: bruja	[bruxa], [bruha]
S-P9: plato	[plato]
S-P10: cruz	[krus], [kru]
S-P11: frio	[frio]
S-P12: flor	[floɾ], [flol]
S-P13: galleta	[gajeta], [gad͡ʒeta], [gaʒeta]
S-P14: elefante	[elefante]
S-P15: bicicleta	[bisikleta]
S-P16: rompecabezas	[rompekaβesas], [rompekaβesa]
S-P17: arroz	[aros], [aro], [axo], [aʀo]
S-P18: perro	[pero], [pexo], [peʀo]
S-P19: guitarra	[gitara], [gitaxa], [gitaʀa]
S-P20: rodilla	[roðija], [xoðija], [ʀoðija]
S-P21: bigote	[biɣote]
S-P22: aguja	[aɣuxa], [aɣuha]
S-P23: agua	[aɣua], [aua], [aβa]
S-P24: mano	[mano]
S-P25: árbol	[arbol]
S-P26: dientes	[dientes], [diente], [diete]
S-P27: cama	[kama]
S-P28: amarillo	[amarijo]

Table A.4. English Phonology

Items	**Acceptable responses**
E-P1: book	[bʊk]
E-P2: thumb	[θʌm], [tʌm]
E-P3: ant	[ænt]
E-P4: toast	[tost], [tos]
E-P5: computer	[kəmpjurɚ]
E-P6: hand	[hænd], [hæn]
E-P7: car	[kɑɚ]
E-P8: pants	[pænts], [pæns]
E-P9: doctor	[dɑktɚ]
E-P10: church	[t͡ʃɝt͡ʃ]
E-P11: thermometer	[θɚmɑmərɚ]
E-P12: ring	[ɹɪŋ]
E-P13: feather	[fɛðɚ], [fɛdɚ]
E-P14: shovel	[ʃʌvəl]
E-P15: bridge	[bɹɪd͡ʒ]
E-P16: umbrella	[əmbɹɛlə]
E-P17: present	[pɹɛsənt], [pɹɛsən]
E-P18: frog	[fɹɑg]
E-P19: stop	[stɑp], [estɑp]
E-P20: plate	[plet]
E-P21: train	[tɹen]
E-P22: screwdriver	[skɹudɹɑ͜ɪvɚ]
E-P23: grape	[gɹep]
E-P24: clown	[klɑ͜ʊn]
E-P25: queen	[kwin]
E-P26: school	[skul]
E-P27: glass	[glæs]
E-P28: helicopter	[hɛləkɑptɚ]
E-P29: nose	[noz]
E-P30: wagon	[wægən], [wæg^ŋ]
E-P31: lollipop	[lɑlipɑp]

Table A.5. Spanish Morphosyntax Cloze items

Items	Acceptable answers	Unacceptable answers
S-M1: Los niños tienen unos carros. ¿Y aquí que tienen los niños? Los niños tienen	**un/el** carro **un/el** coche	una carro unos one car
S-M2: El perrito está mordiendo los zapatos. ¿Y aquí que está mordiendo el perrito? El perrito está mordiendo . . .	**el/un** zapato	un boot el shoe lo zapatos
S-M3: Los panes están en la mesa. ¿Y aquí que está en la mesa?	**el/un pan**	una pan uno un bread
S-M4: María y Juan están dormidos. ¿Y aquí, quienes están dormidos?	**los/unos** gato**s**	los dogs/perros la/lo gato
S-M5: El niño va a leer un cuento. Lo está haciendo ahora. ¿Aquí, que está hacienda? El niño. . .	**está/ta leyendo/lee** un/el cuento **anda leyendo** un libro **está viendo/mirando** el dibujo	está reading is reading está sentado
S-M6: El papa, la mama, y Juan van a ir a comer hamburguesas. Lo están haciendo ahora. ¿Aquí, que están haciendo? El papa, la mama, y Juan. . .	**están/tan comiendo/comen** unas hamburguesas	is eating, está comiendo
S-M7: La mama va a ver televisión. Lo está haciendo ahora. ¿Aquí, que está haciendo? La mama. . .	**está/ta viendo/mirando/ mira/ve** la televisión	are watching, mirar, va a ver la televisión
S-M8: Los niños van a abrir los regales. Y aquí, ¿Que hacen los niños con los regales?	**los** abren/**los** están abriendo/están abriéndo**los** **los** sacan **los** agarran	open it put them on the table la abrieron está abriéndolas

(continued)

Table A.5. *(continued)*

Items	Acceptable answers	Unacceptable answers
S-M9: El niño va a agarras las manzanas. Y aquí, ¿Que hace el niño con las manzanas?	**las** agarra, **las** está agarrando/está agarrándo**las** se **las** quiere comer **las** levanta	ya lo agarro las manzanas la va comer todas la está levantando
S-M10: El perro va a ensuciar a las niñas. Y aquí, ¿Que hace el perro con las niñas?	**las** ensucia/ensucio/mancho, **las** está ensuciando, está ensuciándo**las** **las** salpica/**las** salpico	lo/la ensucio
S-M11: Juan va a asustar a las niñas. Y aquí, ¿Que hace Juan con las niñas?	**Las** asusta/asusto/espanto, **las** está asustando, está asustándo**las**	Hizo get scared, la asusto/ asusta, la está asustando, la niña tiene miedo
S-M12: La mama quiere que se peine. ¿Y aquí que quiere la mama? La mama. . .	quiere que **se lave/limpie** los dientes, quiere que **agarre** el cepillo	su brush her teeth que she brush her teeth quiere que lavar la dientes
S-M13: Juan quiere que se baje del carro. ¿Y aquí que quiere Juan? Juan. . .	quiere que le **dé** el zapato/se lo **dé** quiere que no se **coma** el zapato que **regrese/deje/ ponga/devuelva**	que dame mi zapato quiere la zapatos give him el shoe
S-M14: La mama quiere que pongan la mesa. ¿Y aquí que quiere la mama? La mama. . .	quiere que **coman/tomen** la sopa	quiere este el soup que toma quiere que toman el café
S-M15: La mama quiere que se pongan la pijama. ¿Y aquí que quiere la mama? La mama. . .	quiere que se **acuesten/ duerman/ vayan** a dormir/a la cama quiere que se **quiten** los chongos	que ya se clean up el room, que se duermen, quiere los niños acostan, quiere que se pongan la pijama quiere que se metan a dormir

Table A.6. English Morphosyntax Cloze items

Items	Acceptable items	Unacceptable items
E-M1: Look, this is a girl and this is the girl's umbrella. This is a clown, and this is the. . .	**clown's** umbrella **clown's** **boy's umbrella**	clown umbrella, boy apple, his hat
E-M2: Look, this is a dog and this is the dog's ball. This is a baby, and this is the. . .	**baby's** ball **baby's**	baby ball, ball of the baby
E-M3: Look, this is a puppy and this is the puppy's doll. This is a monkey, and this is the. . .	**monkey's** doll **monkey's**	monkey doll, doll of the monkey
E-M4: Every day these horses jump over the fence. And here, this horse does it, too. What does he do every day? Every day the horse. . .	**jumps** over the fence, **goes** over the fence	comes on to the fence
E-M5: Every day these monkeys eat bananas. And here, this monkey does it, too. What does he do every day? Every day the monkey. . .	**eats/likes** bananas	eat banana
E-M6: Every day they walk the dog. And here, this girl does it, too. What does she do every day? Every day the girl. . .	**walks** the dog, **takes** the dog for a walk, **runs** with the dog	getting him into a walk, walk the dog, is walking the dog
E-M7: Today the man is going to kick the ball. And yesterday, he did it, too. What did the man do yesterday? Yesterday he. . .	**kicked** the ball	kick the ball, threw/throwed the ball
E-M8: Now, the girl is going to jump in the water. And yesterday, she did it, too. What did the girl do yesterday? Yesterday she. . .	**jumped/drowned** in the water, **dove** in the water	jump in the water
E-M9: Look, he is going to drop the balls. And yesterday, he did that, too. What did he do yesterday?	**dropped** the balls, **juggled** the balls, **threw** the balls	drop/drops the balls, throw the balls, drop the baby
E-M10: She has a cat. And here, what does she have?	She has many/lots/a lot of/ two **cats.**	a lot/two/many
E-M11: The girl is buying one orange. And here, what is she buying?	The girl is buying **oranges**.	a whole bunch of 'em

(continued)

Table A.6. *(continued)*

Items	Acceptable items	Unacceptable items
E-M12: There is only one tree. And here?	There are many **trees**.	flowers, a forest
E-M13: Maria and Juan want to skate. They are doing it now. What are they doing here? They. . .	**are skating.**	skating, were skating, was skating, he push him and he want to skate
E-M14: Maria wants to swim. She is doing it now. What is Maria doing here? She. . .	**is swimming.**	swimming, is doing swimming, swims, she jump and then start swimming
E-M15: Yesterday the dogs wanted to eat a bone. Here they were doing it. What were the dogs doing yesterday? Yesterday they. . .	**were eating/chewing/ biting/sharing** a bone.	eating, eat a bone, fighting, were hiding the bone
E-M16: Here Maria is sick. And here Maria and Juan. . .	**are/were** sick.	bored, was sick
E-M17: Here these clothes are dirty. And here the shirt. . .?	**is/was** dirty.	dirty
E-M18: Maria and Juan went to the zoo yesterday. At the zoo, this elephant was big. And these elephants. . .?	**are/were** big, **are/were** little/small, **were** two	is/was little
E-M19: These men wear glasses. And what about them?	They **don't** wear glasses, they **are not** wearing glasses	No/nope, they doesn't
E-M20: She is wearing shoes. And here?	She **is not/isn't** wearing shoes/socks, She **doesn't** have shoes, **She's wearing no shoes**	She not wearing shoes, no/nope
E-M21: The boy wants to eat. And here?	The boy **doesn't/does not** want to eat, The boy **isn't/is not** going to eat.	He don't want to eat, no/nope, he no eat, he no like the food
E-M22: The baby is carried by the mother. What happened to the baby here?	The baby **is/was carried** by the father/dad/daddy.	The dad carried the baby.
E-M23: The window was broken by the boy. What happened to the window here?	The window **is/was broken** by the girl.	The glass broke.
E-M24: The girl is pushed by the boy. What happened to the boy here?	The boy **is/was/got pushed** by the girl.	It's pushed by the girl.

Table A.7. Spanish Semantics

Items	Acceptable answers	Unacceptable answers
S-S1B: Enséñame todas las cosas que se usan para limpiar.	escoba, aspiradora, jabón, balde, trapeador,	
S-S2: ¿Qué se hace con un bate?	jugar al beisbol, pegar la pelota, pegar, jugar, play baseball, hit the ball, hit, play	
S-S3: Enséñame que se hace con una cachucha.	arriba de la cabeza	
S-S4: ¿Para que es un closet?	poner la ropa, guardar la ropa, to put clothes in, to keep clothes in	
S-S5: ¿Para que son estas cosas?	limpiar, barrer, to clean, to sweep	
S-S6: Enséñame para que se usa una escoba.	limpiar, barrer	montar sobre la escoba, jugar al beisbol con la escoba
S-S7: ¿Qué se hace con un cuchillo?	cortar, cortar comida, comer, cut, cut food, eat	
S-S8: Enséñame que se hace con la comida.	comer la comida	
S-S9: Enséñame el perro que es diferente.	perro manchado	cualquier otro perro
S-S10: Dime todos los animales que conoces.	perro, gato, caballo, elefante, tigre, jirafa, león, dog, cat, horse, elephant, tiger, giraffe, lion	
S-S11: Enséñame el resbaladero más bajo.	el resbaladero más bajo	[cualquier de los resbaladeros altos]
S-S12: Dime como es la pelota.	estrellas, circulo, roja, amarilla, stars, circule, red, yellow	
S-S13: Dime todas las cosas que la abuelita necesitaba comprar para limpiar.	escoba, trapeador, aspiradora, jabon, broom, mop, vacuum, soap	
S-S14: Dime, ¿Qué ropa se usa cuando hace frio?	chamarra, guantes, chaqueta, sueter, pantalón, coat, gloves, jacket, sweater, pants	
S-S15: De estas dos chaquetas, enséñame cuales son iguales.	las dos chaquetas verdes	[cualquier otra combinación]

(continued)

Table A.7. *(continued)*

Items	Acceptable answers	Unacceptable answers
S-S16: Dime toda la comida que se puede comer para el lonche/almuerzo.	hamburguesa, pizza, papas, sopa, hamburger, French fries, soup, sandwich	
S-S17: ¿Qué sonidos hace un perrito?	ruf ruf, ladrar, bark, woof woof, arf	
S-S18: Enséñame que fue lo primero que hicieron cuando llegaron los demás.	se lavaron las manos	comieron, sacaron los juguetes del auto, vieron las camionetas
S-S19: Dime que hicieron ellos después de comer.	jugaron, played	se lavaron las manos, abrieron los regales, washed their hands, opened gifts
S-S20: Que tuvo que hacer antes de jugar con sus amigos?	recoger la mesa, clear the table	
S-S21B: Madre va con padre como abuela va con. . .	abuelo, abuelito	madre, bebe
S-S22: Grande va con chiquito como limpio va con. . .	dirty dress	polka-dot dress, striped dress, solid dress
S-S23: Dime todos los animales que se pueden encontrar en el circo.	elefantes, leones, tigres, changos, caballos, elephants, lions, tigers, monkeys, horses	
S-S24: Enséñame donde se encuentran estas cosas.	Escuela	circo, granja, parque, acquario
S-S25: Dile a Miguel donde puede encontrarla.	cerca del resbaladero, near the slide	

Table A.8. English Semantics

Items	Acceptable answers	Unacceptable answers
E-S1. Show me the two that go together.	the two yellow invitations	other combination]
E-S2. Where will Diego take the invitations?	to school, class, friends at school, to the girls and boys, a la escuela, a los amigos de la escuela, a los niños/niñas	mailbox, correo, casa, house
E-S3. Tell me all the toys you can play with in a pool.	dive for rings, water gun, shark, fish out of water, Marco Polo, buscar ruedas, pistola de agua, tiburón	
E-S4. Which picture shows what a party hat is for?	hat on head	hat on cake, hat on child's chin
E-S5. Tell me all the animals you can think of.	dog, cat, bird, fish, monkey, elephant, horse, perro, wua wua, gato, pájaro, pez, pescado, chango, elefante, caballo	
E-S6. Show me another place you would find scissors, pencils, and paper.	school	zoo, circus, park
E-S7. Show me what people do with invitations	mail invitation	tearing invitation, making paper airplane, wearing it on a string around neck
E-S8. What is different about these two invitations?	red/blue, colors, rojo/azul, colores	red, blue, rojo, azul
E-S9. Tell me all the farm animals you can think of.	cow, horse, chicken, rooster, pig, vaca, caballo, gallina, pollo, gallo, marrano, puerco, cochino	flies, ostriches
E-S10. Tell me all the zoo animals you can think of.	zebra, monkey, giraffe, lion, bear, panda, mono, change, girafa, leon, oso	
E-S11. What makes these two gifts go together?	bow, color bow, moño, color de moño	color, size, tamaño
E-S12. What shape is this present?	square, rectangle, cuadrado, rectangular	color, circle, open it, círculo, abrirlo
E-S13. Tell me all the foods you can think of.	egg, cake, hamburger, pizza, hot dog, beans, rice, apple, huevo, pastel, hamburguesa, frijoles, arroz, manzana	

(continued)

Table A.8. *(continued)*

Items	Acceptable answers	Unacceptable answers
E-S14. Show me the picture that finishes this sentence. Sun is to yellow as grass is to ___.	green square	sun, yellow square, grass
E-S15. Show me the piñata that doesn't go with the others.	small piñata	any one of the big piñatas, any combo of more than one piñata
E-S16. What is different about these piñatas?	different number of points	cantidad diferente de puntos
E-S17. Show me who received an invitation last.	teacher	girls, boys, boys and girls
E-S18. Show me the boy in Diego's class with the long striped pants.	boy in long-striped pants	boy in short green pants, boy in long brown pants, boy in short striped pants
E-S19. Show me all the things in this picture you can buy.	pants, socks, shirt, pens	people in love, ear
E-S20. Tell me all the clothes you can think of.	pants, shirt, dress, skirt, T-shirt, sweater, pantalones, camisa, camiseta, vestido, falda, sueter	
E-S21. Show me what you do with a bow.	bow on present	bow on carrot, bow on computer, person stepping on bow
E-S22. Tell Diego where Ana put the present with the big red bow.	under the table, on the floor, debajo de la mesa, en el piso	here, there, aqui, allá, acá
E-S23. Circles, squares, and triangles are all ___.	shapes, forms, figures, formas	circle, square, triangle, círculo, cuadrado, triángulo
E-S24. Tell me all the circus animals you can think of.	lion, tiger, elephant, monkey, bear, dog, leon, tigre, elefante, chango, oso, perro	
E-S25. Look at these two presents. What makes them different?	size, big/little, tamano, grande/chico	big, little, grande, chico

APPENDIX B

Raw Score to Scaled Score Conversions—Spanish Subtests

Table B.1. Spanish Phonology

	Age											
Raw score	**4;0–4;2**	**4;3–4;5**	**4;6–4;8**	**4;9–4;11**	**5;0–5;2**	**5;3–5;5**	**5;6–5;8**	**5;9–5;11**	**6;0–6;2**	**6;3–6;5**	**6;6–6;8**	**6;9–6;11**
1	1	1	1	1	<1	<1	<1	<1	<1	<1	<1	<1
2	2	2	1	1	<1	<1	<1	<1	<1	<1	<1	<1
3	3	2	2	1	1	<1	<1	<1	<1	<1	<1	<1
4	3	3	2	2	1	1	<1	<1	<1	<1	<1	<1
5	4	4	3	2	2	1	1	<1	<1	<1	<1	<1
6	4	4	3	3	2	2	1	<1	<1	<1	<1	<1
7	5	4	4	3	3	2	2	1	<1	<1	<1	<1
8	5	5	4	4	3	3	2	2	1	<1	<1	<1
9	6	5	5	4	4	3	3	2	2	1	<1	<1
10	6	6	5	5	4	4	3	3	2	1	<1	<1
11	6	6	6	5	5	4	4	3	3	2	1	<1
12	7	7	6	6	5	5	4	4	3	2	2	1
13	7	7	7	6	6	5	5	4	4	3	2	2
14	8	8	7	7	6	6	6	5	5	4	3	2
15	8	8	8	7	7	6	6	6	5	4	4	3
16	9	9	8	8	7	7	7	6	6	5	4	4
17	9	9	9	8	8	8	7	7	6	6	5	5
18	**10**	9	9	9	8	8	8	7	7	6	6	5
19	**10**	**10**	**10**	9	9	9	8	8	8	7	6	6
20	**10**	**10**	**10**	**10**	**10**	9	9	8	8	8	7	7
21	11	11	**10**	**10**	**10**	**10**	9	9	9	8	8	7
22	11	11	11	11	11	**10**	**10**	**10**	9	9	8	8
23	12	12	11	11	11	11	11	**10**	**10**	9	9	9
24	12	12	12	12	12	11	11	11	11	**10**	**10**	9
25	13	13	12	12	12	12	12	11	11	11	**10**	**10**
26	13	13	13	13	13	12	12	12	12	11	11	11
27	14	13	13	13	13	13	13	12	12	12	12	12
28	14	14	14	14	14	13	13	13	13	13	13	12

Table B.2. Spanish Morphosyntax—Cloze

	Age											
Raw score	**4;0–4;2**	**4;3–4;5**	**4;6–4;8**	**4;9–4;11**	**5;0–5;2**	**5;3–5;5**	**5;6–5;8**	**5;9–5;11**	**6;0–6;2**	**6;3–6;5**	**6;6–6;8**	**6;9–6;11**
1	3	3	3	3	2	2	2	1	1	<1	<1	<1
2	4	4	4	3	3	3	3	2	2	1	1	1
3	5	5	4	4	4	4	3	3	3	2	2	1
4	6	5	5	5	5	4	4	4	3	3	3	2
5	6	6	6	6	6	5	5	5	4	4	4	3
6	7	7	7	7	6	6	6	6	5	5	5	4
7	8	8	8	8	7	7	7	7	6	6	6	5
8	9	9	9	8	8	8	8	7	7	7	7	6
9	**10**	9	9	9	9	9	9	8	8	8	8	7
10	**10**	**10**	**10**	**10**	**10**	**10**	9	9	9	9	9	8
11	11	11	11	11	11	**10**	**10**	**10**	**10**	**10**	9	9
12	12	12	12	12	12	11	11	11	11	11	**10**	**10**
13	13	13	13	12	12	12	12	12	12	11	11	11
14	14	14	13	13	13	13	13	13	13	12	12	12
15	14	14	14	14	14	14	14	14	13	13	13	13

Table B.3. Spanish Morphosyntax—Sentence Repetition

	Age											
Raw score	**4;0–4;2**	**4;3–4;5**	**4;6–4;8**	**4;9–4;11**	**5;0–5;2**	**5;3–5;5**	**5;6–5;8**	**5;9–5;11**	**6;0–6;2**	**6;3–6;5**	**6;6–6;8**	**6;9–6;11**
1	4	4	4	3	3	3	2	2	1	1	<1	<1
2	5	4	4	4	3	3	2	2	2	1	1	<1
3	5	5	4	4	4	3	3	2	2	1	1	1
4	5	5	5	4	4	4	3	3	2	2	1	1
5	6	5	5	5	4	4	3	3	3	2	2	1
6	6	6	5	5	5	4	4	3	3	2	2	2
7	6	6	6	5	5	5	4	4	3	3	2	2
8	7	6	6	6	5	5	4	4	4	3	3	2
9	7	7	6	6	6	5	5	4	4	4	3	3
10	7	7	7	6	6	6	5	5	4	4	3	3
11	8	7	7	7	6	6	6	5	5	4	4	4
12	8	8	7	7	7	6	6	5	5	5	4	4
13	8	8	8	7	7	7	6	6	5	5	5	4
14	9	8	8	8	7	7	7	6	6	5	5	5
15	9	9	8	8	8	7	7	6	6	6	5	5
16	9	9	9	8	8	8	7	7	6	6	6	5
17	**10**	9	9	9	8	8	8	7	7	6	6	6
18	**10**	**10**	9	9	9	8	8	8	7	7	6	6
19	**10**	**10**	**10**	9	9	9	8	8	8	7	7	6
20	**10**	**10**	**10**	**10**	9	9	9	8	8	7	7	7
21	11	11	11	**10**	**10**	9	9	9	8	8	7	7
22	11	11	11	**10**	**10**	**10**	9	9	9	8	8	7
23	11	11	11	11	**10**	**10**	**10**	9	9	8	8	8
24	12	12	12	11	11	**10**	**10**	**10**	9	9	8	8
25	12	12	12	11	11	11	**10**	**10**	**10**	9	9	9
26	12	12	12	12	11	11	11	**10**	**10**	**10**	9	9
27	13	13	13	12	12	11	11	11	**10**	**10**	**10**	9
28	13	13	13	12	12	12	11	11	11	**10**	**10**	**10**
29	13	13	13	13	12	12	12	11	11	11	**10**	**10**
30	14	14	14	13	13	12	12	12	11	11	11	**10**
31	14	14	14	14	13	13	12	12	12	11	11	11
32	14	14	14	14	14	13	13	12	12	12	11	11
33	15	15	15	14	14	13	13	13	12	12	12	11
34	15	15	15	15	14	14	13	13	13	12	12	12
35	15	15	15	15	15	14	14	13	13	13	12	12
36	16	16	16	15	15	15	14	14	13	13	13	12
37	16	16	16	16	15	15	14	14	14	13	13	13

Table B.4. Spanish Semantics—Receptive

	Age											
Raw score	**4;0–4;2**	**4;3–4;5**	**4;6–4;8**	**4;9–4;11**	**5;0–5;2**	**5;3–5;5**	**5;6–5;8**	**5;9–5;11**	**6;0–6;2**	**6;3–6;5**	**6;6–6;8**	**6;9–6;11**
1	5	4	4	3	2	1	1	<1	<1	<1	<1	<1
2	6	6	5	4	3	3	2	1	<1	<1	<1	<1
3	7	7	6	5	5	4	3	2	1	1	<1	<1
4	9	8	7	7	6	5	4	4	3	2	1	<1
5	**10**	9	9	8	7	7	6	5	4	3	2	1
6	11	**10**	**10**	9	9	8	7	6	6	5	4	3
7	12	12	11	11	**10**	9	9	8	7	6	5	4
8	13	13	13	12	11	11	**10**	9	9	8	7	6
9	14	14	14	13	13	12	11	11	**10**	9	8	7
10	16	15	15	14	14	13	13	12	11	11	**10**	9
11	17	17	16	16	15	15	14	14	13	12	12	11
12	18	18	18	17	17	16	16	15	14	14	13	12

Table B.5. Spanish Semantics—Expressive

	Age											
Raw score	**4;0–4;2**	**4;3–4;5**	**4;6–4;8**	**4;9–4;11**	**5;0–5;2**	**5;3–5;5**	**5;6–5;8**	**5;9–5;11**	**6;0–6;2**	**6;3–6;5**	**6;6–6;8**	**6;9–6;11**
1	5	5	4	3	3	2	1	1	<1	<1	<1	<1
2	6	6	5	5	4	3	3	2	1	<1	<1	<1
3	7	7	6	6	5	5	4	3	2	1	1	<1
4	8	8	7	7	6	6	5	4	4	3	2	1
5	9	9	8	8	7	7	6	6	5	4	3	3
6	11	**10**	9	9	9	8	7	7	6	6	5	4
7	12	11	11	**10**	**10**	9	9	8	8	7	6	6
8	13	12	12	11	11	**10**	**10**	9	9	8	8	7
9	14	13	13	12	12	12	11	11	**10**	**10**	9	9
10	15	14	14	14	13	13	12	12	11	11	**10**	**10**
11	16	15	15	15	14	14	14	13	13	12	12	11
12	17	16	16	16	15	15	15	14	14	14	13	13
13	18	17	17	17	17	16	16	16	15	15	15	14

APPENDIX C

Raw Score to Scaled Score Conversions—English Subtests

Table C.1. English Phonology

	Age											
Raw score	**4;0–4;2**	**4;3–4;5**	**4;6–4;8**	**4;9–4;11**	**5;0–5;2**	**5;3–5;5**	**5;6–5;8**	**5;9–5;11**	**6;0–6;2**	**6;3–6;5**	**6;6–6;8**	**6;9–6;11**
1	1	1	<1	<1	<1	<1	<1	<1	<1	<1	<1	<1
2	2	1	1	<1	<1	<1	<1	<1	<1	<1	<1	<1
3	2	2	1	<1	<1	<1	<1	<1	<1	<1	<1	<1
4	3	2	2	1	<1	<1	<1	<1	<1	<1	<1	<1
5	3	3	2	1	1	<1	<1	<1	<1	<1	<1	<1
6	4	3	2	2	1	1	<1	<1	<1	<1	<1	<1
7	4	4	3	2	2	1	<1	<1	<1	<1	<1	<1
8	5	4	3	3	2	2	1	<1	<1	<1	<1	<1
9	5	5	4	3	3	2	2	1	<1	<1	<1	<1
10	5	5	4	4	3	3	2	2	1	<1	<1	<1
11	6	5	5	4	4	3	3	2	1	<1	<1	<1
12	6	6	5	5	5	4	3	3	2	1	<1	<1
13	7	6	6	5	5	4	4	3	3	2	1	<1
14	7	7	6	6	6	5	4	4	3	3	2	1
15	8	7	7	6	6	6	5	5	4	3	3	2
16	8	8	7	7	7	6	6	5	5	4	3	3
17	9	8	8	7	7	7	6	6	5	5	4	3
18	9	9	8	8	8	7	7	6	6	5	5	4
19	9	9	9	8	8	8	7	7	7	6	6	5
20	**10**	**10**	9	9	9	8	8	8	7	7	6	6
21	**10**	**10**	**10**	9	9	9	9	8	8	7	7	6
22	11	11	**10**	**10**	**10**	9	9	9	8	8	8	7
23	11	11	11	11	**10**	**10**	**10**	**10**	9	9	8	8
24	12	11	11	11	11	11	**10**	**10**	**10**	9	9	9
25	12	12	12	12	11	11	11	11	**10**	**10**	**10**	9
26	13	12	12	12	12	12	12	11	11	11	11	**10**
27	13	13	13	13	13	12	12	12	12	11	11	11
28	13	13	13	13	13	13	13	13	12	12	12	12
29	14	14	14	14	14	13	13	13	13	13	13	13
30	14	14	14	14	14	14	14	14	14	14	13	13
31	15	15	15	15	15	14	14	14	14	14	14	14

Table C.2. English Morphosyntax—Cloze

	Age											
Raw score	**4;0–4;2**	**4;3–4;5**	**4;6–4;8**	**4;9–4;11**	**5;0–5;2**	**5;3–5;5**	**5;6–5;8**	**5;9–5;11**	**6;0–6;2**	**6;3–6;5**	**6;6–6;8**	**6;9–6;11**
1	3	3	3	3	3	3	3	3	3	3	3	3
2	3	3	3	3	3	3	3	3	3	3	3	3
3	4	4	4	4	4	4	4	4	4	4	4	4
4	4	4	4	4	4	4	4	4	4	4	4	4
5	5	5	5	5	5	5	5	5	5	4	4	4
6	5	5	5	5	5	5	5	5	5	5	5	5
7	6	6	6	6	6	6	6	6	5	5	5	5
8	6	6	6	6	6	6	6	6	6	6	6	6
9	7	7	7	7	7	7	7	6	6	6	6	6
10	7	7	7	7	7	7	7	7	7	7	7	7
11	8	8	8	8	8	8	8	7	7	7	7	7
12	8	8	8	8	8	8	8	8	8	8	8	8
13	9	9	9	9	9	9	8	8	8	8	8	8
14	9	9	9	9	9	9	9	9	9	9	9	9
15	**10**	**10**	**10**	**10**	**10**	**10**	9	9	9	9	9	9
16	**10**	**10**	**10**	**10**	**10**	**10**	**10**	**10**	**10**	**10**	**10**	**10**
17	11	11	11	11	11	**10**	**10**	**10**	**10**	**10**	**10**	**10**
18	11	11	11	11	11	11	11	11	11	11	11	**10**
19	12	12	12	12	12	11	11	11	11	11	11	11
20	12	12	12	12	12	12	12	12	12	12	11	11
21	13	13	13	13	13	12	12	12	12	12	12	12
22	13	13	13	13	13	13	13	13	13	13	12	12
23	14	14	14	14	14	13	13	13	13	13	13	13
24	14	14	14	14	14	14	14	14	14	13	13	13

Table C.3. English Morphosyntax—Sentence Repetition

	Age											
Raw score	**4;0–4;2**	**4;3–4;5**	**4;6–4;8**	**4;9–4;11**	**5;0–5;2**	**5;3–5;5**	**5;6–5;8**	**5;9–5;11**	**6;0–6;2**	**6;3–6;5**	**6;6–6;8**	**6;9–6;11**
1	2	2	1	1	1	<1	<1	<1	<1	<1	<1	<1
2	3	2	2	1	1	1	<1	<1	<1	<1	<1	<1
3	3	3	2	2	1	1	1	<1	<1	<1	<1	<1
4	3	3	3	2	2	1	1	<1	<1	<1	<1	<1
5	4	3	3	2	2	2	1	1	<1	<1	<1	<1
6	4	4	3	3	2	2	2	1	1	<1	<1	<1
7	4	4	4	3	3	3	2	2	1	1	<1	<1
8	5	4	4	4	3	3	3	2	2	1	1	<1
9	5	5	4	4	4	3	3	3	2	2	2	1
10	5	5	5	4	4	4	3	3	3	2	2	1
11	6	5	5	5	4	4	4	3	3	3	2	2
12	6	6	5	5	5	4	4	4	3	3	3	2
13	6	6	6	5	5	5	5	4	4	4	3	3
14	6	6	6	6	5	5	5	5	4	4	4	3
15	7	7	6	6	6	6	5	5	5	5	4	4
16	7	7	7	6	6	6	6	6	5	5	5	4
17	7	7	7	7	7	6	6	6	6	6	5	5
18	8	8	7	7	7	7	7	6	6	6	6	5
19	8	8	8	8	7	7	7	7	7	6	6	6
20	8	8	8	8	8	8	7	7	7	7	7	6
21	9	9	8	8	8	8	8	8	7	7	7	7
22	9	9	9	9	8	8	8	8	8	8	8	7
23	9	9	9	9	9	9	9	9	8	8	8	8
24	**10**	9	9	9	9	9	9	9	9	9	9	9
25	**10**	**10**	**10**	**10**	**10**	**10**	9	9	9	9	9	9
26	**10**	**10**	**10**	**10**	**10**	**10**	**10**	**10**	**10**	**10**	**10**	**10**
27	11	**10**	**10**	**10**	**10**	**10**	**10**	**10**	**10**	**10**	**10**	**10**
28	11	11	11	11	11	11	11	11	11	11	11	11
29	11	11	11	11	11	11	11	11	11	11	11	11
30	11	11	11	11	11	11	11	11	12	11	11	12
31	12	12	12	12	12	12	12	12	12	12	12	12
32	12	12	12	12	12	12	12	12	12	12	12	13
33	12	12	13	13	13	13	13	13	13	13	13	13

Table C.4. English Semantics—Receptive

	Age											
Raw score	**4;0–4;2**	**4;3–4;5**	**4;6–4;8**	**4;9–4;11**	**5;0–5;2**	**5;3–5;5**	**5;6–5;8**	**5;9–5;11**	**6;0–6;2**	**6;3–6;5**	**6;6–6;8**	**6;9–6;11**
1	4	4	3	3	2	1	0	<1	<1	<1	<1	<1
2	6	5	5	4	3	2	2	1	1	<1	<1	<1
3	7	6	6	5	5	4	3	3	2	1	1	<1
4	8	7	7	6	6	5	5	4	3	3	2	1
5	9	9	8	8	7	7	6	6	5	4	4	3
6	**10**	**10**	**10**	9	9	8	8	7	7	6	5	5
7	11	11	11	**10**	**10**	**10**	9	9	8	8	7	7
8	12	12	12	12	11	11	11	**10**	**10**	**10**	9	9
9	13	13	13	13	13	13	12	12	12	11	11	**10**
10	14	14	14	14	14	14	14	14	13	13	13	12

Table C.5. English Semantics—Expressive

	Age											
Raw score	**4;0–4;2**	**4;3–4;5**	**4;6–4;8**	**4;9–4;11**	**5;0–5;2**	**5;3–5;5**	**5;6–5;8**	**5;9–5;11**	**6;0–6;2**	**6;3–6;5**	**6;6–6;8**	**6;9–6;11**
1	6	5	5	4	3	3	2	1	<1	<1	<1	<1
2	7	6	5	5	4	4	3	2	1	<1	<1	<1
3	8	7	6	6	5	5	4	3	2	1	1	<1
4	8	8	7	7	6	6	5	4	3	2	2	1
5	9	9	8	8	7	6	6	5	4	4	3	2
6	**10**	9	9	8	8	7	7	6	5	5	4	3
7	11	**10**	**10**	9	9	8	8	7	6	6	5	4
8	12	11	11	**10**	**10**	9	9	8	7	7	6	6
9	12	12	12	11	11	**10**	**10**	9	9	8	7	7
10	13	13	12	12	12	11	11	**10**	**10**	9	8	8
11	14	14	13	13	13	12	12	11	11	**10**	**10**	9
12	15	15	14	14	13	13	13	12	12	11	11	**10**
13	16	16	15	15	14	14	14	13	13	12	12	12
14	17	17	16	16	15	15	15	15	15	15	15	14
15	18	18	18	18	17	17	17	17	16	16	16	16

APPENDIX D

Converting Sum of Scaled Scores to Standard Scores and Percentile Ranks

Use this chart to derive standard scores and percentile ranks for *sum of scaled score* conversions (Morphosyntax and Semantics subtests).

Sum of scaled scores	Standard score	Percentile rank
1	52	<1
2	55	0.1
3	58	0.2
4	60	0.4
5	62	1
6	65	1
7	68	2
8	70	2
9	73	4
10	75	5
11	78	7
12	80	9
13	83	13
14	85	16
15	88	21
16	90	25
17	93	32
18	95	37
19	98	45

Sum of scaled scores	Standard score	Percentile rank
20	**100**	**50**
21	103	58
22	105	63
23	108	70
24	110	75
25	113	81
26	115	84
27	118	88
28	120	91
29	123	94
30	125	95
31	128	97
32	130	98
33	133	99
34	135	99
35	138	99
36	140	>99
37	143	>99
38	145	>99

APPENDIX E

Converting Scaled Scores to Standard Scores and Percentile Ranks

This chart can be used with any subtest.

Standard score	Percentile rank	Scaled score
>145	>99.9	19
145	99.9	19
144	99.8	19
143	99.8	19
142	99.7	18
141	99.7	18
140	99.6	18
139	99.5	18
138	99	18
137	99	17
136	99	17
135	99	17
134	99	17
133	99	17
132	98	16
131	98	16
130	98	16
129	97	16
128	97	16
127	96	15
126	96	15
125	95	15
124	95	15
123	94	15
122	93	14
121	92	14
120	91	14
119	90	14
118	88	14
117	87	13
116	86	13

Standard score	Percentile rank	Scaled score
115	84	13
114	82	13
113	81	13
112	79	12
111	77	12
110	75	12
109	73	12
108	70	12
107	68	11
106	66	11
105	63	11
104	61	11
103	58	11
102	55	**10**
101	53	**10**
100	**50**	**10**
99	47	**10**
98	45	**10**
97	42	9
96	40	9
95	37	9
94	34	9
93	32	9
92	30	8
91	27	8
90	25	8
89	23	8
88	21	8
87	19	7
86	18	7
85	16	7

Standard score	Percentile rank	Scaled score
84	14	7
83	13	7
82	12	6
81	10	6
80	9	6
79	8	6
78	7	6
77	6	5
76	5	5
75	5	5
74	4	5
73	4	5
72	3	4
71	3	4
70	2	4
69	2	4
68	2	4
67	1	3
66	1	3
65	1	3
64	1	3
63	1	3
62	1	2
61	0.5	2
60	0.4	2
59	0.3	2
58	0.2	2
57	0.1	1
56	0.1	1
55	0.1	1
<55	<0.1	1

APPENDIX F

Language Index Composite Scores

Use for *all* ages. To use: find the Semantic subtest standard score in the far left shaded column, then find the Morphosyntax subtest standard score along the top shaded margin; the Language Index composite standard score is at the intersection of those scores.

	Morphosyntax												
Semantics	**55**	**56**	**57**	**58**	**59**	**60**	**61**	**62**	**63**	**64**	**65**	**66**	**67**
55	55	56	56	57	57	58	58	59	59	60	60	61	61
56	55	56	57	57	58	58	59	59	60	60	61	61	62
57	56	56	57	58	58	59	59	60	60	61	61	62	62
58	56	57	57	58	59	59	60	60	61	61	62	62	63
59	57	57	58	58	59	60	60	61	61	62	62	63	63
60	57	58	58	59	59	60	61	61	62	62	63	63	64
61	58	58	59	59	60	60	61	62	62	63	63	64	64
62	58	59	59	60	60	61	61	62	63	63	64	64	65
63	59	59	60	60	61	61	62	62	63	64	64	65	65
64	59	60	60	61	61	62	62	63	63	64	65	65	66
65	60	60	61	61	62	62	63	63	64	64	65	66	66
66	60	61	61	62	62	63	63	64	64	65	65	66	67
67	61	61	62	62	63	63	64	64	65	65	66	66	67
68	61	62	62	63	63	64	64	65	65	66	66	67	67
69	62	62	63	63	64	64	65	65	66	66	67	67	68
70	62	63	63	64	64	65	65	66	66	67	67	68	68

(continued)

	Morphosyntax												
Semantics	**55**	**56**	**57**	**58**	**59**	**60**	**61**	**62**	**63**	**64**	**65**	**66**	**67**
71	63	63	64	64	65	65	66	66	67	67	68	68	69
72	63	64	64	65	65	66	66	67	67	68	68	69	69
73	64	64	65	65	66	66	67	67	68	68	69	69	70
74	64	65	65	66	66	67	67	68	68	69	69	70	70
75	65	65	66	66	67	67	68	68	69	69	70	70	71
76	65	66	66	67	67	68	68	69	69	70	70	71	71
77	66	66	67	67	68	68	69	69	70	70	71	71	72
78	66	67	67	68	68	69	69	70	70	71	71	72	72
79	67	67	68	68	69	69	70	70	71	71	72	72	73
80	67	68	68	69	69	70	70	71	71	72	72	73	73
81	67	68	69	69	70	70	71	71	72	72	73	73	74
82	68	68	69	70	70	71	71	72	72	73	73	74	74
83	68	69	69	70	71	71	72	72	73	73	74	74	75
84	69	69	70	70	71	72	72	73	73	74	74	75	75
85	69	70	70	71	71	72	73	73	74	74	75	75	76
86	70	70	71	71	72	72	73	74	74	75	75	76	76
87	70	71	71	72	72	73	73	74	75	75	76	76	77
88	71	71	72	72	73	73	74	74	75	76	76	77	77
89	71	72	72	73	73	74	74	75	75	76	77	77	78
90	72	72	73	73	74	74	75	75	76	76	77	78	78
91	72	73	73	74	74	75	75	76	76	77	77	78	79
92	73	73	74	74	75	75	76	76	77	77	78	78	79
93	73	74	74	75	75	76	76	77	77	78	78	79	79
94	74	74	75	75	76	76	77	77	78	78	79	79	80
95	74	75	75	76	76	77	77	78	78	79	79	80	80
96	75	75	76	76	77	77	78	78	79	79	80	80	81
97	75	76	76	77	77	78	78	79	79	80	80	81	81
98	76	76	77	77	78	78	79	79	80	80	81	81	82
99	76	77	77	78	78	79	79	80	80	81	81	82	82
100	77	77	78	78	79	79	80	80	81	81	82	82	83
101	77	78	78	79	79	80	80	81	81	82	82	83	83

(continued)

	Morphosyntax												
Semantics	**55**	**56**	**57**	**58**	**59**	**60**	**61**	**62**	**63**	**64**	**65**	**66**	**67**
102	78	78	79	79	80	80	81	81	82	82	83	83	84
103	78	79	79	80	80	81	81	82	82	83	83	84	84
104	79	79	80	80	81	81	82	82	83	83	84	84	85
105	79	80	80	81	81	82	82	83	83	84	84	85	85
106	79	80	81	81	82	82	83	83	84	84	85	85	86
107	80	80	81	82	82	83	83	84	84	85	85	86	86
108	80	81	81	82	83	83	84	84	85	85	86	86	87
109	81	81	82	82	83	84	84	85	85	86	86	87	87
110	81	82	82	83	83	84	85	85	86	86	87	87	88
111	82	82	83	83	84	84	85	86	86	87	87	88	88
112	82	83	83	84	84	85	85	86	87	87	88	88	89
113	83	83	84	84	85	85	86	86	87	88	88	89	89
114	83	84	84	85	85	86	86	87	87	88	89	89	90
115	84	84	85	85	86	86	87	87	88	88	89	90	90
116	84	85	85	86	86	87	87	88	88	89	89	90	91
117	85	85	86	86	87	87	88	88	89	89	90	90	91
118	85	86	86	87	87	88	88	89	89	90	90	91	91
119	86	86	87	87	88	88	89	89	90	90	91	91	92
120	86	87	87	88	88	89	89	90	90	91	91	92	92
121	87	87	88	88	89	89	90	90	91	91	92	92	93
122	87	88	88	89	89	90	90	91	91	92	92	93	93
123	88	88	89	89	90	90	91	91	92	92	93	93	94
124	88	89	89	90	90	91	91	92	92	93	93	94	94
125	89	89	90	90	91	91	92	92	93	93	94	94	95
126	89	90	90	91	91	92	92	93	93	94	94	95	95
127	90	90	91	91	92	92	93	93	94	94	95	95	96
128	90	91	91	92	92	93	93	94	94	95	95	96	96
129	91	91	92	92	93	93	94	94	95	95	96	96	97
130	91	92	92	93	93	94	94	95	95	96	96	97	97
131	91	92	93	93	94	94	95	95	96	96	97	97	98
132	92	92	93	94	94	95	95	96	96	97	97	98	98

(continued)

	Morphosyntax												
Semantics	**55**	**56**	**57**	**58**	**59**	**60**	**61**	**62**	**63**	**64**	**65**	**66**	**67**
133	92	93	93	94	95	95	96	96	97	97	98	98	99
134	93	93	94	94	95	96	96	97	97	98	98	99	99
135	93	94	94	95	95	96	97	97	98	98	99	99	100
136	94	94	95	95	96	96	97	98	98	99	99	100	100
137	94	95	95	96	96	97	97	98	99	99	100	100	101
138	95	95	96	96	97	97	98	98	99	100	100	101	101
139	95	96	96	97	97	98	98	99	99	100	101	101	102
140	96	96	97	97	98	98	99	99	100	100	101	102	102
141	96	97	97	98	98	99	99	100	100	101	101	102	103
142	97	97	98	98	99	99	100	100	101	101	102	102	103
143	97	98	98	99	99	100	100	101	101	102	102	103	103
144	98	98	99	99	100	100	101	101	102	102	103	103	104
145	98	99	99	100	100	101	101	102	102	103	103	104	104
>145	99	99	100	100	101	101	102	102	103	103	104	104	105

	Morphosyntax												
Semantics	**68**	**69**	**70**	**71**	**72**	**73**	**74**	**75**	**76**	**77**	**78**	**79**	**80**
55	62	62	63	63	64	64	65	65	66	66	67	67	68
56	62	63	63	64	64	65	65	66	66	67	67	68	68
57	63	63	64	64	65	65	66	66	67	67	68	68	69
58	63	64	64	65	65	66	66	67	67	68	68	69	69
59	64	64	65	65	66	66	67	67	68	68	69	69	70
60	64	65	65	66	66	67	67	68	68	69	69	70	70
61	65	65	66	66	67	67	68	68	69	69	70	70	71
62	65	66	66	67	67	68	68	69	69	70	70	71	71
63	66	66	67	67	68	68	69	69	70	70	71	71	72
64	66	67	67	68	68	69	69	70	70	71	71	72	72
65	67	67	68	68	69	69	70	70	71	71	72	72	73
66	67	68	68	69	69	70	70	71	71	72	72	73	73
67	68	68	69	69	70	70	71	71	72	72	73	73	74
68	68	69	69	70	70	71	71	72	72	73	73	74	74

(continued)

	Morphosyntax												
Semantics	**68**	**69**	**70**	**71**	**72**	**73**	**74**	**75**	**76**	**77**	**78**	**79**	**80**
69	68	69	70	70	71	71	72	72	73	73	74	74	75
70	69	69	70	71	71	72	72	73	73	74	74	75	75
71	69	70	70	71	72	72	73	73	74	74	75	75	76
72	70	70	71	71	72	73	73	74	74	75	75	76	76
73	70	71	71	72	72	73	74	74	75	75	76	76	77
74	71	71	72	72	73	73	74	75	75	76	76	77	77
75	71	72	72	73	73	74	74	75	76	76	77	77	78
76	72	72	73	73	74	74	75	75	76	77	77	78	78
77	72	73	73	74	74	75	75	76	76	77	78	78	79
78	73	73	74	74	75	75	76	76	77	77	78	79	79
79	73	74	74	75	75	76	76	77	77	78	78	79	80
80	74	74	75	75	76	76	77	77	78	78	79	79	80
81	74	75	75	76	76	77	77	78	78	79	79	80	80
82	75	75	76	76	77	77	78	78	79	79	80	80	81
83	75	76	76	77	77	78	78	79	79	80	80	81	81
84	76	76	77	77	78	78	79	79	80	80	81	81	82
85	76	77	77	78	78	79	79	80	80	81	81	82	82
86	77	77	78	78	79	79	80	80	81	81	82	82	83
87	77	78	78	79	79	80	80	81	81	82	82	83	83
88	78	78	79	79	80	80	81	81	82	82	83	83	84
89	78	79	79	80	80	81	81	82	82	83	83	84	84
90	79	79	80	80	81	81	82	82	83	83	84	84	85
91	79	80	80	81	81	82	82	83	83	84	84	85	85
92	80	80	81	81	82	82	83	83	84	84	85	85	86
93	80	81	81	82	82	83	83	84	84	85	85	86	86
94	80	81	82	82	83	83	84	84	85	85	86	86	87
95	81	81	82	83	83	84	84	85	85	86	86	87	87
96	81	82	82	83	84	84	85	85	86	86	87	87	88
97	82	82	83	83	84	85	85	86	86	87	87	88	88
98	82	83	83	84	84	85	86	86	87	87	88	88	89
99	83	83	84	84	85	85	86	87	87	88	88	89	89
100	83	84	84	85	85	86	86	87	88	88	89	89	90

(continued)

	Morphosyntax												
Semantics	**68**	**69**	**70**	**71**	**72**	**73**	**74**	**75**	**76**	**77**	**78**	**79**	**80**
101	84	84	85	85	86	86	87	87	88	89	89	90	90
102	84	85	85	86	86	87	87	88	88	89	90	90	91
103	85	85	86	86	87	87	88	88	89	89	90	91	91
104	85	86	86	87	87	88	88	89	89	90	90	91	92
105	86	86	87	87	88	88	89	89	90	90	91	91	92
106	86	87	87	88	88	89	89	90	90	91	91	92	92
107	87	87	88	88	89	89	90	90	91	91	92	92	93
108	87	88	88	89	89	90	90	91	91	92	92	93	93
109	88	88	89	89	90	90	91	91	92	92	93	93	94
110	88	89	89	90	90	91	91	92	92	93	93	94	94
111	89	89	90	90	91	91	92	92	93	93	94	94	95
112	89	90	90	91	91	92	92	93	93	94	94	95	95
113	90	90	91	91	92	92	93	93	94	94	95	95	96
114	90	91	91	92	92	93	93	94	94	95	95	96	96
115	91	91	92	92	93	93	94	94	95	95	96	96	97
116	91	92	92	93	93	94	94	95	95	96	96	97	97
117	92	92	93	93	94	94	95	95	96	96	97	97	98
118	92	93	93	94	94	95	95	96	96	97	97	98	98
119	92	93	94	94	95	95	96	96	97	97	98	98	99
120	93	93	94	95	95	96	96	97	97	98	98	99	99
121	93	94	94	95	96	96	97	97	98	98	99	99	100
122	94	94	95	95	96	97	97	98	98	99	99	100	100
123	94	95	95	96	96	97	98	98	99	99	100	100	101
124	95	95	96	96	97	97	98	99	99	100	100	101	101
125	95	96	96	97	97	98	98	99	100	100	101	101	102
126	96	96	97	97	98	98	99	99	100	101	101	102	102
127	96	97	97	98	98	99	99	100	100	101	102	102	103
128	97	97	98	98	99	99	100	100	101	101	102	103	103
129	97	98	98	99	99	100	100	101	101	102	102	103	104
130	98	98	99	99	100	100	101	101	102	102	103	103	104
131	98	99	99	100	100	101	101	102	102	103	103	104	104
132	99	99	100	100	101	101	102	102	103	103	104	104	105

(continued)

	Morphosyntax												
Semantics	**68**	**69**	**70**	**71**	**72**	**73**	**74**	**75**	**76**	**77**	**78**	**79**	**80**
133	99	100	100	101	101	102	102	103	103	104	104	105	105
134	100	100	101	101	102	102	103	103	104	104	105	105	106
135	100	101	101	102	102	103	103	104	104	105	105	106	106
136	101	101	102	102	103	103	104	104	105	105	106	106	107
137	101	102	102	103	103	104	104	105	105	106	106	107	107
138	102	102	103	103	104	104	105	105	106	106	107	107	108
139	102	103	103	104	104	105	105	106	106	107	107	108	108
140	103	103	104	104	105	105	106	106	107	107	108	108	109
141	103	104	104	105	105	106	106	107	107	108	108	109	109
142	104	104	105	105	106	106	107	107	108	108	109	109	110
143	104	105	105	106	106	107	107	108	108	109	109	110	110
144	104	105	106	106	107	107	108	108	109	109	110	110	111
145	105	105	106	107	107	108	108	109	109	110	110	111	111
>145	105	106	106	107	108	108	109	109	110	110	111	111	112

	Morphosyntax												
Semantics	**81**	**82**	**83**	**84**	**85**	**86**	**87**	**88**	**89**	**90**	**91**	**92**	**93**
55	69	69	70	70	71	71	72	72	73	73	74	74	75
56	69	70	70	71	71	72	72	73	73	74	74	75	75
57	69	70	71	71	72	72	73	73	74	74	75	75	76
58	70	70	71	72	72	73	73	74	74	75	75	76	76
59	70	71	71	72	73	73	74	74	75	75	76	76	77
60	71	71	72	72	73	74	74	75	75	76	76	77	77
61	71	72	72	73	73	74	75	75	76	76	77	77	78
62	72	72	73	73	74	74	75	76	76	77	77	78	78
63	72	73	73	74	74	75	75	76	77	77	78	78	79
64	73	73	74	74	75	75	76	76	77	78	78	79	79
65	73	74	74	75	75	76	76	77	77	78	79	79	80
66	74	74	75	75	76	76	77	77	78	78	79	80	80
67	74	75	75	76	76	77	77	78	78	79	79	80	81
68	75	75	76	76	77	77	78	78	79	79	80	80	81

(continued)

	Morphosyntax												
Semantics	**81**	**82**	**83**	**84**	**85**	**86**	**87**	**88**	**89**	**90**	**91**	**92**	**93**
69	75	76	76	77	77	78	78	79	79	80	80	81	81
70	76	76	77	77	78	78	79	79	80	80	81	81	82
71	76	77	77	78	78	79	79	80	80	81	81	82	82
72	77	77	78	78	79	79	80	80	81	81	82	82	83
73	77	78	78	79	79	80	80	81	81	82	82	83	83
74	78	78	79	79	80	80	81	81	82	82	83	83	84
75	78	79	79	80	80	81	81	82	82	83	83	84	84
76	79	79	80	80	81	81	82	82	83	83	84	84	85
77	79	80	80	81	81	82	82	83	83	84	84	85	85
78	80	80	81	81	82	82	83	83	84	84	85	85	86
79	80	81	81	82	82	83	83	84	84	85	85	86	86
80	81	81	82	82	83	83	84	84	85	85	86	86	87
81	81	82	82	83	83	84	84	85	85	86	86	87	87
82	81	82	83	83	84	84	85	85	86	86	87	87	88
83	82	82	83	84	84	85	85	86	86	87	87	88	88
84	82	83	83	84	85	85	86	86	87	87	88	88	89
85	83	83	84	84	85	86	86	87	87	88	88	89	89
86	83	84	84	85	85	86	87	87	88	88	89	89	90
87	84	84	85	85	86	86	87	88	88	89	89	90	90
88	84	85	85	86	86	87	87	88	89	89	90	90	91
89	85	85	86	86	87	87	88	88	89	90	90	91	91
90	85	86	86	87	87	88	88	89	89	90	91	91	92
91	86	86	87	87	88	88	89	89	90	90	91	92	92
92	86	87	87	88	88	89	89	90	90	91	91	92	93
93	87	87	88	88	89	89	90	90	91	91	92	92	93
94	87	88	88	89	89	90	90	91	91	92	92	93	93
95	88	88	89	89	90	90	91	91	92	92	93	93	94
96	88	89	89	90	90	91	91	92	92	93	93	94	94
97	89	89	90	90	91	91	92	92	93	93	94	94	95
98	89	90	90	91	91	92	92	93	93	94	94	95	95
99	90	90	91	91	92	92	93	93	94	94	95	95	96
100	90	91	91	92	92	93	93	94	94	95	95	96	96

(continued)

	Morphosyntax												
Semantics	**81**	**82**	**83**	**84**	**85**	**86**	**87**	**88**	**89**	**90**	**91**	**92**	**93**
101	91	91	92	92	93	93	94	94	95	95	96	96	97
102	91	92	92	93	93	94	94	95	95	96	96	97	97
103	92	92	93	93	94	94	95	95	96	96	97	97	98
104	92	93	93	94	94	95	95	96	96	97	97	98	98
105	93	93	94	94	95	95	96	96	97	97	98	98	99
106	93	94	94	95	95	96	96	97	97	98	98	99	99
107	93	94	95	95	96	96	97	97	98	98	99	99	100
108	94	94	95	96	96	97	97	98	98	99	99	100	100
109	94	95	95	96	97	97	98	98	99	99	100	100	101
110	95	95	96	96	97	98	98	99	99	100	100	101	101
111	95	96	96	97	97	98	99	99	100	100	101	101	102
112	96	96	97	97	98	98	99	100	100	101	101	102	102
113	96	97	97	98	98	99	99	100	101	101	102	102	103
114	97	97	98	98	99	99	100	100	101	102	102	103	103
115	97	98	98	99	99	100	100	101	101	102	103	103	104
116	98	98	99	99	100	100	101	101	102	102	103	104	104
117	98	99	99	100	100	101	101	102	102	103	103	104	105
118	99	99	100	100	101	101	102	102	103	103	104	104	105
119	99	100	100	101	101	102	102	103	103	104	104	105	105
120	100	100	101	101	102	102	103	103	104	104	105	105	106
121	100	101	101	102	102	103	103	104	104	105	105	106	106
122	101	101	102	102	103	103	104	104	105	105	106	106	107
123	101	102	102	103	103	104	104	105	105	106	106	107	107
124	102	102	103	103	104	104	105	105	106	106	107	107	108
125	102	103	103	104	104	105	105	106	106	107	107	108	108
126	103	103	104	104	105	105	106	106	107	107	108	108	109
127	103	104	104	105	105	106	106	107	107	108	108	109	109
128	104	104	105	105	106	106	107	107	108	108	109	109	110
129	104	105	105	106	106	107	107	108	108	109	109	110	110
130	105	105	106	106	107	107	108	108	109	109	110	110	111
131	105	106	106	107	107	108	108	109	109	110	110	111	111
132	105	106	107	107	108	108	109	109	110	110	111	111	112

(continued)

	Morphosyntax												
Semantics	**81**	**82**	**83**	**84**	**85**	**86**	**87**	**88**	**89**	**90**	**91**	**92**	**93**
133	106	106	107	108	108	109	109	110	110	111	111	112	112
134	106	107	107	108	109	109	110	110	111	111	112	112	113
135	107	107	108	108	109	110	110	111	111	112	112	113	113
136	107	108	108	109	109	110	111	111	112	112	113	113	114
137	108	108	109	109	110	110	111	112	112	113	113	114	114
138	108	109	109	110	110	111	111	112	113	113	114	114	115
139	109	109	110	110	111	111	112	112	113	114	114	115	115
140	109	110	110	111	111	112	112	113	113	114	115	115	116
141	110	110	111	111	112	112	113	113	114	114	115	116	116
142	110	111	111	112	112	113	113	114	114	115	115	116	117
143	111	111	112	112	113	113	114	114	115	115	116	116	117
144	111	112	112	113	113	114	114	115	115	116	116	117	117
145	112	112	113	113	114	114	115	115	116	116	117	117	118
>145	112	113	113	114	114	115	115	116	116	117	117	118	118

	Morphosyntax												
Semantics	**94**	**95**	**96**	**97**	**98**	**99**	**100**	**101**	**102**	**103**	**104**	**105**	**106**
55	75	76	76	77	77	78	78	79	79	80	80	81	82
56	76	76	77	77	78	78	79	79	80	80	81	81	82
57	76	77	77	78	78	79	79	80	80	81	81	82	82
58	77	77	78	78	79	79	80	80	81	81	82	82	83
59	77	78	78	79	79	80	80	81	81	82	82	83	83
60	78	78	79	79	80	80	81	81	82	82	83	83	84
61	78	79	79	80	80	81	81	82	82	83	83	84	84
62	79	79	80	80	81	81	82	82	83	83	84	84	85
63	79	80	80	81	81	82	82	83	83	84	84	85	85
64	80	80	81	81	82	82	83	83	84	84	85	85	86
65	80	81	81	82	82	83	83	84	84	85	85	86	86
66	81	81	82	82	83	83	84	84	85	85	86	86	87
67	81	82	82	83	83	84	84	85	85	86	86	87	87
68	82	82	83	83	84	84	85	85	86	86	87	87	88

(continued)

	Morphosyntax												
Semantics	**94**	**95**	**96**	**97**	**98**	**99**	**100**	**101**	**102**	**103**	**104**	**105**	**106**
69	82	83	83	84	84	85	85	86	86	87	87	88	88
70	82	83	84	84	85	85	86	86	87	87	88	88	89
71	83	83	84	85	85	86	86	87	87	88	88	89	89
72	83	84	84	85	86	86	87	87	88	88	89	89	90
73	84	84	85	85	86	87	87	88	88	89	89	90	90
74	84	85	85	86	86	87	88	88	89	89	90	90	91
75	85	85	86	86	87	87	88	89	89	90	90	91	91
76	85	86	86	87	87	88	88	89	90	90	91	91	92
77	86	86	87	87	88	88	89	89	90	91	91	92	92
78	86	87	87	88	88	89	89	90	90	91	92	92	93
79	87	87	88	88	89	89	90	90	91	91	92	93	93
80	87	88	88	89	89	90	90	91	91	92	92	93	94
81	88	88	89	89	90	90	91	91	92	92	93	93	94
82	88	89	89	90	90	91	91	92	92	93	93	94	94
83	89	89	90	90	91	91	92	92	93	93	94	94	95
84	89	90	90	91	91	92	92	93	93	94	94	95	95
85	90	90	91	91	92	92	93	93	94	94	95	95	96
86	90	91	91	92	92	93	93	94	94	95	95	96	96
87	91	91	92	92	93	93	94	94	95	95	96	96	97
88	91	92	92	93	93	94	94	95	95	96	96	97	97
89	92	92	93	93	94	94	95	95	96	96	97	97	98
90	92	93	93	94	94	95	95	96	96	97	97	98	98
91	93	93	94	94	95	95	96	96	97	97	98	98	99
92	93	94	94	95	95	96	96	97	97	98	98	99	99
93	94	94	95	95	96	96	97	97	98	98	99	99	100
94	94	95	95	96	96	97	97	98	98	99	99	100	100
95	94	95	96	96	97	97	98	98	99	99	100	100	101
96	95	95	96	97	97	98	98	99	99	100	100	101	101
97	95	96	96	97	98	98	99	99	100	100	101	101	102
98	96	96	97	97	98	99	99	100	100	101	101	102	102
99	96	97	97	98	98	99	100	100	101	101	102	102	103
100	97	97	98	98	99	99	100	101	101	102	102	103	103

(continued)

	Morphosyntax												
Semantics	**94**	**95**	**96**	**97**	**98**	**99**	**100**	**101**	**102**	**103**	**104**	**105**	**106**
101	97	98	98	99	99	100	100	101	102	102	103	103	104
102	98	98	99	99	100	100	101	101	102	103	103	104	104
103	98	99	99	100	100	101	101	102	102	103	104	104	105
104	99	99	100	100	101	101	102	102	103	103	104	105	105
105	99	100	100	101	101	102	102	103	103	104	104	105	106
106	100	100	101	101	102	102	103	103	104	104	105	105	106
107	100	101	101	102	102	103	103	104	104	105	105	106	106
108	101	101	102	102	103	103	104	104	105	105	106	106	107
109	101	102	102	103	103	104	104	105	105	106	106	107	107
110	102	102	103	103	104	104	105	105	106	106	107	107	108
111	102	103	103	104	104	105	105	106	106	107	107	108	108
112	103	103	104	104	105	105	106	106	107	107	108	108	109
113	103	104	104	105	105	106	106	107	107	108	108	109	109
114	104	104	105	105	106	106	107	107	108	108	109	109	110
115	104	105	105	106	106	107	107	108	108	109	109	110	110
116	105	105	106	106	107	107	108	108	109	109	110	110	111
117	105	106	106	107	107	108	108	109	109	110	110	111	111
118	106	106	107	107	108	108	109	109	110	110	111	111	112
119	106	107	107	108	108	109	109	110	110	111	111	112	112
120	106	107	108	108	109	109	110	110	111	111	112	112	113
121	107	107	108	109	109	110	110	111	111	112	112	113	113
122	107	108	108	109	110	110	111	111	112	112	113	113	114
123	108	108	109	109	110	111	111	112	112	113	113	114	114
124	108	109	109	110	110	111	112	112	113	113	114	114	115
125	109	109	110	110	111	111	112	113	113	114	114	115	115
126	109	110	110	111	111	112	112	113	114	114	115	115	116
127	110	110	111	111	112	112	113	113	114	115	115	116	116
128	110	111	111	112	112	113	113	114	114	115	116	116	117
129	111	111	112	112	113	113	114	114	115	115	116	117	117
130	111	112	112	113	113	114	114	115	115	116	116	117	118
131	112	112	113	113	114	114	115	115	116	116	117	117	118
132	112	113	113	114	114	115	115	116	116	117	117	118	118

(continued)

	Morphosyntax												
Semantics	**94**	**95**	**96**	**97**	**98**	**99**	**100**	**101**	**102**	**103**	**104**	**105**	**106**
133	113	113	114	114	115	115	116	116	117	117	118	118	119
134	113	114	114	115	115	116	116	117	117	118	118	119	119
135	114	114	115	115	116	116	117	117	118	118	119	119	120
136	114	115	115	116	116	117	117	118	118	119	119	120	120
137	115	115	116	116	117	117	118	118	119	119	120	120	121
138	115	116	116	117	117	118	118	119	119	120	120	121	121
139	116	116	117	117	118	118	119	119	120	120	121	121	122
140	116	117	117	118	118	119	119	120	120	121	121	122	122
141	117	117	118	118	119	119	120	120	121	121	122	122	123
142	117	118	118	119	119	120	120	121	121	122	122	123	123
143	118	118	119	119	120	120	121	121	122	122	123	123	124
144	118	119	119	120	120	121	121	122	122	123	123	124	124
145	118	119	120	120	121	121	122	122	123	123	124	124	125
>145	119	119	120	121	121	122	122	123	123	124	124	125	125

	Morphosyntax												
Semantics	**107**	**108**	**109**	**110**	**111**	**112**	**113**	**114**	**115**	**116**	**117**	**118**	**119**
55	82	83	83	84	84	85	85	86	86	87	87	88	88
56	83	83	84	84	85	85	86	86	87	87	88	88	89
57	83	84	84	85	85	86	86	87	87	88	88	89	89
58	83	84	85	85	86	86	87	87	88	88	89	89	90
59	84	84	85	86	86	87	87	88	88	89	89	90	90
60	84	85	85	86	87	87	88	88	89	89	90	90	91
61	85	85	86	86	87	88	88	89	89	90	90	91	91
62	85	86	86	87	87	88	89	89	90	90	91	91	92
63	86	86	87	87	88	88	89	90	90	91	91	92	92
64	86	87	87	88	88	89	89	90	91	91	92	92	93
65	87	87	88	88	89	89	90	90	91	92	92	93	93
66	87	88	88	89	89	90	90	91	91	92	93	93	94
67	88	88	89	89	90	90	91	91	92	92	93	94	94
68	88	89	89	90	90	91	91	92	92	93	93	94	95

(continued)

	Morphosyntax												
Semantics	**107**	**108**	**109**	**110**	**111**	**112**	**113**	**114**	**115**	**116**	**117**	**118**	**119**
69	89	89	90	90	91	91	92	92	93	93	94	94	95
70	89	90	90	91	91	92	92	93	93	94	94	95	95
71	90	90	91	91	92	92	93	93	94	94	95	95	96
72	90	91	91	92	92	93	93	94	94	95	95	96	96
73	91	91	92	92	93	93	94	94	95	95	96	96	97
74	91	92	92	93	93	94	94	95	95	96	96	97	97
75	92	92	93	93	94	94	95	95	96	96	97	97	98
76	92	93	93	94	94	95	95	96	96	97	97	98	98
77	93	93	94	94	95	95	96	96	97	97	98	98	99
78	93	94	94	95	95	96	96	97	97	98	98	99	99
79	94	94	95	95	96	96	97	97	98	98	99	99	100
80	94	95	95	96	96	97	97	98	98	99	99	100	100
81	95	95	96	96	97	97	98	98	99	99	100	100	101
82	95	96	96	97	97	98	98	99	99	100	100	101	101
83	95	96	97	97	98	98	99	99	100	100	101	101	102
84	96	96	97	98	98	99	99	100	100	101	101	102	102
85	96	97	97	98	99	99	100	100	101	101	102	102	103
86	97	97	98	98	99	100	100	101	101	102	102	103	103
87	97	98	98	99	99	100	101	101	102	102	103	103	104
88	98	98	99	99	100	100	101	102	102	103	103	104	104
89	98	99	99	100	100	101	101	102	103	103	104	104	105
90	99	99	100	100	101	101	102	102	103	104	104	105	105
91	99	100	100	101	101	102	102	103	103	104	105	105	106
92	100	100	101	101	102	102	103	103	104	104	105	106	106
93	100	101	101	102	102	103	103	104	104	105	105	106	107
94	101	101	102	102	103	103	104	104	105	105	106	106	107
95	101	102	102	103	103	104	104	105	105	106	106	107	107
96	102	102	103	103	104	104	105	105	106	106	107	107	108
97	102	103	103	104	104	105	105	106	106	107	107	108	108
98	103	103	104	104	105	105	106	106	107	107	108	108	109
99	103	104	104	105	105	106	106	107	107	108	108	109	109
100	104	104	105	105	106	106	107	107	108	108	109	109	110

(continued)

	Morphosyntax												
Semantics	**107**	**108**	**109**	**110**	**111**	**112**	**113**	**114**	**115**	**116**	**117**	**118**	**119**
101	104	105	105	106	106	107	107	108	108	109	109	110	110
102	105	105	106	106	107	107	108	108	109	109	110	110	111
103	105	106	106	107	107	108	108	109	109	110	110	111	111
104	106	106	107	107	108	108	109	109	110	110	111	111	112
105	106	107	107	108	108	109	109	110	110	111	111	112	112
106	107	107	108	108	109	109	110	110	111	111	112	112	113
107	107	108	108	109	109	110	110	111	111	112	112	113	113
108	107	108	109	109	110	110	111	111	112	112	113	113	114
109	108	108	109	110	110	111	111	112	112	113	113	114	114
110	108	109	109	110	111	111	112	112	113	113	114	114	115
111	109	109	110	110	111	112	112	113	113	114	114	115	115
112	109	110	110	111	111	112	113	113	114	114	115	115	116
113	110	110	111	111	112	112	113	114	114	115	115	116	116
114	110	111	111	112	112	113	113	114	115	115	116	116	117
115	111	111	112	112	113	113	114	114	115	116	116	117	117
116	111	112	112	113	113	114	114	115	115	116	117	117	118
117	112	112	113	113	114	114	115	115	116	116	117	118	118
118	112	113	113	114	114	115	115	116	116	117	117	118	119
119	113	113	114	114	115	115	116	116	117	117	118	118	119
120	113	114	114	115	115	116	116	117	117	118	118	119	119
121	114	114	115	115	116	116	117	117	118	118	119	119	120
122	114	115	115	116	116	117	117	118	118	119	119	120	120
123	115	115	116	116	117	117	118	118	119	119	120	120	121
124	115	116	116	117	117	118	118	119	119	120	120	121	121
125	116	116	117	117	118	118	119	119	120	120	121	121	122
126	116	117	117	118	118	119	119	120	120	121	121	122	122
127	117	117	118	118	119	119	120	120	121	121	122	122	123
128	117	118	118	119	119	120	120	121	121	122	122	123	123
129	118	118	119	119	120	120	121	121	122	122	123	123	124
130	118	119	119	120	120	121	121	122	122	123	123	124	124
131	119	119	120	120	121	121	122	122	123	123	124	124	125
132	119	120	120	121	121	122	122	123	123	124	124	125	125

(continued)

	Morphosyntax												
Semantics	**107**	**108**	**109**	**110**	**111**	**112**	**113**	**114**	**115**	**116**	**117**	**118**	**119**
133	119	120	121	121	122	122	123	123	124	124	125	125	126
134	120	120	121	122	122	123	123	124	124	125	125	126	126
135	120	121	121	122	123	123	124	124	125	125	126	126	127
136	121	121	122	122	123	124	124	125	125	126	126	127	127
137	121	122	122	123	123	124	125	125	126	126	127	127	128
138	122	122	123	123	124	124	125	126	126	127	127	128	128
139	122	123	123	124	124	125	125	126	127	127	128	128	129
140	123	123	124	124	125	125	126	126	127	128	128	129	129
141	123	124	124	125	125	126	126	127	127	128	129	129	130
142	124	124	125	125	126	126	127	127	128	128	129	130	130
143	124	125	125	126	126	127	127	128	128	129	129	130	131
144	125	125	126	126	127	127	128	128	129	129	130	130	131
145	125	126	126	127	127	128	128	129	129	130	130	131	131
>145	126	126	127	127	128	128	129	129	130	130	131	131	132

	Morphosyntax												
Semantics	**120**	**121**	**122**	**123**	**124**	**125**	**126**	**127**	**128**	**129**	**130**	**131**	**132**
55	89	89	90	90	91	91	92	92	93	93	94	95	95
56	89	90	90	91	91	92	92	93	93	94	94	95	96
57	90	90	91	91	92	92	93	93	94	94	95	95	96
58	90	91	91	92	92	93	93	94	94	95	95	96	96
59	91	91	92	92	93	93	94	94	95	95	96	96	97
60	91	92	92	93	93	94	94	95	95	96	96	97	97
61	92	92	93	93	94	94	95	95	96	96	97	97	98
62	92	93	93	94	94	95	95	96	96	97	97	98	98
63	93	93	94	94	95	95	96	96	97	97	98	98	99
64	93	94	94	95	95	96	96	97	97	98	98	99	99
65	94	94	95	95	96	96	97	97	98	98	99	99	100
66	94	95	95	96	96	97	97	98	98	99	99	100	100
67	95	95	96	96	97	97	98	98	99	99	100	100	101
68	95	96	96	97	97	98	98	99	99	100	100	101	101

(continued)

	Morphosyntax												
Semantics	**120**	**121**	**122**	**123**	**124**	**125**	**126**	**127**	**128**	**129**	**130**	**131**	**132**
69	96	96	97	97	98	98	99	99	100	100	101	101	102
70	96	97	97	98	98	99	99	100	100	101	101	102	102
71	96	97	98	98	99	99	100	100	101	101	102	102	103
72	97	97	98	99	99	100	100	101	101	102	102	103	103
73	97	98	98	99	100	100	101	101	102	102	103	103	104
74	98	98	99	99	100	101	101	102	102	103	103	104	104
75	98	99	99	100	100	101	102	102	103	103	104	104	105
76	99	99	100	100	101	101	102	103	103	104	104	105	105
77	99	100	100	101	101	102	102	103	104	104	105	105	106
78	100	100	101	101	102	102	103	103	104	105	105	106	106
79	100	101	101	102	102	103	103	104	104	105	106	106	107
80	101	101	102	102	103	103	104	104	105	105	106	107	107
81	101	102	102	103	103	104	104	105	105	106	106	107	108
82	102	102	103	103	104	104	105	105	106	106	107	107	108
83	102	103	103	104	104	105	105	106	106	107	107	108	108
84	103	103	104	104	105	105	106	106	107	107	108	108	109
85	103	104	104	105	105	106	106	107	107	108	108	109	109
86	104	104	105	105	106	106	107	107	108	108	109	109	110
87	104	105	105	106	106	107	107	108	108	109	109	110	110
88	105	105	106	106	107	107	108	108	109	109	110	110	111
89	105	106	106	107	107	108	108	109	109	110	110	111	111
90	106	106	107	107	108	108	109	109	110	110	111	111	112
91	106	107	107	108	108	109	109	110	110	111	111	112	112
92	107	107	108	108	109	109	110	110	111	111	112	112	113
93	107	108	108	109	109	110	110	111	111	112	112	113	113
94	108	108	109	109	110	110	111	111	112	112	113	113	114
95	108	109	109	110	110	111	111	112	112	113	113	114	114
96	108	109	110	110	111	111	112	112	113	113	114	114	115
97	109	109	110	111	111	112	112	113	113	114	114	115	115
98	109	110	110	111	112	112	113	113	114	114	115	115	116
99	110	110	111	111	112	113	113	114	114	115	115	116	116
100	110	111	111	112	112	113	114	114	115	115	116	116	117

(continued)

	Morphosyntax												
Semantics	**120**	**121**	**122**	**123**	**124**	**125**	**126**	**127**	**128**	**129**	**130**	**131**	**132**
101	111	111	112	112	113	113	114	115	115	116	116	117	117
102	111	112	112	113	113	114	114	115	116	116	117	117	118
103	112	112	113	113	114	114	115	115	116	117	117	118	118
104	112	113	113	114	114	115	115	116	116	117	118	118	119
105	113	113	114	114	115	115	116	116	117	117	118	119	119
106	113	114	114	115	115	116	116	117	117	118	118	119	120
107	114	114	115	115	116	116	117	117	118	118	119	119	120
108	114	115	115	116	116	117	117	118	118	119	119	120	120
109	115	115	116	116	117	117	118	118	119	119	120	120	121
110	115	116	116	117	117	118	118	119	119	120	120	121	121
111	116	116	117	117	118	118	119	119	120	120	121	121	122
112	116	117	117	118	118	119	119	120	120	121	121	122	122
113	117	117	118	118	119	119	120	120	121	121	122	122	123
114	117	118	118	119	119	120	120	121	121	122	122	123	123
115	118	118	119	119	120	120	121	121	122	122	123	123	124
116	118	119	119	120	120	121	121	122	122	123	123	124	124
117	119	119	120	120	121	121	122	122	123	123	124	124	125
118	119	120	120	121	121	122	122	123	123	124	124	125	125
119	120	120	121	121	122	122	123	123	124	124	125	125	126
120	120	121	121	122	122	123	123	124	124	125	125	126	126
121	120	121	122	122	123	123	124	124	125	125	126	126	127
122	121	121	122	123	123	124	124	125	125	126	126	127	127
123	121	122	122	123	124	124	125	125	126	126	127	127	128
124	122	122	123	123	124	125	125	126	126	127	127	128	128
125	122	123	123	124	124	125	126	126	127	127	128	128	129
126	123	123	124	124	125	125	126	127	127	128	128	129	129
127	123	124	124	125	125	126	126	127	128	128	129	129	130
128	124	124	125	125	126	126	127	127	128	129	129	130	130
129	124	125	125	126	126	127	127	128	128	129	130	130	131
130	125	125	126	126	127	127	128	128	129	129	130	131	131
131	125	126	126	127	127	128	128	129	129	130	130	131	132
132	126	126	127	127	128	128	129	129	130	130	131	131	132

(continued)

	Morphosyntax												
Semantics	**120**	**121**	**122**	**123**	**124**	**125**	**126**	**127**	**128**	**129**	**130**	**131**	**132**
133	126	127	127	128	128	129	129	130	130	131	131	132	132
134	127	127	128	128	129	129	130	130	131	131	132	132	133
135	127	128	128	129	129	130	130	131	131	132	132	133	133
136	128	128	129	129	130	130	131	131	132	132	133	133	134
137	128	129	129	130	130	131	131	132	132	133	133	134	134
138	129	129	130	130	131	131	132	132	133	133	134	134	135
139	129	130	130	131	131	132	132	133	133	134	134	135	135
140	130	130	131	131	132	132	133	133	134	134	135	135	136
141	130	131	131	132	132	133	133	134	134	135	135	136	136
142	131	131	132	132	133	133	134	134	135	135	136	136	137
143	131	132	132	133	133	134	134	135	135	136	136	137	137
144	132	132	133	133	134	134	135	135	136	136	137	137	138
145	132	133	133	134	134	135	135	136	136	137	137	138	138
>145	132	133	134	134	135	135	136	136	137	137	138	138	139

	Morphosyntax												
Semantics	**133**	**134**	**135**	**136**	**137**	**138**	**139**	**140**	**141**	**142**	**143**	**144**	**145**
55	96	96	97	97	98	98	99	99	100	100	101	101	102
56	96	97	97	98	98	99	99	100	100	101	101	102	102
57	97	97	98	98	99	99	100	100	101	101	102	102	103
58	97	98	98	99	99	100	100	101	101	102	102	103	103
59	97	98	99	99	100	100	101	101	102	102	103	103	104
60	98	98	99	100	100	101	101	102	102	103	103	104	104
61	98	99	99	100	101	101	102	102	103	103	104	104	105
62	99	99	100	100	101	102	102	103	103	104	104	105	105
63	99	100	100	101	101	102	103	103	104	104	105	105	106
64	100	100	101	101	102	102	103	104	104	105	105	106	106
65	100	101	101	102	102	103	103	104	105	105	106	106	107
66	101	101	102	102	103	103	104	104	105	106	106	107	107
67	101	102	102	103	103	104	104	105	105	106	107	107	108
68	102	102	103	103	104	104	105	105	106	106	107	108	108

(continued)

	Morphosyntax												
Semantics	**133**	**134**	**135**	**136**	**137**	**138**	**139**	**140**	**141**	**142**	**143**	**144**	**145**
69	102	103	103	104	104	105	105	106	106	107	107	108	109
70	103	103	104	104	105	105	106	106	107	107	108	108	109
71	103	104	104	105	105	106	106	107	107	108	108	109	109
72	104	104	105	105	106	106	107	107	108	108	109	109	110
73	104	105	105	106	106	107	107	108	108	109	109	110	110
74	105	105	106	106	107	107	108	108	109	109	110	110	111
75	105	106	106	107	107	108	108	109	109	110	110	111	111
76	106	106	107	107	108	108	109	109	110	110	111	111	112
77	106	107	107	108	108	109	109	110	110	111	111	112	112
78	107	107	108	108	109	109	110	110	111	111	112	112	113
79	107	108	108	109	109	110	110	111	111	112	112	113	113
80	108	108	109	109	110	110	111	111	112	112	113	113	114
81	108	109	109	110	110	111	111	112	112	113	113	114	114
82	109	109	110	110	111	111	112	112	113	113	114	114	115
83	109	110	110	111	111	112	112	113	113	114	114	115	115
84	109	110	111	111	112	112	113	113	114	114	115	115	116
85	110	110	111	112	112	113	113	114	114	115	115	116	116
86	110	111	111	112	113	113	114	114	115	115	116	116	117
87	111	111	112	112	113	114	114	115	115	116	116	117	117
88	111	112	112	113	113	114	115	115	116	116	117	117	118
89	112	112	113	113	114	114	115	116	116	117	117	118	118
90	112	113	113	114	114	115	115	116	117	117	118	118	119
91	113	113	114	114	115	115	116	116	117	118	118	119	119
92	113	114	114	115	115	116	116	117	117	118	119	119	120
93	114	114	115	115	116	116	117	117	118	118	119	120	120
94	114	115	115	116	116	117	117	118	118	119	119	120	121
95	115	115	116	116	117	117	118	118	119	119	120	120	121
96	115	116	116	117	117	118	118	119	119	120	120	121	121
97	116	116	117	117	118	118	119	119	120	120	121	121	122
98	116	117	117	118	118	119	119	120	120	121	121	122	122
99	117	117	118	118	119	119	120	120	121	121	122	122	123
100	117	118	118	119	119	120	120	121	121	122	122	123	123

(continued)

	Morphosyntax												
Semantics	**133**	**134**	**135**	**136**	**137**	**138**	**139**	**140**	**141**	**142**	**143**	**144**	**145**
101	118	118	119	119	120	120	121	121	122	122	123	123	124
102	118	119	119	120	120	121	121	122	122	123	123	124	124
103	119	119	120	120	121	121	122	122	123	123	124	124	125
104	119	120	120	121	121	122	122	123	123	124	124	125	125
105	120	120	121	121	122	122	123	123	124	124	125	125	126
106	120	121	121	122	122	123	123	124	124	125	125	126	126
107	121	121	122	122	123	123	124	124	125	125	126	126	127
108	121	122	122	123	123	124	124	125	125	126	126	127	127
109	121	122	123	123	124	124	125	125	126	126	127	127	128
110	122	122	123	124	124	125	125	126	126	127	127	128	128
111	122	123	123	124	125	125	126	126	127	127	128	128	129
112	123	123	124	124	125	126	126	127	127	128	128	129	129
113	123	124	124	125	125	126	127	127	128	128	129	129	130
114	124	124	125	125	126	126	127	128	128	129	129	130	130
115	124	125	125	126	126	127	127	128	129	129	130	130	131
116	125	125	126	126	127	127	128	128	129	130	130	131	131
117	125	126	126	127	127	128	128	129	129	130	131	131	132
118	126	126	127	127	128	128	129	129	130	130	131	132	132
119	126	127	127	128	128	129	129	130	130	131	131	132	133
120	127	127	128	128	129	129	130	130	131	131	132	132	133
121	127	128	128	129	129	130	130	131	131	132	132	133	133
122	128	128	129	129	130	130	131	131	132	132	133	133	134
123	128	129	129	130	130	131	131	132	132	133	133	134	134
124	129	129	130	130	131	131	132	132	133	133	134	134	135
125	129	130	130	131	131	132	132	133	133	134	134	135	135
126	130	130	131	131	132	132	133	133	134	134	135	135	136
127	130	131	131	132	132	133	133	134	134	135	135	136	136
128	131	131	132	132	133	133	134	134	135	135	136	136	137
129	131	132	132	133	133	134	134	135	135	136	136	137	137
130	132	132	133	133	134	134	135	135	136	136	137	137	138
131	132	133	133	134	134	135	135	136	136	137	137	138	138
132	133	133	134	134	135	135	136	136	137	137	138	138	139

(continued)

	Morphosyntax												
Semantics	**133**	**134**	**135**	**136**	**137**	**138**	**139**	**140**	**141**	**142**	**143**	**144**	**145**
133	133	134	134	135	135	136	136	137	137	138	138	139	139
134	133	134	135	135	136	136	137	137	138	138	139	139	140
135	134	134	135	136	136	137	137	138	138	139	139	140	140
136	134	135	135	136	137	137	138	138	139	139	140	140	141
137	135	135	136	136	137	138	138	139	139	140	140	141	141
138	135	136	136	137	137	138	139	139	140	140	141	141	142
139	136	136	137	137	138	138	139	140	140	141	141	142	142
140	136	137	137	138	138	139	139	140	141	141	142	142	143
141	137	137	138	138	139	139	140	140	141	142	142	143	143
142	137	138	138	139	139	140	140	141	141	142	143	143	144
143	138	138	139	139	140	140	141	141	142	142	143	144	144
144	138	139	139	140	140	141	141	142	142	143	143	144	145
145	139	139	140	140	141	141	142	142	143	143	144	144	145
>145	139	140	140	141	141	142	142	143	143	144	144	145	145

APPENDIX G

Age Equivalents for Raw Scores

Table G.1. Spanish subtests

Phonology	
Raw score	**Age equivalent**
0–18	<4;0
19	4;0
20	4;5
21	5;0
22	5;5
23	5;11
24	6;6
25	6;10
26+	>7;0

Morphosyntax—cloze	
Raw score	**Age equivalent**
0–9	<4;0
10	4;9
11	5;11
12	6;11
13+	>7;0

Morphosyntax—sentence repetition	
Raw score	**Age equivalent**
0–17	<4;0
18	4;0
19	4;3
20	4;7
21	4;10
22	5;1
23	5;4
24	5;6
25	5;9
26	6;0
27	6;3
28	6;6
29	6;9
30+	>6;11

Semantics—receptive	
Raw score	**Age equivalent**
0–4	<4;0
5	4;0
6	4;6
7	5;0
8	5;6
9	6;0
10	6;6
11	7;0
12	>7;0

Semantics—expressive	
Raw score	**Age equivalent**
0–5	<4;0
6	4;4
7	4;10
8	5;6
9	6;1
10	6;9
11+	>7;0

Table G.2. English subtests

Phonology	
Raw score	**Age equivalent**
0–20	<4;0
21	4;4
22	4;7
23	5;3
24	5;6
25	6;4
26	6;11
27+	>7;0

Morphosyntax—cloze	
Raw score	**Age equivalent**
0–15	<4;0
16	5;6
17	6;8
18+	>7;0

Morphosyntax—sentence repetition	
Raw score	**Age equivalent**
0–25	<4;0
26	5;0
27	7;0
28+	>7;0

Semantics—receptive	
Raw score	**Age equivalent**
0–5	<4;0
6	4;0
7	5;0
8	6;0
9	7;0
10	>7;0

Semantics—expressive	
Raw score	**Age equivalent**
0–5	<4;0
6	4;0
7	4;5
8	4;11
9	5;4
10	5;7
11	6;4
12+	7;0

APPENDIX H

Percentage of Consonants, Vowels, and Segments Correct

To use: Find the language of comparison (English or Spanish). In that section, find the child's age group in the shaded column. Then find the typically developing (TD) and phonologically impaired (PI) comparisons for percentage consonants correct, percentage vowels correct, and percentage segments correct. Use this information to determine whether the child's performance is more consistent with TD or PI for each measure. Note that only the child's better language should be used in determining a phonological impairment.

English							
Age group		Percentage consonants correct		Percentage vowels correct		Percentage segments correct	
Typically developing	4	94.23%	(4.84)	97.94%	(2.60)	95.51%	(3.79)
	5	94.64%	(4.89)	97.55%	(4.48)	95.68%	(4.37)
	6	95.47%	(3.82)	98.62%	(1.94)	96.58%	(2.91)
Phonologically impaired	4	74.31%	(6.70)	91.00%	(8.21)	80.06%	(6.48)
	5	77.65%	(10.04)	91.28%	(8.28)	82.46%	(8.55)
	6	78.30%	(7.23)	91.28%	(8.28)	82.46%	(8.55)
Spanish							
Age group		Percentage consonants correct		Percentage vowels correct		Percentage segments correct	
Typically developing	4	94.65%	(5.12)	98.61%	(1.77)	96.42%	(3.30)
	5	95.04%	(4.93)	99.08%	(1.45)	96.85%	(3.01)
	6	96.62%	(4.14)	99.32%	(1.34)	97.84%	(2.61)
Phonologically impaired	4	74.17%	(8.21)	94.58%	(6.15)	83.35%	(5.81)
	5	76.09%	(10.76)	96.34%	(3.80)	85.24%	(7.08)
	6	80.61%	(7.19)	98.54%	(1.04)	88.75%	(4.28)

APPENDIX I

Factor Loadings—BESA Items

Table I.1. Spanish items

	Component			
	Morphosyntax	**Phonology**	**Semantics**	**Pragmatics**
Span. Sem. 1	0.241	0.066	**0.534**	–0.011
Span. Sem. 2	0.042	0.043	**0.536**	0.072
Span. Sem. 3	0.027	0.142	**0.561**	–0.127
Span. Sem. 4	0.175	0.098	**0.489**	0.110
Span. Sem. 5	0.164	0.155	**0.477**	0.142
Span. Sem. 6	0.212	0.250	**0.472**	–0.023
Span. Sem. 7	0.196	0.157	**0.407**	0.115
Span. Sem. 8	0.070	0.075	**0.58**	–0.039
Span. Sem. 9	0.127	0.198	**0.453**	–0.073
Span. Sem. 10	0.248	0.097	**0.585**	0.098
Span. Sem. 11	0.203	0.173	**0.397**	–0.033
Span. Sem. 12	0.171	0.030	**0.356**	0.116
Span. Sem. 13	0.352	0.136	**0.404**	0.064
Span. Sem. 14	0.201	0.169	**0.524**	0.073
Span. Sem. 15	0.148	0.242	**0.438**	–0.112
Span. Sem. 16	0.203	0.218	**0.458**	–0.016
Span. Sem. 17	0.148	0.090	**0.483**	–0.038
Span. Sem. 18	0.080	0.175	**0.366**	0.034
Span. Sem. 19	0.247	0.046	**0.400**	0.026

(continued)

Table I.1. *(continued)*

	Component			
	Morphosyntax	**Phonology**	**Semantics**	**Pragmatics**
Span. Sem. 20	**0.335**	**0.234**	0.190	–0.015
Span. Sem. 21	0.184	0.032	**0.367**	–0.033
Span. Sem. 22	0.109	0.085	**0.395**	0.025
Span. Sem. 23	0.225	0.131	**0.480**	0.040
Span. Sem. 24	0.186	0.014	**0.374**	0.015
Span. Sem. 25	**0.282**	0.076	**0.295**	–0.014
Cloze 1	**0.459**	0.034	0.104	–0.016
Cloze 2	**0.340**	0.068	0.085	0.026
Cloze 3	**0.399**	0.198	0.094	0.148
Cloze 4	**0.371**	0.183	0.085	0.022
Cloze 5	**0.290**	0.146	0.088	0.164
Cloze 6	**0.386**	0.099	–0.129	0.181
Cloze 7	**0.258**	0.133	–0.068	0.143
Cloze 8	**0.491**	0.275	0.016	–0.085
Cloze 9	**0.498**	0.298	–0.049	–0.042
Cloze 10	**0.552**	0.255	–0.113	–0.002
Cloze 11	**0.546**	0.245	–0.063	0.059
Cloze 12	**0.480**	0.143	0.103	–0.015
Cloze 13	**0.292**	0.178	0.114	–0.031
Cloze 14	**0.526**	0.121	0.147	0.005
Cloze 15	**0.416**	0.194	0.056	0.087
Sent. Rep. 1	**0.588**	0.122	0.299	0.100
Sent. Rep. 2	**0.555**	0.055	0.258	0.158
Sent. Rep. 3	**0.455**	0.198	0.301	0.049
Sent. Rep. 4	**0.460**	0.194	0.331	0.145
Sent. Rep. 5	**0.535**	0.193	0.215	0.069
Sent. Rep. 6	**0.490**	0.148	0.196	0.093
Sent. Rep. 7	**0.578**	0.115	0.178	0.167
Sent. Rep. 8	**0.511**	0.140	0.229	0.092
Sent. Rep. 9	**0.428**	0.108	0.172	0.243
Sent. Rep. 10	**0.523**	0.197	0.243	0.070
Sent. Rep. 11	**0.411**	0.157	0.342	0.209

Table I.1. *(continued)*

	Component			
	Morphosyntax	**Phonology**	**Semantics**	**Pragmatics**
Sent. Rep. 12	**0.483**	0.102	0.167	0.005
Sent. Rep. 13	**0.590**	0.084	0.216	0.073
Sent. Rep. 14	**0.625**	0.132	0.332	0.073
Sent. Rep. 15	**0.621**	0.124	0.200	−0.100
Sent. Rep. 16	**0.628**	0.120	0.139	−0.073
Sent. Rep. 17	**0.589**	0.123	0.251	0.051
Sent. Rep. 18	**0.642**	0.064	0.146	−0.117
Sent. Rep. 19	**0.568**	0.051	0.130	0.036
Sent. Rep. 20	**0.513**	0	0.161	0.047
Sent. Rep. 21	**0.594**	0.094	0.158	0.094
Sent. Rep. 22	**0.578**	0.050	0.235	−0.083
Sent. Rep. 23	**0.455**	0.051	0.163	−0.023
Sent. Rep. 24	**0.647**	0.068	0.143	−0.039
Sent. Rep. 25	**0.619**	0.032	0.224	−0.034
Sent. Rep. 26	**0.555**	0.243	0.111	0.016
Sent. Rep. 27	**0.489**	0.206	0.019	0.100
Sent. Rep. 28	**0.643**	0.047	0.259	−0.039
Sent. Rep. 29	**0.531**	0.090	0.175	−0.005
Sent. Rep. 30	**0.378**	0.041	0.136	−0.127
Sent. Rep. 31	**0.507**	0.082	0.116	−0.005
Sent. Rep. 32	**0.555**	0.118	0.296	0.071
Sent. Rep. 33	**0.578**	0.004	0.168	0.009
Sent. Rep. 34	**0.478**	0.197	0.012	0.082
Sent. Rep. 35	**0.588**	0.119	0.164	−0.032
Sent. Rep. 36	**0.632**	0.062	0.160	−0.126
Sent. Rep. 37	**0.485**	−0.009	0.159	0.091
Phon. 1	0.104	**0.571**	0	0.026
Phon. 2	0.189	**0.604**	0.032	0.077
Phon. 3	−0.007	**0.363**	0.055	0.129
Phon. 4	0.098	**0.598**	0.076	0.048
Phon. 5	0.097	**0.651**	0.228	0.073
Phon. 6	0.067	**0.544**	0.197	0.043

(continued)

Table I.1. *(continued)*

	Component			
	Morphosyntax	**Phonology**	**Semantics**	**Pragmatics**
Phon. 7	0.019	**0.467**	0.171	0.044
Phon. 8	0.096	**0.666**	0.105	0.120
Phon. 9	–0.005	**0.527**	0.211	0.123
Phon. 10	0.167	**0.596**	0.179	0.034
Phon. 11	0.153	**0.660**	0.184	0.094
Phon. 12	0.065	**0.666**	0.118	–0.013
Phon. 13	0.074	**0.336**	–0.134	–0.176
Phon. 14	0.172	**0.387**	0.163	0.077
Phon. 15	0.106	**0.494**	0.184	0.096
Phon. 16	0.181	**0.458**	0.121	0.019
Phon. 17	0.198	**0.502**	0.115	–0.010
Phon. 18	0.073	**0.632**	0.051	0.018
Phon. 19	0.176	**0.566**	0.139	0.105
Phon. 20	0.267	**0.541**	0.072	–0.030
Phon. 21	0.201	**0.472**	0.082	0.014
Phon. 22	0.170	**0.409**	–0.028	0.052
Phon. 23	0.061	**0.088**	0.056	–0.097
Phon. 24	0.066	**0.024**	0.063	0.116
Phon. 25	0.271	**0.547**	0.149	–0.010
Phon. 26	0.147	**0.422**	0.139	–0.073
Phon. 27	0.037	**0.304**	0.103	–0.044
Phon. 28	0.322	**0.501**	0.104	0.035
Prag. 1	0.051	0.022	0.071	**0.501**
Prag. 2	0	0.027	–0.101	**0.354**
Prag. 3	0.016	–0.013	–0.027	**0.444**
Prag. 4	0.035	–0.058	0.258	**0.446**
Prag. 5	0.007	0.094	–0.023	**0.585**
Prag. 6	0.053	0.053	0.131	**0.545**
Prag. 7	0.025	0.164	0.032	**0.579**
Prag. 8	0.067	0.032	0.049	**0.429**
Prag. 9	0.031	–0.019	–0.046	**0.448**
Prag. 10	–0.037	0.121	–0.003	**0.438**

Table I.2. English items

	Component				
	Morphosyntax sentence repetition	**Morphosyntax cloze**	**Semantics**	**Phonology**	**Pragmatics**
Eng. Sem. 1	0.128	0.194	**0.467**	−0.013	−0.011
Eng. Sem. 2	0.183	0.262	**0.295**	0.064	0.079
Eng. Sem. 3	0.121	−0.094	**0.433**	0.036	0.037
Eng. Sem. 4	0.162	0.130	**0.538**	0.08	0.071
Eng. Sem. 5	0.135	0.015	**0.58**	0.064	0.045
Eng. Sem. 6	0.097	0.193	**0.513**	0.07	0.043
Eng. Sem. 7	0.058	0.056	**0.374**	0.099	−0.025
Eng. Sem. 8	0.114	0.085	**0.571**	0.063	−0.100
Eng. Sem. 9	0.200	0.310	**0.430**	0.138	0.03
Eng. Sem. 10	0.164	0.231	**0.536**	0.118	0.078
Eng. Sem. 11	0.318	0.112	**0.382**	0.057	−0.025
Eng. Sem. 12	0.269	0.219	**0.477**	0.194	0.064
Eng. Sem. 13	0.243	0.062	**0.533**	0.062	0.026
Eng. Sem. 14	0.087	0.215	**0.28**	−0.053	0.026
Eng. Sem. 15	0.222	0.163	**0.484**	0.124	−0.115
Eng. Sem. 16	0.219	0.251	**0.473**	0.041	−0.054
Eng. Sem. 17	0.139	0.162	**0.413**	0.063	−0.034
Eng. Sem. 18	0.184	0.207	**0.422**	0.004	0.113
Eng. Sem. 19	0.093	0.206	**0.549**	0.143	−0.098
Eng. Sem. 20	0.140	0.137	**0.579**	0.100	0.052
Eng. Sem. 21	0.092	0.109	**0.533**	0.152	0.126
Eng. Sem. 22	0.232	0.119	**0.413**	−0.025	−0.006
Eng. Sem. 23	0.178	0.235	**0.41**	0.091	0.061
Eng. Sem. 24	0.104	0.031	**0.534**	0.021	0.007
Eng. Sem. 25	0.147	0.154	**0.490**	0.099	0.047
Eng. Cloze 1	0.238	**0.614**	0.159	0.225	0.03
Eng. Cloze 2	0.232	**0.549**	0.113	0.171	0.002
Eng. Cloze 3	0.262	**0.615**	0.165	0.183	0.024
Eng. Cloze 4	0.310	**0.546**	0.115	0.165	0.015
Eng. Cloze 5	0.208	**0.625**	0.193	0.177	0.060
Eng. Cloze 6	0.250	**0.601**	0.151	0.201	0.074

(continued)

Table I.2. *(continued)*

	Component				
	Morphosyntax sentence repetition	**Morphosyntax cloze**	**Semantics**	**Phonology**	**Pragmatics**
Eng. Cloze 7	0.202	**0.422**	0.147	0.192	0.053
Eng. Cloze 8	0.223	**0.497**	0.135	0.132	0.022
Eng. Cloze 9	0.185	**0.486**	0.130	0.078	0.049
Eng. Cloze 10	0.117	**0.349**	0.237	0.161	–0.021
Eng. Cloze 11	0.157	**0.518**	0.151	0.074	–0.006
Eng. Cloze 12	0.184	**0.320**	0.216	0.154	–0.124
Eng. Cloze 13	0.083	**0.540**	0.174	0.055	0.004
Eng. Cloze 14	0.157	**0.543**	0.147	0.175	0.022
Eng. Cloze 15	0.087	**0.529**	0.087	0.079	0.116
Eng. Cloze 16	0.123	**0.484**	0.243	0.188	0.041
Eng. Cloze 17	0.198	**0.421**	0.219	0.016	–0.14
Eng. Cloze 18	0.261	**0.528**	0.061	0.138	0.065
Eng. Cloze 19	0.265	**0.44**	0.075	0.154	0.031
Eng. Cloze 20	0.283	**0.579**	0.230	0.167	0.031
Eng. Cloze 21	0.297	**0.631**	0.118	0.193	0.085
Eng. Cloze 22	0.281	**0.503**	0.202	0.044	–0.006
Eng. Cloze 23	0.230	**0.575**	0.202	0.070	0.012
Eng. Cloze 24	0.228	**0.564**	0.197	0.116	0.08
Eng. Sent. Rep. 1	**0.382**	–0.006	0.339	0.293	–0.032
Eng. Sent. Rep. 2	**0.531**	0.285	0.140	0.106	0.020
Eng. Sent. Rep. 3	**0.406**	0.146	0.260	–0.001	0.065
Eng. Sent. Rep. 4	**0.670**	0.201	0.084	0.229	0.092
Eng. Sent. Rep. 5	**0.559**	0.100	0.215	0.212	0.010
Eng. Sent. Rep. 6	**0.627**	0.143	0.125	0.067	0.058
Eng. Sent. Rep. 7	**0.580**	0.183	0.031	0.094	0.127
Eng. Sent. Rep. 8	**0.595**	0.276	0.116	0.141	–0.037
Eng. Sent. Rep. 9	**0.584**	0.169	0.209	0.161	–0.004
Eng. Sent. Rep. 10	**0.563**	0.139	0.134	0.150	0.043
Eng. Sent. Rep. 11	**0.601**	0.181	0.147	0.163	–0.104
Eng. Sent. Rep. 12	**0.647**	0.164	0.092	–0.007	–0.018
Eng. Sent. Rep. 13	**0.468**	0.233	0.184	0.147	–0.044

Table I.2. *(continued)*

	Component				
	Morphosyntax sentence repetition	**Morphosyntax cloze**	**Semantics**	**Phonology**	**Pragmatics**
Eng. Sent. Rep. 14	**0.636**	0.221	0.190	0.049	−0.090
Eng. Sent. Rep. 15	**0.551**	0.159	0.139	0.038	−0.146
Eng. Sent. Rep. 16	**0.396**	0.206	0.152	0.123	−0.005
Eng. Sent. Rep. 17	**0.501**	0.269	0.082	0.207	0.015
Eng. Sent. Rep. 18	**0.460**	0.418	0.209	0.228	0.039
Eng. Sent. Rep. 19	**0.616**	0.202	0.312	0.102	0.023
Eng. Sent. Rep. 20	**0.536**	0.187	0.191	0.163	−0.009
Eng. Sent. Rep. 21	**0.553**	0.179	0.185	0.108	0.095
Eng. Sent. Rep. 22	**0.539**	0.184	0.128	0.046	0.105
Eng. Sent. Rep. 23	**0.464**	0.262	0.076	0.043	0.126
Eng. Sent. Rep. 24	**0.527**	0.287	0.208	0.184	0.108
Eng. Sent. Rep. 25	**0.554**	0.238	0.115	0.226	−0.038
Eng. Sent. Rep. 26	**0.351**	0.381	0.037	0.117	−0.151
Eng. Sent. Rep. 27	**0.461**	0.426	0.226	0.085	0.077
Eng. Sent. Rep. 28	**0.622**	0.064	0.288	0.089	0.05
Eng. Sent. Rep. 29	**0.631**	0.143	0.215	0.034	0.038
Eng. Sent. Rep. 30	**0.631**	0.179	0.251	0.091	0.022
Eng. Sent. Rep. 31	**0.566**	0.343	0.157	0.147	−0.071
Eng. Sent. Rep. 32	**0.518**	0.146	0.215	0.031	0.035
Eng. Sent. Rep. 33	**0.558**	0.178	0.199	−0.043	0.035
Eng. Phon. 1	−0.011	0.176	0.068	**0.279**	0.003
Eng. Phon. 2	0.154	0.319	−0.012	**0.282**	0.042
Eng. Phon. 3	0.073	0.191	0.103	**0.124**	−0.155
Eng. Phon. 4	0.195	0.215	0.032	**0.236**	0.029
Eng. Phon. 5	0.150	0.245	0.07	**0.450**	−0.032
Eng. Phon. 6	0.072	0.039	0.105	**0.164**	−0.098
Eng. Phon. 7	0.064	0.071	−0.024	**0.452**	−0.019
Eng. Phon. 8	0.022	0.049	0.108	**0.303**	−0.176
Eng. Phon. 9	0.125	0.137	−0.012	**0.502**	0.109
Eng. Phon. 10	0.120	0.221	−0.083	**0.429**	0.036
Eng. Phon. 11	0.127	0.317	0.006	**0.24**	0.036

(continued)

Table I.2. *(continued)*

	Component				
	Morphosyntax sentence repetition	**Morphosyntax cloze**	**Semantics**	**Phonology**	**Pragmatics**
Eng. Phon. 12	–0.025	0.042	–0.036	**0.596**	0.034
Eng. Phon. 13	0.180	0.294	0.127	**0.395**	–0.098
Eng. Phon. 14	0.155	0.308	0.057	**0.461**	0.109
Eng. Phon. 15	0.114	0.300	–0.015	**0.552**	–0.009
Eng. Phon. 16	0.155	0.278	0.099	**0.542**	–0.035
Eng. Phon. 17	0.144	0.017	0.107	**0.618**	0.028
Eng. Phon. 18	0.134	0.042	–0.008	**0.626**	0.005
Eng. Phon. 19	0.030	0.106	0.111	**0.476**	0.072
Eng. Phon. 20	0.044	0.084	0.171	**0.416**	0.077
Eng. Phon. 21	0.040	0.068	0.039	**0.559**	0.135
Eng. Phon. 22	0.186	0.022	0.127	**0.636**	0.063
Eng. Phon. 23	0.204	0.331	–0.072	**0.349**	–0.001
Eng. Phon. 24	0.047	0.118	0.172	**0.404**	0.044
Eng. Phon. 25	0.232	–0.033	0.144	**0.438**	–0.055
Eng. Phon. 26	0.023	0.142	0.063	**0.512**	0.023
Eng. Phon. 27	0.061	0.004	0.165	**0.537**	0.021
Eng. Phon. 28	0.120	0.266	–0.002	**0.503**	–0.054
Eng. Phon. 29	–0.052	0.089	0.028	**0.418**	0.004
Eng. Phon. 30	0.147	0.011	0.160	**0.355**	–0.095
Eng. Phon. 31	0.061	0.333	0.179	**0.322**	–0.018
Eng. Prag. 1	–0.011	–0.077	0.107	0.072	**0.516**
Eng. Prag. 2	0.063	–0.078	0.105	–0.027	**0.383**
Eng. Prag. 3	0.000	–0.036	0.086	–0.067	**0.503**
Eng. Prag. 4	0.001	0.106	0.143	0.087	**0.465**
Eng. Prag. 5	0.082	–0.011	–0.113	0.059	**0.620**
Eng. Prag. 6	0.090	0.106	0.086	–0.001	**0.532**
Eng. Prag. 7	–0.024	0.083	0.010	0.065	**0.590**
Eng. Prag. 8	0.061	0.063	–0.087	0.095	**0.460**
Eng. Prag. 9	0.120	0.097	–0.031	–0.146	**0.379**
Eng. Prag. 10	–0.147	0.106	–0.080	0.085	**0.460**

Index

References to tables and figures are indicated with a *t* and *f*, respectively.

Ordering Guide

Bilingual English-Spanish Assessment (BESA)

BESA is a valid and reliable assessment that specifically responds to the needs of young Spanish-English bilingual children, ages 4 through 6 years.
BESA KIT INCLUDES: Test Manual, stimulus book, protocols in English and Spanish, BIOS forms, and ITALK forms | Stock #: 52797 | ISBN: 978-1-68125-279-7

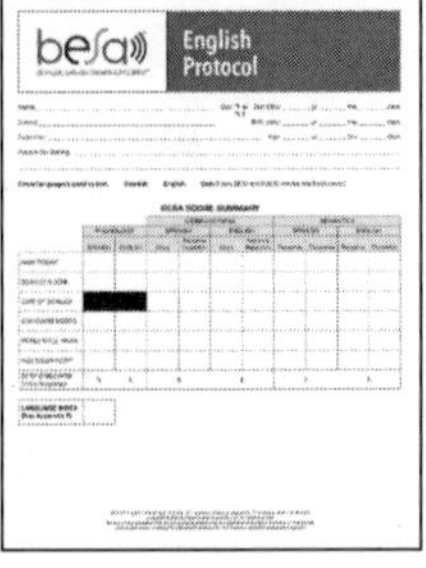

BESA Protocol, English

Sold in a package of 20 forms, the English subtests take about 15 minutes each and address the key domains of pragmatics, morphosyntax, semantics, and phonology.

BESA Protocol, English: Sold in a package of 20 forms | Stock #: 52827 | ISBN: 978-1-68125-282-7

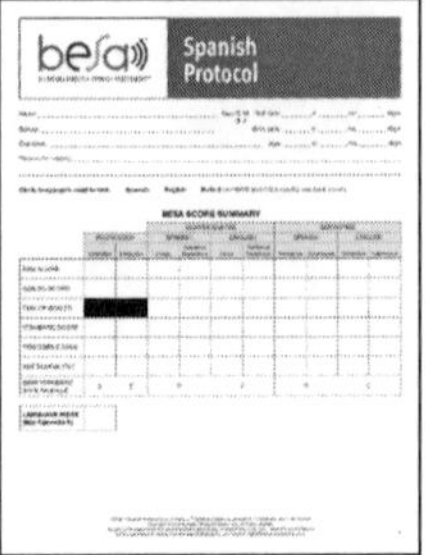

BESA Protocol, Spanish

Sold in a package of 20 forms, the Spanish subtests take about 15 minutes each and address the key domains of pragmatics, morphosyntax, semantics, and phonology.

BESA Protocol, Spanish: Sold in a package of 20 forms | Stock #: 52834 | ISBN: 978-1-68125-2834

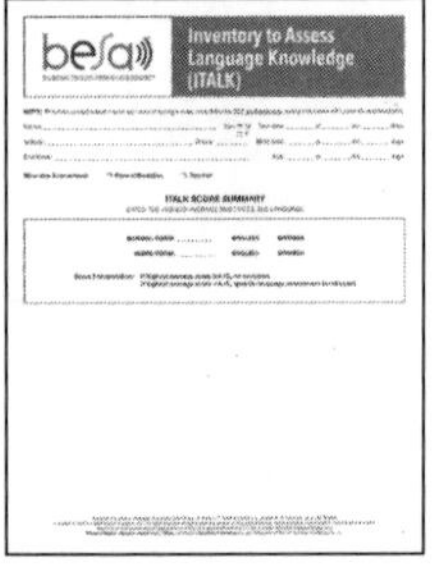

Inventory to Assess Language Knowledge (ITALK)

Completed by the examiner as a parent and teacher interview, the 10-minute ITALK addresses relative use of a child's two languages and five areas of speech and language development (vocabulary, grammar, sentence production, comprehension, and phonology) in both Spanish and English.

ITALK: Sold in package of 20 forms | Stock #: 52858 | ISBN: 978-1-68125-285-8

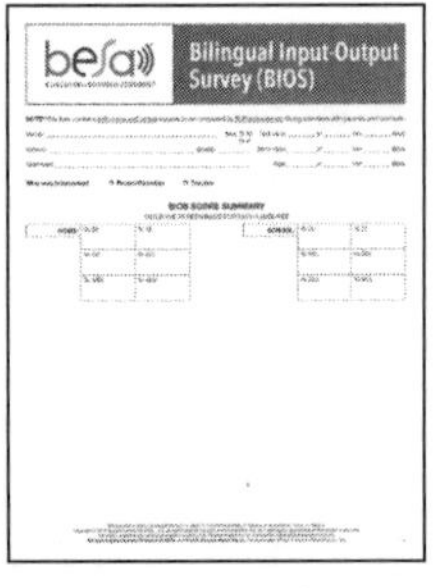

Bilingual Input-Output Survey (BIOS)

Completed by the examiner as a parent and teacher survey, the BIOS helps uncover when and in what context each of the child's two languages were used on a year-to-year basis.

BIOS: Sold in package of 20 forms | Stock #: 52841 | ISBN: 978-1-68125-284-1